PLAY LIKE A MAN

MUSIC IN AMERICAN LIFE

PLAY LIKE A MAN

MY LIFE IN POSTER CHILDREN

ROSE MARSHACK

UNIVERSITY OF
ILLINOIS PRESS
Urbana, Chicago, and Springfield

Publication was supported by a grant from
Illinois State University.

Library of Congress Cataloging-in-Publication Data
Names: Marshack, Rose, 1965– author.
Title: Play like a man : my life in Poster Children /
    Rose Marshack.
Description: Urbana: University of Illinois Press,
    2023. | Series: Music in American life | Includes
    bibliographical references and index.
Identifiers: LCCN 2022036528 (print) | LCCN
    2022036529 (ebook) | ISBN 9780252044861
    (hardback) | ISBN 9780252086960 (paperback) |
    ISBN 9780252054013 (ebook)
Subjects: LCSH: Marshack, Rose, 1965– | Women
    bass guitarists—United States—Biography. |
    Women alternative rock musicians—United States—
    Biography. | Bass guitarists—United States—
    Biography. | Alternative rock musicians—United
    States—Biography. | Poster Children (Musical
    group) | BISAC: MUSIC / Genres & Styles / Punk |
    BIOGRAPHY & AUTOBIOGRAPHY / Music
Classification: LCC ML419.M314 A3 2023 (print) |
    LCC ML419.M314 (ebook) | DDC 787.87/166092
    [B]—dc23/eng/20220804
LC record available at https://lccn.loc.gov/2022036528
LC ebook record available at https://lccn.loc.gov/2022036529

With help from Rick, Gram, and Dao

"We don't have a future, we don't have a past."

—Rick Valentin, "Zero Stars"

Contents

PART ONE. 1980S: COLLEGE

PART TWO. 1987–1992: PRE–MAJOR LABEL LIFE

PART THREE. 1993–1996: MAJOR LABEL LIFE

PART FOUR. 1997: POST–MAJOR LABEL

List of Tour Reports

PART THREE. 1993–1996: MAJOR LABEL LIFE

PART FOUR. 1997: POST–MAJOR LABEL

Preface

Driving down the highway on the lookout for the cops,
Breaking every limit we're the band that never stops,
80 miles an hour and 500 miles a day,
After two weeks every exit starts to look the same.
—Rick Valentin, "Zero Stars"

Rick Valentin is responsible for my active participation in the post-1890s
music scene. A thing of beauty, clothed in a mustard suit-jacket and with
shoulder-length blond-to-me hair, he lived next door to my group of geek-
friends in Allen Hall, he was an engineer, and he had an electric guitar. As
a classically trained piano player and violinist, I'd never met someone who
played an electric guitar, and as a girl from the north suburbs of Chicago, I'd
not yet met any engineers. The first time I saw him as I passed by his door,
I looked at him sadly, as one might regard an expensive car, and thought,
"Well, there's something I'll never have."

From the Poster Children website archive, by Rick Valentin:

Rick and Rose formed Poster Children with drummer Shannon Drew
in September of 1987 in Champaign–Urbana, home of the University of
Illinois. Rick and Rose had met a few years earlier at Allen Hall, a dorm
on campus. Rick was playing guitar in a band called Penguin Dust and
when the bass player quit, Rose was suggested as a replacement. Everyone
thought it was a good idea except Rick, who pointed out that Rose had

never played the bass before. Thankfully he was outvoted and Rose became a member of the band, renamed Cries and Whispers.

Rick patiently shepherded me, his brother, and the rest of the Poster Children alumni through our careers, always knowing how to plan ahead, what path came next, all the time with longevity and humility in mind. He wrote all the lyrics to all our songs and later, when he had appropriate tools, recorded and mixed the records and filmed and edited the videos. His ideas drove our band. The only reason that he is not writing this book is that he is a perfectionist. But it was his idea for me to write and publish my tour reports on the web in 1995, and it is for that reason that I have written this book.

Poster Children at Café Du Nord. Left to right, Jim, Rose, Rick, and Matt. Photograph by Patric Carver, @pc.photo.rock.

Preface

Acknowledgments

Thank you to my family: Rick, Gram, and Dao; Mom and Dad; Carla and Sara; MomV, DadV, and JimV.

Also thanks to:

Laurie Matheson, Michael Roux, and UI Press for their patience.

Tony Sanfilippo, Steve Fast, Chris Corpora, ML and Skip, Ellen Stewart.

Steve Albini for being a sport, Ian MacKaye for being a friend.

Sarah Garibaldi (my Breast Bitch), Chris Garibaldi, and Lotuspool Records.

Heidi Ore, Barb Schilf, Candice Belanoff, Rachel Switzky, Kim Coletta.

The Poster Children alumni, the pkids-listers and community.

The Champaign–Urbana scene.

All the bands who played with us and asked us to play with them.

Grand Master Namsoo Hyong, Lillian Hoddeson (my martial arts sister), and Peter.

Contramestre Deni and Professora Aisha Chiaramonte, Santanu Rahman, Frances Reedy, Seth Fein, Rick Powers.

Kevin Hamilton, Michael Azerrad, Jon Fine, Howie Klein, Peter Shershin, Al Smith.

Sara Hudson, Lisa BK, Linda Duke, Ming Kuo, Donna Cox.

The Prairie Sangha.
My Illinois State University family.
All those who I forgot to mention here.
And You.

PLAY LIKE A MAN

PART ONE

1980s
College

"Where's my five bucks?" an audience member yelled from the back of the church. "Up my ass, with your wristwatch, where you left it last week," drawled Mr. Steve Albini, from the stage. He was taking too long to tune his guitar, a red Strat-shaped object with the words "that's the thing" on it, attached to him by a thick leather strap wrapped around his waist. He'd worn his guitar in this fashion since high school, no conventional guitar strap across his chest. His thin waist supported his entire instrument, leaving both his arms free.

It was 1986, October 19, and I was in what I'd later come to call the PRU, the People's Republic of Urbana, Illinois, in college, standing with about a hundred other students in a dimly lit, box-shaped, high-ceilinged structure where religious groups sometimes met, about a thousand steps away from my dorm room in Allen Hall. If you were here, at Channing-Murray Foundation, on Monday nights, you could eat Hare Krishna food, yellow and peanuty, at the Red Herring vegetarian restaurant in the basement. But tonight, the main, dusty cathedral floor hosted a different type of group, here to witness an all-ages punk rock show put on by Josh Gottheil,[1] a teenaged townie, loved and renowned for bringing bands from all over the world to the Champaign–Urbana scene. This was one of the first all-ages punk rock

SUBVERSIVE SOUNDS PRODUCTIONS & RECORD SWAP PRESENT

BIG
BLACK

URGE OVERKILL   DIDJITS

ClubCrack

SUNDAY OCT. 19, 1986

THE CHANNING MURRAY
FOUNDATION CORNER OF OREGON &
MATHEWS - CAMPUS

TICKETS $5
AVAILABLE AT
RECORD SWAP
RECORD SERVICE
THAT'S RENTERTAINMENT

ALL AGES - DOORS OPEN AT 7:00

Subversive Sounds/Record Swap present

BIG BLACK URGE OVERKILL
THE DIJITS   CLUB CRACK

Channing-Murray Foundation Sun., Oct. 19, 1986

All ages   Doors open at 7 p.m. $5

151

SUBVERSIVE SOUNDS
SUBVERSIVE SOUNDS PRODUCTIONS
P.O. BOX 3356
URBANA, IL 61801

Flier for Big Black Show at
Channing-Murray Foundation.
Collection of Jim Proefrock.

shows I'd see at my university: two local bands: Club Crack, then Didjits, followed by Chicago's Big Black.[2] Afterward I'd go back to the dorm to finish my computer programming homework, coding 8086 assembler to create a two-digit multiplication machine. The punk-rock equivalent of computer programming languages—low-level, straightforward, and minimal. Base.

There were no more outbursts from the audience, and it continued to wait patiently as Steve used his free hands to finish attending to Roland, the drummer in the band. Steve was on the short side with black, cropped hair and spectacles, dressed as a working engineer. Roland was acting up, delaying the show, probably because Roland was a drum machine, and may have needed to be restarted due to the humidity in the room. Finally, Roland emitted some gunshots and Big Black started into a song, which sounded like an avalanche of noise with a nonchalant monotone speaking over it, teaching us of the inadequacies and inequalities in the world. This spectacle, and contemplating how a wristwatch would end up inside someone's ass, along with the growl of songs about lighting people on fire, child molestation, and a song titled "Passing Complexion" (which is how I learned about passing complexions) was how I first remember becoming aware of Mr. Steve Albini. He was nearly arrested that evening for setting off firecrackers onstage before the show. And I was thinking about all this now, because I'd just pressed the doorbell to his house. I was going to record a record with him.

CHAPTER 1

Origin Story

How did I get here? I was a white, privileged Jewish American Princess from the Chicago suburbs, had classical music lessons, ballet lessons, and a nose job growing up. I was a geek who loved role-playing games and knitted Dr. Who scarves in high school. I was the quintessential rule-follower and would cry and beg if I scored an A– on a quiz. But now, I'd discovered punk rock, and I was helping write it, and I'd convinced myself, with my heart and soul, that the two bass notes (E and F-sharp) that comprised our song "If You See Kay" formed just as complete and essential a composition as the entire Beethoven *Pathetique* that I'd learned in high school. Minimalism. It felt like holy writ now, that a song only requires one or two chords, three if you need a crutch. The Chopin Etude in C-sharp minor I was now toying with on the piano was as bloated as a Primus song.

Rick likes to joke that I only know music from before 1890 and after 1980, and he seems proud of that fact, which makes me love him more. A friend, and devoted fan Mike from New Jersey/Hawaii, recently tested me through Rick. "Would Rose know Wings?" he asked. Rick answered, "The 1977 date is shorthand for punk, so Wings, even though they were active at that time, are not included." Rick continued, "For example, Rose would only know Journey from the *TRON* soundtrack." That is correct.

I had no relationship to rock in my childhood—my dad, a huge influence on my life, hated anything pedestrian or manipulative. To him, rock music was lazy and he called it "hillbilly music." Dad played jazz trumpet, and my whole life, at least one night a week, he'd be gone playing a "gig" in Chicago after he finished up at the office. Dad's license plate says "Day Gig" because that is what musicians must have if they are not good enough to make a living playing music, he explained to me, laughingly. His "day gig" was dentistry, so the cars that bore that license plate were usually Mercedes or BMWs. He was beloved in both worlds, medicine and music, and when I'd be with him in public, he'd always be greeted cordially as "Doc" by his musician friends, and at restaurants his former dental students would run up to him and hug him.

Dad is inspirational in his ethics, his drive, and his generosity. He embodies all the major traits of the "Silent Generation," especially discipline. He simply does what he needs to do, without question, angst, or worry. In his nineties, he still adheres to a strict workout and practice schedule, regardless of whether he has gigs scheduled. He also keeps a list of all his activities and times spent on them, handwritten on paper, which, to me, looks like artwork. He practices trumpet fifty-five minutes every other day—"because I don't want to practice the last five minutes," he says, both seriously and with a slight smile. Charles Marshack, his father, born in 1899, had intended to become a doctor (probably at his parents' request) but dropped out of college after a year and became a music teacher. He was a saxophonist, but he taught practically every instrument. My grandma Bea was a year or two younger, and I always remember her playing the piano. Music was a given in my family.

Dad joined the Musicians Union at fifteen, under the age limit, so he had to bring an instrument and perform as part of the application. "I took my trumpet and played half of 'Blue Skies,'" he remembers, "and they let me in." His first job, at fifteen, was with a piano player, at Six Corners in Chicago, Cicero Avenue, Irving Park Boulevard and Milwaukee Avenue, at the American Legion. "It was terrible! We were supposed to go until one a.m., and at midnight they stopped us, gave us twelve dollars each, and said we could go home early." Dad then went over to Green Mill where his father was playing saxophone with Elmer Kaiser's band, old standards; people were dancing. "When they took a break, my father asked, 'What are you doing here, Poo Poo? You were supposed to play 'til one a.m.!' and I said, 'They let us go early' and the whole band was screaming with laughter."

Growing up, Mom chose to play violin, but could only practice in her house when people weren't watching TV, so she wouldn't disturb anyone. She says there was no question that her children would be given music lessons. "Even if Dad wasn't a musician, I'd still have made you play. Music is just so important," she says. So, my two younger sisters and I had piano lessons first, and then were able to choose a second instrument. I chose violin, Mom's instrument, since Dad was so harsh on me at the piano. The middle sister, Carla, chose trumpet, apparently not knowing how intense Dad could get. In high school she attempted to get out of practicing because her braces hurt her gums, but Dad forced the orthodontist to hasten her treatment and remove the braces earlier so she could continue playing. To encourage him, Dad says, he threatened to stop sending him referrals. I imagine that at the time, Carla didn't have a problem with getting her braces off early. Sara, our youngest sister, chose cello, an instrument whose sound she loved, but also an instrument that neither of our parents played, and it was at that time that both Carla and I realized her brilliance.

So my knowledge of music pre-1890 is a result of my parents. Being forced to play violin enabled me to pick up a bass without lessons, and I'm convinced that I have my job as a professor in a school of music because, in my preliminary interview, speaking so reverently of my dad's jazz career lent some legitimacy to my punk rock background. As I raise my children, friends ask what types of guitars and basses to buy their children, to give them a seemingly more relevant practice in music. My children are being trained in the Suzuki method by the strictest violin teacher on the planet, and being forced to practice, just as I was. I don't even bother saying, "Someday you'll thank me." I didn't understand what it meant when my dad said it to me, but I eventually did just that, thanking him many times from the stage, pointing and waving at him while he stood proudly, six-foot, three-inches tall, and fifty years older than most of the audience.

Thursday May 6, 1999, Iowa City, Iowa, with Mercy Rule

INDIE RADIO INTERVIEWS ARE SO MUCH BETTER THAN COMMERCIAL ONES

We had a radio interview with a future serial-killer from the northern Chicago suburbs tonight, on a station with a listenership of five people. Howie, our drummer, actually said on the radio, interrupting him, "You're pretty cynical for a young man your age." Rick said, "I'm going to tell my school counselor about you." He was going on and on about how competitive the Iowa City Music Scene is, which made us laugh. What would you compete for, in Iowa City? Or, anywhere?

Is there some sort of throne? Anyway, this guy was from Highland Park, Illinois, part of the rich, privileged, white suburban area north of Chicago. When he found out Howie was from nearby Wilmette, he beamed and clapped. Howie is family. When he found out I'm from Deerfield, the rival next-door town of Highland Park, he screamed, jumped up and down, and pounded on the radio console, causing the mics to all go out. About five minutes of dead air ensued while he ranted about our pitiful growings-up in the suburbs, until he calmed down and noticed that the mics were off. What an angry young man, but what a great interview! Rick tried to convince him to start his own radio show on the internet. He's very talented.

Radio was my primary access to music from the current century, but to me, that music was conflated with the interspersed commercials. I couldn't tell the difference and I figured it was all there to sell me stuff. But malls and sports were the main culture in the north suburbs of Chicago, so consumption was comforting to me. I'd awaken many times in the middle of the night, terrified of nukes and tornadoes, and turn on the radio to assure myself that there were still people alive and buying in the world. Voices from a broadcast, cars on the road, these were signs that everyone probably wasn't dead yet.

On the other side of the radio was the Steve Dahl and Garry Meier talk show on WLUP in Chicago, a show I loved, mainstream media spewing "non-conventional ideas." Dahl was a radio DJ shock jock who was earlier and more midwestern than Howard Stern, more substance and much less trash, and he partnered with Garry Meier and created as countercultural a movement as possible for a Chicago suburban teenager to experience. I was a regular listener, and sometimes even audiotaped it on cassette while I listened, so I could later play it for my dad. I saved a cassette of Steve and Garry making a prank call to an "Islamic Fried Chicken," ordering a variety of fast food for the hostages.[1] I thought their stamina was amazing. They created material to keep me entertained for four hours a day, five days a week!

During this time, Dahl led a movement against disco, scratching (as in, trying to destroy) and blowing up disco records on the air. (He'd been fired from an earlier Chicago radio station that had changed genres overnight to disco, goes the story.) On July 12, 1979, he ran an event at Chicago's Comiskey Park during a White Sox double-header, inviting tens of thousands of fans to riot in between games, blowing up disco records and destroying the field. "Disco Demolition Night" turned into a public mob scene, a gathering of people to protest a type of music and lifestyle. Other protests I'd seen or been involved with were political; I had attended a simultaneous rally against a Nazi Party march in Skokie. This event, at a White Sox game, was tens of thousands of people protesting a genre of music. The narrative is problematic now as viewed through the lens of racism, but at the time, I was fourteen years old, and amazed that people could get so angry and violent about music, and thrilled that, in doing so, they'd disrupted a major league ball game.[2]

In high school, I begrudgingly attended a KISS concert with a friend, and all I remember from it was that I was informed that the people behind us were smoking pot (probably the 5,000 people behind us were smoking pot). This had compelled me to borrow five dollars to purchase a giant, glossy KISS concert program. I needed the giant program because I wanted proof, for social capital, not that I'd been to a KISS concert, but that I'd been to a place where people had been smoking pot. Another time, I was given an Eagles record and a STYX record as a birthday present from a school friend. I played them once to air out the vinyl smell. The only record I ever remember liking was a live album, *Cheap Trick at Budokan*. I liked the power in the music, and I liked how the chords resolved. I liked how "Surrender" mentioned "Mom and Dad"—I remember being quite happy that the singer was singing about his parents enjoying the same music as he was. He seemed like a nice boy, and also from the Midwest.

Once in a while, though, kids from the suburbs would have stumbled upon little glimpses, windows into the larger scene. Near the end of high school, I could drive the forty-five minutes down to the city, go museum-hopping near the lake to get some culture in, and then end up at Punkin' Donuts (as we called it), making fun of kids with spikey mohawks who we also figured were from the suburbs. Then up to Wax Trax record store, to ogle the tiny one-inch buttons with band names and scratchy logos in the glass cases, flags for new, unexplored auditory empires. It was thrilling to hang out in Chicago and come back alive—of course, never having been in any real danger. There were also momentary lapses of the status quo on regular TV, as teenage Rick discovered. There, safe at home in your pajamas, you'd see the Clash performing on Tom Snyder's show in 1981, Fear on *Saturday Night Live*, or Devo or the Jam, just a couple of weeks after Jefferson Starship and Jimmy Buffet, who occupied the very same screen, and you'd think, as Rick did, "What the hell did I just see?"

CHAPTER 2

The Scene at College

People Hanging Around Outside Talking

The Big Black show was the first of many shows I would see in college. As thrilling as it was to stand a couple of feet away from rock stars and fireworks, I enjoyed even more the hanging around outside, talking. Growing up, I'd normally avoided playground crowds, but here in the tiny parking lot surrounded by giant trees in the middle of campus, I felt safe. A secret community, borne of older kids, even grad students (teaching assistants!), where shared show experiences and lyrics made it easier to converse, to discuss social issues, politics, and learn about the world around us. Later I would learn from UIUC researchers the importance of learning outside, and how greenspace and the architecture of this landscape affects everything from our health to how we communicate.

One warm night, I stood outside a venue named House of Chin, listening to people talking about other bands who'd come through town. "Did you see Tad? Yeah! It was amazing! He was *so* big!" (nothing about the music). "Didjits got banned from Mabel's again last week!" Then someone asked me, "Did you see 13 Nightmares?" I'd missed that show, and was treated to a rundown of the night, including a description of a bass player from Lincoln,

Nebraska, who rocked more, jumped higher, played faster, sang louder and sweeter than any other bass player imaginable and, also, she was a woman! I knew at some point I'd get to meet Heidi Ore, but for now, I had this notion of a force of nature, a woman who could inspire awe and admiration in the context of punk rock, and that made me decide that it was important for me to do the same.

Heidi Ore, of Mercy Rule. Taken on April 4, 1995, at the Bottom of the Hill in San Francisco. Photograph by Peter Ellenby.

The Quaker

Tuesday was the day that new records were released. We would pilgrimage from the Engineering Campus down Green Street where a stretch of black sidewalk sparkled in the daylight and stank of beer. Through a windowed door covered with fliers, up the staircase to the second floor, we'd enter Record Swap. There we'd find The Quaker, a legendary figure in the Champaign rock scene. Six-foot-tall with waist-long black hair flowing down the sides of his head, he'd be standing at the counter, playing "fetch the paper wad" with Fazer and Marley, when they weren't asleep atop the record bins. All good record stores have cats. Jared, the owner of Waiting Room Records in Normal, Illinois, says that a cat makes you feel comfortable in a record store, where you might feel intimidated being surrounded by a world of obscure records, knowable only by the extent of your research efforts.

If you hung out and petted the cats, you'd learn a lot. The Quaker and his good friend Bob Diener, the owner of Record Swap, took turns playing records in the store. Bob would play reggae (his preference) and then The Quaker would play noise or punk. He remembers, "Once, I put on the new Einsterzende Neubauten album while [Bob] was standing at the back of the store under the speakers. After a few minutes, he stomped up to the stereo, ripped off the LP (literally) and put a reggae album on. Never said a word!"

The Quaker is a gentle man with a great sense of humor who shaped the Champaign scene through handwritten dots. Each Tuesday there'd be a garden crop of twenty or thirty newly released, brightly colored twelve-inch records to pick off the wall. Names and sounds of bands were not always obvious from their cover art, and from Vaughan Oliver's 4AD covers to the artwork of Peter Saville, every record cover was gorgeous, so you might not know which album you wanted to buy. That is where the dots came in. For each new release, The Quaker would place a vertical line of four or five sticky fluorescent dots along the side of the plastic sleeve, and he'd write in cursive, "Dark, driving, post-punk reminiscent of Hüsker Dü" or something like that. If he had more to write, there would be more dots. One day I walked into the store and there was a blue album with scraggly orange writing on it that said, "Volcano Suns," and double dots going vertically down the album sleeve; in fact, sometimes The Quaker would run out of room and have to do two columns of writing. If I saw lots of dots, I'd pay attention. And if I saw those particular words—"dark, driving," etc.—on an album, I would grab it immediately. That was the sound I liked.

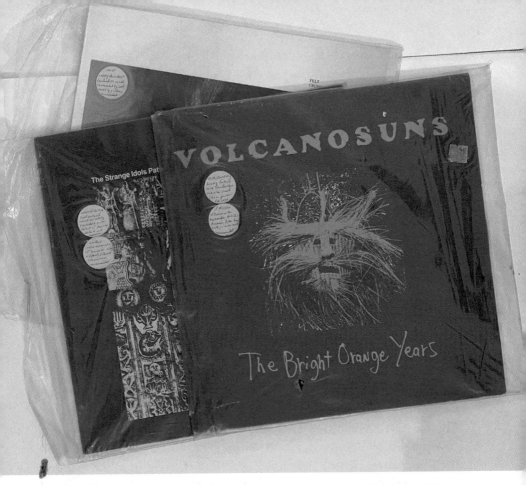

Record reviews on sticky dots by The Quaker. Albums by Volcano Suns and Felt. Photograph by Gram Valentin.

Scene Bands Who Had Already Made It

I had also grabbed a record with a photo of three lovely gentlemen dressed in button-up shirts and cardigans on the cover, with a seemingly incongruous title in stampy blood-red letters, *Holding the Grenade Too Long,* by the Outnumbered, on Homestead Records, one of the top indie labels at the time. This record was very special to me because the Outnumbered were from Champaign, and they'd been on tour and MTV! Somehow this record had started out here and made it all the way to the Dutch East India Trading Company, Homestead's distributor, a name that sounded exotic and worldly to me. In my hands, the record required extra reverence. I remember looking at the friendly faces on the cover—they just looked like normal guys—and marveling that someone across the world could be holding this same printed cover right now, looking at these same friendly faces—but that I could also run into them at the food store! I loved the jangly-pop juxtaposed with dangerous words. And I had come across Paul Budin and John Ginoli (who later founded the pioneering Queerpunk band Pansy Division) and the others in Champaign and they were always very sweet.

There were other predecessors in the scene. A couple of years before this, the Last Gentlemen had a hit single "One Possession" in 1984, and records out on indies and Zoo Entertainment. The Elvis Brothers and the Vertebrats were local favorites. Before this, Screams had gone to the UK and been stranded by their major record label, and before that, REO Speedwagon had left one of their members alone in a cornfield and driven off, to greater fame and fortune.

Hypotenuse Save My Ass

In the late 1980s, Champaign–Urbana had a good number of local venues. One of the most easily accessible was House of Chin, in the middle of Campustown, nestled between normal-people bars. The first floor housed a Chinese restaurant where I'd never eaten, and the second had fancy, shared cocktails (Volcanos), which I'd never drunk. The third floor was a tiny room, the size of three couches, or enough room to stand around the Flaming Lips' drumkit and not step on the Christmas lights on the floor, admire their mirrored ball hanging off the drum stand, shooting stars within reach because it's indie rock, and marvel at how loud a noise can sound inside a square room, a noise that can make you see fuzz.

George Chin, who owned House of Chin, had a famous saying: "Money talk, bullshit walk," though younger, unknown bands had a better chance of playing there than other, larger (100–300-seat) venues like Trito's, Treno's, and Mabel's. Of the many folkloric tales about George Chin in Champaign, there is one that sums up everything I love about the Champaign–Urbana music scene. It goes like this: George Chin was getting noise complaints from a local church, which took him to court citing an ordinance that put the venue too close to the church. Chin brought a mathematician to court with him who argued that Chin's music venue was on the third floor of the building, and then showed the calculation of distance between that room and the church, a descending diagonal line to the street. Chin won the case,

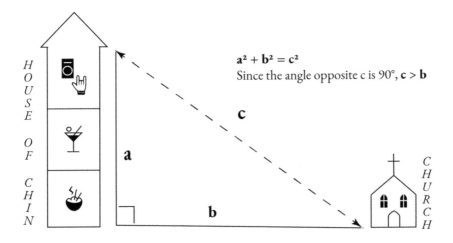

$$a^2 + b^2 = c^2$$

Since the angle opposite c is 90°, $c > b$

Hypotenuse Save My Ass.

and upon exit of the court, his quote to the local media was "Hypotenuse save my ass."

Saturday, October 18, 1997, Princeton University, NJ

SALARYMAN OPENS FOR POSTER CHILDREN IN PRINCETON

Well, so we're playing Princeton again, at a dining club. It's like a frat, but it's a bit different. I didn't really inquire into how one gets accepted into the club; I want to believe you just apply and are accepted. This particular club is pretty far out there; there were punker students sitting in the cafeteria. Peter the promoter told us there was a naked guy yesterday. He just walked around the hall naked all day. No one cared, Peter said.

This place is historically hard for us to play, because the show is free, we get paid a lot of money, but no one ever shows up. The amount we're paid is usually inversely proportional to how many people show up, and how much fun a show is to play. Tonight was really different, however, because a bunch of students from Pennsylvania, our friends (the brilliant kids!) drove up to Princeton. Timmy Bowers even drove up from Washington, DC! So there was a nice crowd there to watch us play our guts out, Salaryman opening for Poster Children!!

We had a pretty intense discussion about being driven, as students. The students at Princeton are those kids who are still driven, even after high school. I never made it past my junior year of high school. I cracked during that year, and I attribute it to a Satanic English teacher. Rick had the same experience too; I guess he ran into a bad teacher somewhere in his high school career. It's a wonder that anyone makes it intact through high school. What stopped us both up was realizing how much a person's grades depend upon the whim of a high school teacher. Rick talks a lot about being stamped as a young child, you're either stamped "Gifted" or "Normal" or "Troublesome" and you turn out the way you are stamped, because the teachers treat the "Gifted" students better than they treat the rest.

I don't mean to say that we dropped out of high school. We just sort of stopped driving ourselves so hard.

CHAPTER 3

Punk Bands in Dorms

"Looks like it's University of Illinois," shrugged Tom Cruise, high above us on a screen, and a hundred Gen-X freshmen yelled out a whoop of delight in unison. If you graduated from a suburban Chicago high school and didn't make it into Harvard or MIT, you went to U of I, as documented in the movie *Risky Business*, released the exact month that I left for college. That wasn't so bad. At this time, the University of Illinois was one of the top engineering schools in the United States. On my first night at Allen Hall, scared, lonely, but sitting butt-to-butt with all the other freshmen who also "weren't ivy-league material," on the tennis court outside the dorm amid giant bowls of ice cream, I knew I was home.

Allen Hall was known as the dorm for "creative" people at that time, since it had extra-hippie classes and a pottery studio in the basement, but when I first arrived with my boxes in fall 1983, the foyer looked to me like a 1970s old folks' home: beige, linoleum floor, mailboxes, a TV set, and couches, complete with people wandering around aimlessly, incoherent—grown-up children living inside a giant institutional equivalent of khaki pants. Engineering students played Dungeons & Dragons, downed liter-sized wax-paper cartons of Coke through giant straws from the "Junk Food Jungle" in the basement, listened to the Police on WPGU-FM, and did their homework and drugs in the communal, brown tweed living areas. On the way from the main-floor PLATO computer lounge to the Junk Food Jungle to the basement music practice room, the predecessor to Poster Children formed.

You Needed Another Person

In the 1980s, most people had tiny TV sets in their rooms and some fortunate ones had VCRs. Music came on a mix of CDs and albums. The cafeteria was a great big warehouse full of tables and students, and since there were no personal mobile devices to stare at, you'd be forced to navigate and talk to people who were around you all the time; there was no escape from the faces. Bands would start this way. And there were hardly any consumer-grade automated music-making machines. To get coherent sound, you needed another person.

Rick arrived at Allen Hall in 1984, as a mechanical engineering major, with a black Squire Stratocaster. "I was writing indie-rock Hüsker-Dü-y stuff, social commentary. People would go to college with a guitar, and if somebody brought a guitar to college, they probably wanted to play music. The advantage of a dorm is you're getting a concentration of eighteen-to-twenty-year-olds, and you're going to find people who like the same music as you and it's obvious if someone's playing guitar in their room, they like music. You don't have to go looking for people; it's like a shopping mall for collaborators." I'd spent the year before he arrived learning Taekwondo, playing violin in the University of Illinois Orchestra, knitting Dr. Who scarves, and hiding from my bullies. The story of how we finally started going out involves a fight with my former boyfriend, who lived in the room next door, leaving Rick with crushed vertebrae. I would love to think they were fighting over me, but I think Rick would say they were fighting over a principle.

In a WCIA (local TV station) interview outside the Red Lion in Champaign, March 1977, kids described the new rock as "young, fast, and scientific" (referencing another NYC band, the Dictators), and also, "what rock 'n' roll is supposed to be, it's fun!"[1] It would make sense that students were looking for a reprieve from the stresses of college, because when I was there, UIUC was an assemblage of students who'd gotten As their whole lives without studying, all suddenly experiencing Cs, Ds, and lower for the first time. We'd all grown up before "grit," in a period when you were praised for being "smart." Nowadays, the *work* is praised, not the talent, because repeated affirmations of intelligence make kids believe that any ability they have was bestowed upon them by luck, and when challenged with something they cannot easily complete, they do not know how to work, nor do they think work will do any good. I remember having to learn to work in college. In my higher-level math classes (like real analysis, complex analysis, or game theory), it was not uncommon for the curve to yield As at 30 percent and above. I remember one test where a 13 percent was an A, and I was in single digits. So we needed a release. "Fun."

There were a couple of factions of punk-rock-playing bands in the dorms, most notably badflannel, whose members also included engineering students, but from a different dorm. With similar roots, they began as a cover band at FAR (Florida Avenue Residence Hall), playing 1980s angry, "dark, driving" alternative indie music, with props like a fifty-five-gallon oil drum and a bullhorn. Gordon Pellegrinetti says,

> In school we may have been rebelling against the predictability of those people that spend all of their time just on their studies. Breaking down expectations and people's preconceived notions for what it meant to be successful, or even acceptable. There was something fun about showing up for class with the hair and the clothes and the attitude, and then killing it on the tests. . . . And still leaving plenty of time for the music, which was just us trying to play what we liked to listen to at the time . . . Flaming Lips, Einstürzende Neubauten, Butthole Surfers, Big Black, Union Carbide. All rolled together, except that we didn't know how to play at all, so we simplified things. Started with Led Zeppelin, but only the verses. Ramones. And Flipper.[2]

Badflannel's comedic antics onstage countered their intense UIUC engineering discipline. They'd spend until five p.m. for coursework and then would go down to the practice room where they had crammed their instruments and spent the rest of the evening "being idiots." "It was all performance art. Andy Kaufman goes to college," Gordon says. They had two drummers and Balthazar de Ley, their bass player, was the first person I ever saw with a toilet paper roll attached to his bass, although apparently that was a "thing" and had been done in other places, too.

Meanwhile, on the "creative" end of campus, Matt Golosinski of Hardcore Barbie says:

> My mom had bought me a Fender Precision bass from a priest while I was in high school. I dinked around on it at home trying to play along with the radio and Oingo Boingo etc., and by the time I got to Urbana I was eager to

connect with the local scene. My musical journey in Champaign–Urbana started with me putting up posters on campus looking for like-minded souls who wanted to create a band inspired by Roxy Music, Iggy Pop, the Police, Joe Jackson, Psychedelic Furs, P-Funk, and the Jam. I ended up getting called by REM nerds! Larry Thompson (later of Steakdaddy Six) and Darin Strack (later of Sixteen Tons). Great guys.

Rolf [Langsjoen] and I met in our first year there and lived as roommates at the Six Pack dorms. When we weren't blaring Def Leppard or defiling those marshmallow Easter Peeps by nailing them to our dorm door, he and I practiced in the "music room" (a ten-by-twelve blank space downstairs near the cafeteria). Rolf—who was and is a fantastic jazz player, born and raised in CU but now living for many years in Paris and Brussels—would bring either his trumpet or guitar down there. This would have been spring of 1985. Soon thereafter we started practicing at Larry Thompson's tiny two-bedroom apartment—kitty-corner from Tugrik House behind the Krannert Center for the Arts.

The band's name came about as Rolf and I were almost certainly stoned in the dorm talking about Klaus Barbie (the infamous Nazi) and rather childishly attaching that grim vibe to the poor ultra-popular Barbie doll. I suppose we thought we were making some parallel between the tyranny of the marketplace and authoritarianism. For all that, the band's sound wasn't really "hardcore," but somehow channeled VU and the Stooges through a kind of Jonathan Richman lens. That's probably why we ended up playing with Lonely Trailer, like, four times a month, including random house parties where someone would ask us a day or two before if we were available and interested in performing. We rarely said no, because we loved the scene, the people, the energy so much.[3]

Our good friend and roommate Andy Switzky, co-founder of the band Hum, remembers one distinct party where our generation's music scene coalesced, in spring 1987. badflannel, Tugrik Dhugugrik, and Gutter Poets, all from different sides of campus, played and everyone heard each other and realized there were musicians in town who were interested in more than just REM. A new community formed.

The Privileged Have an Obligation

There's an innate legitimacy to any punk band from a down-and-out LA suburb or bombed-out ex-factory town like Rockford, Illinois, but what right do angry engineers, English or biopsychology majors living in "posh" dorm rooms have to be commenting on society? As John Mohr from the great Chicago band Tar noted (its predecessor Blatant Dissent emerged in the eighties from the Grant North and Stevenson South dorms while Mohr was studying business at Northern Illinois University), "What right? I think it's an obligation, a responsibility." He adds, "I was the first person in my family to graduate from college, so the blue-collar concerns, ethos, and ethics are very much with me."[4]

Rick from Poster Children would write his political lyrics sometimes the day before recording, watching CNN on TV, getting angrier and angrier at the news and the current state of politics, the media, and any other injustice called to his attention. He'd inherited his ethics from a lineage of Chicago Democrats and especially his father, an engineer, who was "always interested in politics." Rick came to college listening to the Clash, Gang of Four, and Minutemen records. He says, "Just being able to make art is a luxury. Being a musician, you make a choice to be poor. Our society does not reward artists financially, so by default you're going to be sympathetic."

I feel a certain teaching component in the way that punk rock challenges people's expectations. It's the detournement of strict engineering discipline into raunchy, noisy rock music, this evolving into a fight for social justice. I also love the communication of ideas in nonstandard ways. Marda Kirn, founding director of EcoArts Connections, says, "Artists can scream, scientists can't"—in combining this quote with the work translating science into fictional narrative of another of my UIUC mentors, Richard Powers, I find direction in life.

A giant campus, UIUC is rich with opportunities. I entered thinking I'd chosen dentistry over law. In four years I wove a path from liberal arts to bioengineering, through math. I took fencing, logic, mythology, Japanese aesthetics, operating systems, and swimming. I studied the East Asian tea ceremony, code optimization, and landscape architecture. I met my future husband. Following him, I switched into the computer science major at UIUC. That same year, I bought my first bass.

CHAPTER 4

Computers

The campus police approached me as I was crossing the Boneyard Creek after my Computer Science 265 class, carrying my homework, a large metal cage bulging with wires and chip cards. I was stopped and questioned. Had I stolen this box? What was I going to do with it? At the time, I figured I was detained because I was dressed vaguely punk but, in retrospect, it was probably because I was a girl carrying a jumbled computer that looked a little like a bomb. After explaining with enough technical terms to bore the security guards, I was allowed on my way with my prized circuit-logic homework, relieved, and a bit indignant from the interaction. Just as the resistance of punk rock became available to me in college, so did the world of computers.

In my household, computers weren't for girls. Dad certainly wasn't a techie, and Mom hadn't yet discovered her inherent understanding of computers. I'd only touched a TRS-80 Model III computer at our high school, when my friend Mary showed me how to alter what was in the memory location that displayed the cursor, and from that point I was enraptured. Typing POKE 16419,196 would change (or detourn!) the common white three-by-two pixeled rectangle into a smiley-face. Putting 255 in that same location would yield a rocket ship.[1] Already a way to mess with the status quo! My other favorite thing to do with computers was to write 10 print

"Hello World"; 20 goto 10, which resulted in repeatedly scrolling the message of choice up the screen. In this way you could issue a seemingly infinite, uninterrupted proclamation, a virtual prayer flag,[2] or an automated swearing machine. So I already knew computers were powerful and could be easily controlled, but hadn't had the opportunity to explore them until I left for college. There in the entryway of my dorm, new digital opportunities awaited.

PLATO

The numbers are incomplete, but it is probable that people interacting with other people represented at least half of all PLATO usage. This is remarkable considering that the designers of PLATO never envisioned that communication between people would play more than an incidental role.[3]

In 1983, Allen Hall housed one of the few PLATO labs on campus, three murky-black touch screens with words glowing in jeweled orange, next to the Cyber terminal (2400 baud), which was connected to a mainframe that didn't allow you to save filenames with swear words in them (I tried). PLATO terminals were the only way students could access their online instruction (nobody had personal computers back then), but there were also networked games accessible through these terminals. There were plenty of rumors about students flunking out of school due to addiction to PLATO. The danger was real.

Interactive online course delivery was experimental at this time. While my Greek mythology class was taught by a man who dressed up as the Greek god Apollo on Fridays and predicted the football scores (not interactive), and my Chemistry 102B class was taught by a television set that was wheeled to the front of the 200-seat theater (also not interactive), the "electronic" section of Physics 106 was taught through PLATO terminals, and these were interactive. The lessons incorporated quizzes and there would be instant gratification if you touched the correct part of the screen. The framework also had a spectacular offshoot—a forum ("notesfile") where students could ask their teaching assistant (TA) questions—and this was fantastic, because you didn't need to be in the room with, or even working at the same time as your TA. You could ask the question anytime, and the TAs could answer it at their convenience. You'd find a present—the answer—waiting for you the next time you logged in. For the common folk, quick, text-based asynchronous communication was unheard-of at the time.

Now, this notesfile, ostensibly only there for physics question help, had to be "cleared out" constantly because the comment threads would veer off-topic into current events discussions, flame wars, or local cultural announcements. Students were beginning to learn to communicate with each other online, and instructors and authorities were becoming usurped. A community of student junior-programmers was employed to create the online courses (gods to me!), and they would come in at night and read all the requests and comments for new projects and fix them overnight. During the day, the professors and students would test the fixes and generate more requests. This asynchronous process begat an online community, as programmers explored new ways of leaving work communications for each other, and then discovered the other types of messages that would interest the community.

For me, PLATO yielded access to actual, globally networked games, instant and personal messaging, discussion forums, synchronous chat, and presence-awareness, allowing me to communicate with people around the world whom I'd never met and who couldn't see or judge my face, body, or voice. I spoke (not wrote)[4] to these people with my fingers, through term-talk, in short, snarky ten-word messages, displayed in orange, jeweled pixels. I left messages for them, read their jokes and rants, and critiqued their diatribes on public forums. I was addicted to this world, to the notesfiles, and already to the asynchronous and synchronous self-validation, to social networking in 1986, and to the digital repository where I learned about the different ways laughter and cynicism were expressed throughout the world.

Later on, this practice of instant DIY broadcasting enabled me to start writing the tour reports that are the basis for this book.

April 1995

ROTE FABRIK, ZURICH, SWITZERLAND— FIRST POSTER CHILDREN EUROPEAN TOUR

Switzerland has too much money and the people are too beautiful.

In Zurich, we played at Rote Fabrik, an amazing club that I know is good 'cuz Fugazi's gonna play there next month. This night I hated our show, though, and after it, I sat outside next to the lake on the dock and felt sorry for myself, almost crying. Here I am in one of the most beautiful places on earth, I think, and we can't even play a good show. As I lay on my back, listening to chimes off in the distance across the lake, staring at the sky, thinking about the stars, half-crying, I heard this weird shuffling noise and looked up and there was the biggest, fluffiest white swan I'd ever seen, floating down the lake, blue in the moonlight. Every so often you need a jolt to remind you that you're still alive. The swan looked like a merry-go-round seat. ML (our manager) says that it is spring and they are looking for mates.

In 2010, the Computer History Museum (CHM) in Mountain View, California, hosted a "PLATO @ 50" event. In session 6, titled "An Early Online Community: People Plus Computing Grows Communities,"[5] you can hear very soft-spoken programmers answering questions about how their notes-files and p-notes systems developed. Most important is that the community grew out of an asynchronous *topic-based*, not individual-based, communications. No one on PLATO had a personal profile page where they could boast about their background, their favorite TV shows, vacations, records, or books. If you were known as an individual (and some were, in fact, famous), it was because of your interactions, your critique or influence spread about in discussion forums. Your online presence existed not for your own benefit, but for that of the community, and the goal of the community was education.

Years later, as I watch the programmers in that video talk about their experiences, I am struck by how emphatic they are about community existing first for the *work* (*education*). Then the notesfiles were developed out of a need to communicate about how to fix problems, and lastly, the p (personal)-note system was developed for one-on-one communication. It's like a 1960s *Star Trek* episode, where the lesson is that the initial use for the invention was for the benefit of the community, not the individual. I realize now that Rick and I got our inspiration for our pioneering online communities, blog-writing, and podcasting from PLATO and its very community-minded programmers.

CHAPTER 5

Play Like a Man

Unbeknownst to me at the time, there were not a lot of women in computer science, possibly because I couldn't detect gender through textual, screen representations of people. Little by little, I had slight awakenings, irritations. There was only one women's restroom in the Electrical Engineering building, and it was in the far corner of the giant, three-story building, near the office, ostensibly for the secretaries, so if there was an intermission in a lecture, I'd have to run both ways to get back in time. I had a job writing database dumps on PLATO that I was most proud of, but my boss would rest his hand on my bare knee when I showed him my work, so, during the hot summer, I had to remember to wear pants during that job. These things were just daily inconveniences, reroutings that I never thought about again. I once went to the office hours of my chip design professor for help, early in the semester. As I introduced myself at his door, he didn't even offer me a seat. He looked at me straight in the eye, in 1985, and told me, "This class isn't good for women." I left and dropped the class. I figured he was probably right. A couple of days later, only then becoming aware, I looked around in another programming class and realized that I was one of three girls in a class of over one hundred students.

Rose and Rick at Poster Children concert at Johnny Brenda's, Philadelphia, October 1, 2016. Photograph by Scott Nichol.

Growing up, I'd been keenly unaware of my gender. Computer science wasn't the only mostly male space I'd occupied. I'd been doing martial arts for a while, having identified with the bullied male protagonist of *Karate Kid*, and, with wonderfully supportive instructors, had never noticed there were few women in the dojang. I'd also been playing role-playing games with groups of male friends. *Star Wars* was a big part of my life, and the character I'd most aligned with was Luke Skywalker, who, albeit not the most traditionally manliest of males, was still not female. Mr. Saavik, the female character in the movie *Star Trek II*, always gave me happy chills, because she was addressed as "Mister." Consolidating the separate titles of Miss, Ms., or Mrs., which essentially ended the separation of the female, felt appropriate to me.

Ignoring gender norms had always felt like achieving equality to me. I have vivid memories of practicing the piano when I was young, my dad proctoring the session. I usually fought with him, talking back until he'd reciprocate physically. I was learning Chopin, giant five-fingered chords too big for my hands, when Dad shouted, "Play like a man!" He could tell with his eyes closed, he said, if it was a woman playing the piano. This time I didn't argue with him. I separated my shoulder blades and rounded my back, diverting more strength into arms and fingers and played louder. I took up more space, giving myself more bandwidth for expression. I did not find this message insulting. It was the 1970s and I felt like my dad was telling me that women could be equal to men.

So I never considered my femininity when playing bass, and I'm really embarrassed about it. I was a couple of years too early and a bit too east to be a Riot Grrrl. I was also never mentioned in the *Women in Rock* zine issues. I forfeited my one opportunity to get on stage with Ian MacKaye and sing Fugazi's antirape anthem, "Suggestion," because I actually didn't know all the words.[1] The song didn't feel like my personal story, and I worried I wouldn't do it justice for my fellow women.[2] I even feel fraudulent for not singing or contributing lyrics to our band, as though I'm muting myself and setting women back.

Not proudly, I have chosen to ignore the many times when I've been helped or hindered by being female. One of our earliest reviews mentioned me as the "stalwart female bass player" and I had always hated that review. Though "stalwart" is a respectable word—I looked it up many times—it felt diminutive and unflattering, as though I was a loyal supporter and a ubiquitous female bass player, and also, it contains the word "wart." In my mind, gender is a construct, a fluid spectrum of traits, and pigeonholing some as female and others as male shortchanges the human experience.

I have support in my beliefs. In media, separate treatment of women in rock contributes to other systemic issues. In *Gender in the Music Industry*, Marion Leonard warns, "The exposé-style coverage often afforded to female rock performers tends to erase the history of women who have spent many years working in the music industry as practising musicians. The periodic articles on 'women in rock' in the music press present female performers as both notable and a topic for debate."[3] This, of course, is very disagreeable to me, as women have been playing and performing music for my whole life. Now, that there was an actual "presence" of female bass players in indie-rock bands in the nineties cannot be argued. In a study on women's "overrepresentation" on bass guitar, Mary Ann Clawson's interviews with pop-scene working musicians provide disconcerting reasons for the "ubiquity" of female bass players in nineties alternative rock. "It's an easier instrument to play; there are only 4 strings and you only have to play one note at a time. Men 'let' women play bass because it's the least desirable position in the band, no man really wants to just play one note over and over again," and—according to women in one study—bass is rhythmic and women are earthy.[4] Yes, we are tethered holistically to the world by our periods.

The male rock-critic narrative of the female bass player usually dramatizes the mythology of the star female avant-garde bass player (Tina Weymouth, Kim Gordon) descending from the heavens, leading future bass sisters to believe that we, too, can rock. My story is not a top-down anointing of bass princesses, it's a grassroots uprising where people happen upon interesting music, musical instruments, and a community of open-minded musicians, and create their own paths. I picked up a bass because the bass player in Rick's band kept quitting. I offered to fill in for as long as necessary. Yes, I hadn't played that particular instrument before, but I have perfect pitch, so the chords I hear translate to alphabet letters in my head, and I can just play the matching note. (Or decide not to). My sole purpose for buying a bass was to help out with the community and keep the music going.

Upon asking my fellow midwestern indie-rock bass sisters how they first started, I found similar stories. Barb Schilf (House of Large Sizes, Cedar Falls, Iowa), like me, first picked up a bass because Dave, the guitarist, needed a bass player in his band. Heidi Ore (Mercy Rule, Lincoln, Nebraska) was given a short-scale Fender bass and Peavey combo amplifier for Valentine's Day by her then boyfriend, now husband, Jon Taylor. She started 13 Nightmares with Jon and Gregg Cosgrove, and learned to play on the job.

Candice Belanoff (Walt Mink, Minneapolis, Minnesota) saw Joey Warronker and John Kimbrough playing a show without a bass player and was prodded by other scenesters into jamming with them. A classically trained pianist who began to find her way into drum-circles and world music ensembles at Macalester College, she had picked up bass because she wanted to play bass-heavy music. Commenting on gender, she relates that at an early age she found herself more drawn to male-gender social roles and trappings. "I liked everything that boys had—their expectation of assertiveness, their sports equipment, their Matchbox cars, and never, ever having to wear a dress or painful shoes. I wanted that kind of personal power—even though I was raised in the middle of second-wave feminism in NYC in the 70s and was told I could be any kind of woman." When she took up the bass, she did not want to be seen as a girl bass player. "I knew there were great woman players out there—but it was annoying to be told that I played 'pretty good for a girl.' I just wanted to be a great bass player. My parents were classical musicians, so I did not grow up hearing that Alicia de Larrocha was a 'pretty good pianist for a girl.' For fuck's sake. . . ."

I at first noticed a common thread here, that the women all joined bands to support the men, and worried that this belied an inherent female impulse, but almost all the musicians in the alternative bands were men (so anyone would be joining to support the men), and second, it's also common practice for men to join bands to help out. Part of me still feels like the support I endeavored to give was more of a caretaking role. I wanted the boys to be able to continue their band, so I would fill in while their bass player took a break.

It took a few years later for the self-actualization necessary to start an all-girls punk band in Champaign. Violinist and double-bassist Rachel Switzky was coerced into buying an electric bass by her older brother Andy. Rachel had begun playing double bass because of an obsession with Sting and the Police song "Every Breath You Take." She'd also been booking bands and running her own production company since high school, because "I was bored, and I knew one could do that." Already prepared in college with a bass and punk-rock experience, she'd been aware enough to find the UIUC scene male-dominated, and as a reaction, had co-formed the all-girl band Corndolly, "to get back at our boyfriends who had dumped us."

Regarding the "ubiquity" of female bass players in indie rock bands—in my experience, the bass player is the entry-level position in a band. It is the seat most likely to be vacated due to some aspiring musician whose ego requires more strings. Bass players are a necessity, second guitarists aren't. Something Mike Watt (bass player from the Minutemen/Firehose) once said to me echoes in my head. "The bass player is the least important member of the band. Lowest man on the totem-pole," he said. Just gotta keep the band together. That was the only meaningful encounter I ever really had with him.

Candice Belanoff. Photograph by Chris Butler.

Afterward, I decided he must have a weird sense of humor. But perhaps he's just bragging about the humility required to play indie-rock bass.

Barb mentions that it was seeing both male and female bass players in punk/alternative bands that made her think, "I could do that." Heidi says, "While I was out touring I certainly noticed when there was a girl in the band—you could go a week without seeing one. That's why it was important to play—it certainly was a permission. That's not the only reason a person plays in a band, though."[5] So while we didn't pay close attention to our gender in our own playing, we did feel a responsibility to uphold our position and promote it across the land. "You can do this, too!" Heidi shouts from the stage. Permission granted.

The Doorbell

It's 1990. Chicago. Albini's house. Time to make a record. I stand with my finger hovering over Steve's doorbell, and I am allowing myself to acknowledge that I am, in fact, scared. The rest of the guys in the band have now backed away and are cowering behind me. I am a Girl Shield, I think, because no one would hit a girl. I'm the one who has to ring the doorbell. What if he swears at me, I ask? Do you think he'll be wearing his porkpie hat, I try to joke? I hope he'll be wearing his porkpie hat.

DING DONG. Steve opens the door, welcomes us with a friendly smile and a businesslike hello, and I make a nervous joke about how happy I am to see that he is wearing his hat. He explains to me that he has a ridge on his head, displays it, and tells us all the technical name for it: sagittal crest, and says that this, actually, is why he wears a hat. Rick tells me now that he is pretty sure that was a joke. I don't think it was. Steve doesn't joke about science.

We set up our instruments in Steve's basement, and he has to run back and forth and up the stairs to push record. He is overly accommodating, extremely professional, and very to-the-point. When you record with him, you are to record your true sound; you record live, all at the same time, and raw energy and integrity are more important than any fancy overdubs you think you should put in your song.

I actually hate recording, and Steve makes it palatable for me. On tape, you can't see me jump, pound my fist into my bass, smile or fall. In turn, I can't see you and feed off your energy. I also hate the idea that something is fixed on tape forever, a moment in time, a mistake, an unsolvable bug trapped in amber. Something that could have been more perfect. Now I know that someone can trap a perfect sound on tape, like the feedback on a Bitch Magnet album, but I don't know if we've ever done it. Perhaps we have, but I've never seriously relistened to any of our records to find it. That would feel decadent and vain, like Googling myself.

For Steve, the act of recording is an act of documentation. You play earnestly, your music, your sound, and he scribes it onto two-inch analog tape. No funny business. The first time we recorded with Steve, there was so much energy in the room. His persona and bands are so strong and we are so impressed with him that I don't think we wanted to come across as weak. Around Steve, Rick seemed to have more energy and more power in his vocals—and I always feel like fear is a part of it.

Steve has something called a Dietz cabinet, a wooden one-by-fifteen-foot cabinet that looks like it's been thrown around but is built like it's indestructible. There is a thick metal grating in front of the speaker. I feel like throwing a basketball at it just to see how it would bounce back. He sets it up for me to play my bass through. He suggests using his Traynor 100-watt tube amp, a type of amp that I seek out and buy used, the following month, for seventy-five dollars at Guitar Center, an amp I've used ever since. He puts two microphones in front of the speaker, one closer, and one farther away. My bass sound has both treble and bass in it. I like it to enunciate clearly.

Guitars are set up in another room; similarly, we tune, and then we blow through our songs. Afterward, Rick has to do vocals over his scratch vocals he'd recorded while we recorded the basic tracks. Quick, move on to the next song! Rick completes vocals on many songs in one take, with Steve's coercion. In fact, he sings through half of "Thinner, Stronger," a song we'd never performed live, and bungles the words, voice caught in a knot, then screams in frustration. "Good job, what's next?" shouts Steve. "He's not done with the song yet," I say politely, "he messed up the words and hasn't finished the last verse or chorus." "Sounds finished to me," Steve says. "Let's move on!" We have to implore him to restart the take from Rick's scream. We reasoned with Steve that Rick had gone to all the trouble to write the rest of the words to the song—and I actually had to show him the lyric sheet to prove it—so he should probably sing them onto the tape. "Thinner, Stronger" (which Bob our drummer at the time named after a condom) may have been a bit too much of a funk song for Steve.

In between playing sessions, there would be food and lecture-discussion. By the end of our session with him, Steve had taught us everything we'd ever need to know about the music industry, and almost everything I'd need to know to get started teaching music business as a professor.

Amazing things I have learned from Steve Albini, in order of importance:

- It doesn't matter what your recording contract states. You may have "complete control" but if your label refuses to honor it, you can say "We'll sue" but then you have to find and pay a lawyer. You must sue in New York or Los Angeles. This is prohibitively expensive for a band, and while you wait for your lawyer to sue, you're basically unable to make money. If you're waiting for a record to come out, you cannot play shows. People will get tired of your "oldies" and you don't want to wear out your new music before the release.

- Steve is an ENGINEER. He does not change your sound. He merely documents it. He does not like to be called a producer.
- The money that the record label is paying you will always come out of the money that you make from the records. That means if you get tour support for a bus, or, for instance, say the label (let's call it "Sire") has to pay another label (for example, "Twin/Tone") to buy out your contract, that is *your* money that Sire is using (let's say, $60,000) and it's recoupable from your records.
- Any "producer" who takes (percentage) points off an album is no longer a neutral party in the documentation of a band. The producer becomes invested creating an album that will sell more, because his or her payment is tied to sales of the album. For this reason, Steve will never take a percentage of an album's royalties.
- For your band photographs or your band videos, your record label may choose people *they* enjoy working with, and use *your* money to hire these people. There may be nothing special about these people; they are just "friends" of the label who would also like some of your money. Since it's not really the label's money, they have nothing to lose by just giving it away. In this way the label also is able to forge relationships with people for free.
- Stuffed animals may be blown up by creating a small hole in the middle with a knife and inserting firecrackers. Having a container full of old stuffed animals can yield an afternoon of entertainment at a July Fourth barbeque.
- The green stuff in the homemade salsa is called "cilantro." It looks like a little bush. You wash it and you can put it in salsa. It flavors many types of foods. (This was my introduction to cilantro, and I would go on to become a big fan after we recorded.)
- Do not use the shiny broken drumsticks in the barbeque firepit. They have lacquer on them, and that is poisonous. But you can soak the unshiny broken drumsticks in a bucket of water for a long time, and then you can put them in the barbeque, and your meat will be hickory-smoked because the drumsticks are made of hickory wood.
- Having good, expensive microphones is the key to recording. Steve has an amazing array of very expensive microphones. Once I was in

the microphone room at Electrical Audio and microphones were taken out and displayed to me as if I was in a Buddhist temple and the scrolls were being shown off, one by one. But to me, the prices were as impressive as the microphones.

- Studio A at Electrical Audio has a quadratic diffuser in the ceiling of the area behind the sound engineer position. This is because there would have been a flat area, due to an unavoidable change in ceiling height, and it would have caused sound reflections back to the listener. This would be bad. The diffuser takes away this problem. It is divided into cells, which can be thought of as one unit in a plot. Essentially it looks like a wooden sculpture broken up into depths that are relative to a power of the square root of 2. I get overly excited when people talk math. It was my first love. But this diffuser is art too, math, sound, art. When you look at it, you can see the parabola, and when you run your hand across it, you can both hear and feel the parabola.
- The Pixies did not have the beginnings and endings of the songs on / figured out before they recorded with him.
- A vagina can fart.[6]

PART TWO

1987–1992
Pre–Major Label Life

It was our first East Coast tour. We packed up a minivan and drove from Illinois to New York City and parked at the door of Woody's Bar in Manhattan. We arrived an hour early, even with the type of traffic I'd only ever seen on movie screens. I blasted open the door and sauntered triumphantly down Woody's stairs and, arms spread wide, announced loudly into the room, "Hello! We are Poster Children and we are playing here at this bar tonight!"

A lone bartender looked up from the counter he was wiping and replied, "So?" He went back to wiping his counter. I had assumed the proprietors of the establishment would be pleased we were so early, having driven for fourteen hours. I had expected them to at least inquire about our journey. Had we encountered any obstacles? What, as midwesterners, were our first impressions of their fine city? Were we hungry? New Yorkers don't give a shit about you and also, they've met midwesterners before. "Well, I, uh, was just wondering where we should load in," I quickly replied and readjusted my attitude. It was just like playing Dungeons & Dragons, and I was prepared.

CHAPTER 6

The Indie Code of Ethics

How did an unknown indie-rock band from Champaign, Illinois, get its first show in New York City, and at a bar co-owned by Ron Wood of the Rolling Stones? I attribute it to the kindness and support that embodied the Champaign punk and indie-rock scene during our time. When the band Thin White Rope, from Davis, California, was traveling through Champaign, April 19, 1988, and played at Mabel's, we had the opening slot. Apparently at that show, Thin White Rope loved us so much that they invited us to open for them in New York City. More accurately, Thin White Rope just had a really great time in our town. ML Compton, their manager (and our future manager) confirms this. "The Champaign show was packed and people were going crazy," even though they were thousands of miles from their home, with no UIUC indie-rock college radio station at the time and no internet to help spread the word. It was also their first time playing in Champaign. Perhaps it was The Quaker's dot-reviews on their albums at Record Swap that drew people to the show. But for us, the invitation to play with them in New York City was an incredibly generous move, something that happened a lot in indie-rock circles, and a tradition we carried on.

Maybe it seems precious to thank our local scene, but in my time there, it was lovely, and no one seemed arrogant. The local bands that we'd met were always very friendly. Maybe we were just really friendly to everyone. There also wasn't really much to fight over. In addition, we'd heard that the Chicago scene was very contentious and we wanted ours to be different. We made certain all projects we touched were equitable and generous to everyone.

Positive Punk

On January 17, 1989, another Mabel's show changed my life. The seminal punk-rock band 7 Seconds, from Reno, Nevada, was coming through town. Our fellow locals badflannel were slated to play first and we were supposed to play afterward, right before 7 Seconds, but badflannel were such huge 7 Seconds fans, they asked to have the middle slot. We agreed. We loved badflannel and wanted to show them off too.

At 9 p.m., Mabel's was a dark, cavernous, and very empty 300-capacity campus bar with a balcony on the far end and heavy-metal band promo photos all over dark-painted walls. We were already accustomed to playing our hardest and most energetic regardless of the audience, so it didn't really matter. This show, we'd just play for ourselves, enjoying our own energy and passion.

A couple of songs into our set, I happily noticed that a few people had materialized in front of the stage, and one guy was directly in front of me, shaking his long hair and dancing and pumping his fist, jumping up and down, smiling as we played. He had transcended the "Circle of Death"—our name for the empty moat that occurs when people are backed against the wall as you perform. Another similarly cool-looking guy was dancing in front of Rick. Who could these people be, I wondered? What an incredible feeling it is, to be playing one of your first shows on such a tall (waist-high!) stage and to be seeing people reacting in this way to your music! Later, I found out, these two people were Kevin Seconds and Steve Youth, of the headlining band, dancing and smiling and supporting the first band on the bill. I vowed to forever carry that energy forward.

What You Already Have

The Indie Code of Ethics reads like a handbook on the midwestern work ethic—"an unwaveringly pragmatic and dogmatic belief that hard work and perseverance rooted in quiet humility pays off in the long run."[1] In indie rock, you helped others out, did things yourself, were (mostly) humble, and questioned everything.

The rulebook is widespread and existed long before the internet, transmitted by word of mouth, record, and zine, between touring bands, their labels, talent buyers, booking agents, recording engineers, and audiences. We learned proper behavior (like, even though you were invited to stay on at Lollapalooza for one more day, you had to honor the show you had already booked in Tennessee, which would be empty) from our booking agent. If you didn't uphold the code of ethics, people knew about it; booking agents wouldn't book at your club; people would boycott your shows.

The underground scene, with entities such as Dischord Records, Touch & Go Records, and Electrical Audio among many others, placed a high emphasis on being fair and conscientious. The driving force behind these indie labels and studios was not money, but community. Greed was already on the wane as a style, and possibly a reaction to the hippie-turned-sociopath Baby Boomers and their legacy.[2] Indie ethics now focused on self-sufficiency, frugality, and strength for sustenance. In an interview found not in *Maximum Rock and Roll* or *Punk Planet* but in *Psychology Today* about punk rock ethics in business, Steve Albini is quoted, "You deal with what you actually have, and not some aspiration for what you might someday have, and not some expectation of what someday you will be given or earn."[3] Comprised of outsiders, indie communities strove to be inclusive. Steve says inclusivity and helping others are simply survival skills. "It had to be inclusive, because there weren't enough people that you could afford to exclude anybody."[4]

Ian MacKaye

So I was going to get to meet the great Ian MacKaye, or at least, be in the same room as him. We were opening for Fugazi, in Champaign, June 6, 1991, at Latzer Hall YMCA, the same room where I got my brown belt in Taekwondo.

MacKaye co-founded Dischord Records in Washington, DC, for only DC-area bands. He set up shows without using booking agents, insisting on a low cover charge. He made sure the shows were all-ages accessible, which led him to search out unconventional venues.

In maybe his biggest influence on my own life, he questioned why the rock lifestyle necessitated drinking alcohol. He wrote songs about this that resonated for people like me, making it safe for people to not drink at shows (and beyond). As I am someone who always wants to be present and experience everything life has to offer, it made perfect sense, and felt wonderful to know I had company. For me, Ian is like a god, and every encounter with him is rich, thought-provoking, and meaningful.

Fugazi shows are intense, because even if the band wants to be solely about its music, it never is. Everyone wants to join in on the conversation. At this show, there were skinheads from Peoria who were angry that Fugazi had sold out. (Ian's previous band Minor Threat had allowed slamdancing, but at this point, Fugazi was more interested in their audience's safety, thus "selling out.") After the show, someone stole one of Fugazi's monitors. People were milling around outside in the parking lot, while Bob, our goofy drummer at the time, was panhandling. I remember we were trying to explain to Ian why Bob was panhandling. Amid all this, they were all still so nice to us. Then they put on a show that blew my mind. Such rhythms, such intensity. I could stand up close and not get hurt. I hoped to be able to see them and talk to them again. This is all I remember from that night. I have now had thirty years of intense, sporadic conversations with Ian MacKaye, but I do not remember our first meeting. In fact I don't remember ever not knowing Ian MacKaye.

Gratitude

I spend a lot of time thinking about gratitude, something I picked up practicing martial arts, tea ceremony, and Buddhism. In tea rituals, especially, the entire practice revolves around generosity and gratitude and attention to your environment. Research on happiness states that gratitude enhances one's life.[5] Though positive punk and indie rock ethics embrace social awareness, one can also act "inherently good" as a practice for one's own being, even when there isn't anyone else around. As a martial artist, I practice alone in order to be able to perform skillfully when I am engaged with others. There is also about a zero percent chance that I will ever be in an actual fight with someone—and in that case, every lineage I belong to instructs me to run to avoid conflict—yet I've practiced for more than three decades the precise arc, acceleration, and placement of my body parts. In Buddhism, karma works the same way. It is energy you put out into the system. You are not necessarily going to see the outcome of all your work, but your practice is conditioning your heart. And even in minuscule amounts, I believe good work spreads.

THREE SWANS AT 90 MPH

Jim notes that people who live in the mountains and hills just don't take advantage of the beauty of their surroundings. He points to various shacks situated in the hills along the road; they have a house in the midst of all this beauty and they will usually have about fifteen old rusted cars and car parts and other pieces of junk laying out in their front yard. I always thought that was part of the beauty of these areas, that the junk is part of the charm, that the land is so beautiful that it overpowers the rusted riding mowers and old Quonset hut pieces fenced in with the rest of the garbage. But it's neat to hear an unsolicited opinion from Jim about something like this, because he's usually just so laid back and quiet.

We've been here in Missoula so many times, once home of Steve Albini and David Lynch. I still feel like it's so surreal to be in a town, to know a couple of parts of a town so well, a town so far from home. To stand on a bridge outside a restaurant we've been to before, and be recognized. I love that feeling. I love the mountains, and I wish I had taken a picture of the student union here, because it's a huge building with trees growing inside it. It's gorgeous. You can climb the big yellow mountain with the big "M" on it just outside the union—our promoter tells us that in the summer, people climb the zigzag path up the mountain wearing white shirts and it looks like some sort of religious procession.

Thursday, May 13, 1997, Boise, ID

IDAHO REST AREA

What is it about Idaho that makes the sunset turn the land gold? I think that my favorite mountains are the yellow grassy foothills in the middle of Idaho. I'll bet I'm the only person on earth who feels that way. They are so odd, distinct, sparse, and uniform! This area contains my most favorite drive of all, a drive that no one in the van could be persuaded to take today. In fact, many people asked us last night how we were going to get to Boise from Missoula, and when I asked them about the smaller roads, they all shook their heads and said, ominously, "I'd stay on the interstate for as LONG AS YOU CAN."

So, no cutting through Idaho for us today, like I did last time. No Arco, the First City of Atomic Power, and no "Craters of the National Moon" monument, and no West Yellowstone blizzard, and no driving straight up to a big yellow grassy mountain and then, at the last second, the road cutting around it, onward through more yellow grasslands. No "Do Not Go Down This Road—SINKHOLES" signs and no "Road Closed—US Government Chemical Station" signs. Someone will stay up to make sure I don't take a short cut.

The interstate-west sweeps dumbly in an anticlockwise curve around the bottom of Idaho, steering us far away from the mysterious forest center of Idaho and the "Frank Church River of No Return Wilderness Area" (that's what it says on our map). So instead, following the interstate, we got lots and lots of cows, sheep, farmland, Taco Muertes, and McDonald's. We did hit one blizzard on a mountain pass, and we saw an exotic Kentucky Fried Chicken/Casino Gas Station. There was one or two miles that had a preview of "Craters of the Moon" National Monument—all of a sudden for no apparent reason, the brown shrub desert on either side of the road turns into huge volcanic black rocks—then goes back to grasslands. The farmlands near the end of the day all were being irrigated, hundreds of rotating sprinklers spraying silver water on a bright green field set in the golden mountains. At one point, above the sprinklers I noticed a huge TA gas station sign, off in the distance, and underneath the sprinklers and sign, three white swans on the green lawn, which we drove by at ninety miles an hour.

Walking in Champaign

I stayed an extra semester at UIUC and graduated with an extra undergraduate degree in computer science (this time from the Engineering College), because I really didn't want to leave Champaign. I was also terrified to look for a computer programming job, for a really weird reason—I had never actually turned *on* a computer. All the computers we used in our classes were terminals connected to a mainframe. UIUC was a big place. I'd spent four years coding search algorithms and operating systems, calculating optimizations, and circumventing the "computer classes that were bad for women," and somehow, through it all, had never actually seen a power switch. And I was legitimately scared that at a job interview, I'd be put in a room with a computer that hadn't been turned on. So I got a job at Espresso Royale, a coffee shop, even though I'd never drunk coffee. I really wanted to prove to myself that I didn't need much money to live in Champaign, and I wanted to see how far this band "thing" would go.

At that time, I was learning about the Walkable City, something I'd become more aware of as we toured. Champaign-Urbana seemed like another planet from my hometown. Continuing its manufacture of shopping malls and sports fans, Deerfield, Illinois, was also still constructing large, "convenient" car parking lots in front of its public gathering areas, thus rendering them useless as far as community goes. Joel Garreau's *Edge City: Life on the New Frontier*, one of the favorite Poster Children van-study books, came out September 1, 1992, but in practice, I already knew I wanted to live where I could coffee-shop-hop, and where there were museums next to bookstores next to music venues, and where anytime you'd run into someone (walking, on the sidewalk) you could converse about their research, instead of the latest sportsball scores. I'd learned from roommate Andy Switzky that in strolling through Champaign, campus, and Urbana, you'd run into another person you knew every couple of minutes, and this would yield spontaneous and sublime conversations (like in the movie *Slacker*). Later I learned this was *dérive*, the act of drifting, a game Situationists played, slow-motion parkour, but here, traversing community as environment, people as edifices, with knowledge and research gained from movement. Punks in this scene valued learning and books. I couldn't go back home.

Sunday, May 16, 1999

PORTLAND, OR–EUGENE OR

Today we did laundry and then walked around the Powell's (Burnside Street) area of Portland. Powell's is a block-long bookstore that features used books next to the new ones on the shelves; you can find a new copy of Don DeLillo's *Underworld* right next to a used one, for half the price! It's always been an amazing place in Portland, and a hangout for freaks. Howie says the freaks in Portland are a bit sloppier than the freaks in Seattle; the Seattle freaks look much more stylish and kept up.

I walked around in Powell's for a while and then decided I wasn't going to buy anything; it's cheaper to take books out of the library. So I went outside and walked around for a bit. The street is full of punks. I went into a couple of used clothing stores, full of way-too-expensive used clothes; then went into a couple more hip bookstores. Everyone around this area looks like they're ready to appear on a talk show as a Punk Rocker Rebel. I finally started getting so sick of the hipness, I had to walk out of a couple of stores. I took one look at a guy behind a counter listening to a band that kind of sounded like Sonic Youth, wearing sunglasses inside, and I had to walk out of the store. I swore that the next guy that came walking past me with metal in his face and a black t-shirt on with some sort of punk band that played their last show before he was born, I was going to punch. I kept going, "Ok, not this guy; I'll punch the next guy." But they just kept coming!

Later, we saw *Election*, with Reese Witherspoon. This is a good movie. It's about a teacher (Matthew Broderick) who tries to hold back an overachieving little girl, and it's really funny. The whole movie is really a commentary on how teachers' ineptness and hypocriticism conspire to keep any kind of independent sparks of creativity under control in a school. I've read reviews that extend the metaphor to politics, and life in general. Rick was beside himself—he had a good day today. He is like a kid in a candy store when he knows he's going to see a movie. That, and he found a bunch of Nixon and spy books at Powell's. One of the books is called *Nixon* but he's got it laying upside down all the time, so it looks like "Noxin" whenever I see it. *(Note: three days later, Rick spent the entire time we waited in line for the premiere of* The Phantom Menace, *in a small Nevada town, reading his Nixon book.)*

Wednesday, May 26, 1999
AUSTIN, TX, BUT FIRST, DALLAS

We drove through Dallas and had some time, and Howie's reading the Don DeLillo book about the Kennedy assassination, so we stopped at the Grassy Knoll, and went up into the Book Depository, where Lee Harvey Oswald "allegedly" shot JFK. The Grassy Knoll is pretty small; it's just a little area between where a lot of cars drive. Its name definitely sounds a lot more majestic than it actually appears.

On the sixth floor of the Texas Book Depository, there is a museum. You have to pay six dollars to get in, and you have to check your camera—they allow *no* pictures whatsoever, due to copyright laws, they say. We thought it was probably a really cheesy museum, but when you walk into the main floor and look at the panels they have up, it sort of lets you know that it's gonna be higher class than what you were thinking. [A long description of the museum follows; see my online tour reports for more].

Walking around on the sixth floor was the closest I'd ever felt to history. Even though JFK wasn't *my* president, I still felt some reverence, and being in a place like this where an event that made such a huge impact on society happened was probably the closest I've ever felt to being in a church. If you look out the windows on the sixth floor, at the road below, you can see a painted white X in the middle of one of the lanes. That X marks the spot where Kennedy was shot.

And, actually, the most intense thing I saw in the whole museum was a child's drawing; they had a couple up on the wall. This one was black and white I think, and depicted a plane with the stairway extended down. At the bottom of the stairway were stick figures of Jackie Kennedy holding the children, all looking very sad. On the way up the staircase was a flushed-looking JFK, sort of smiling, and at the top of the plane's staircase, extending his hand, was what looked like Abraham Lincoln, helping JFK up the staircase. At least it was either Abraham Lincoln, or maybe it was God, with a black beard. I wish I could see that picture again, or at least have a copy of it.

As you leave the museum, outside, stuck to the wall, is a bottle of Coke. (If you remember, Oswald stopped in the second-floor cafeteria after he allegedly shot Kennedy, to buy a Coke.)

Friday, July 25, 1997
VAN FUN, DRIVING TO DAYTON

We're sitting in the van making fun of Howie for reading Nietzsche. "You're reading NIETZSCHE?" I yell. Rick from the back of the van, "OH GOD." "YOU POSER!" I yell (standard Poster Children acknowledgment to anyone in the band who is doing something blatantly highbrow). "Hey shut up," Howie whines. "This stuff would do you some good," sarcastically. "Maybe I will loan it to you after I'm done. Yes, in fact, I will loan it to you when I'm done." Rick, laying in the back of the van reading the newest Amtrak National Timetable pamphlet, "Nites-Chee (intentionally mispronouncing it)—what was that book? 'I AM GOD?' Something like that? I AM THE CENTER OF THE UNIVERSE? He was one of those misunderstood Germans, wasn't he? Like Hitler."

1987: Champaign Lore, Econo, and a Place in the Canon

By 1987 we had stopped changing our band name, had moved out of our dorm rooms and into local band houses, and sat around bragging about how cheap it was to live in Champaign because there was nothing to do, and therefore, nothing to pay for. Rick and I lived and practiced in Urbana, in the Tugrik Dhugugrik house (now a parking lot across from Spurlock Museum of World Cultures), down a couple of streets from the Ten Shitty Guys house (now a Korean and European coffee shop), where the Bowery Boys lived, with future Champaign mayor Don Gerard. In Champaign, there was Rock City, which housed the Didjits, and the ¡Ack Ack! Hotel, which housed ¡Ack Ack! From the Honorable Don Gerard, drummer of the Bowery Boys:

> Ten Shitty Guys originated at 1102 West Nevada (although, it looked a *lot* more like 1313 Mockingbird Lane). Our landlord was Fred Krauss and Viktor Krauss told me as kids he and Alison Krauss would ask to drive by "that crazy guy" house if they were out to dinner or whatever. We then moved briefly to 1008 West Nevada and finally to the dump (still standing) on Springfield Avenue. There were skateboard ramps at all locations.

After band practice, we'd go see shows. During this time, small, independent bands crossed the country in vans, played on campuses on weeknights to Monday crowds of thirty, Thursday crowds of fifty, and we got to see them. I fantasized, listening to the hypnotic, repeated riff of the Minutemen's *Tour Spiel* (1984) of following that path, stopping at all the towns, standing on the different stages across the country, but on our own terms, making our own decisions, small, "econo." We never had the big, commercial dreams. We just wanted longevity and to tour.

SST, Homestead Records, Touch & Go, Twin/Tone, Amphetamine Reptile, and Dischord logos festooned the backs of our vinyl record covers. These were the most well-known independent record labels for midwesterners. I learned that each label had a personality. SST was for famous, harder-edged bands; Homestead was for famous, jangly, poppier bands. Touch & Go and Quarterstick were for my tough-guy Chicago heroes. One day, we thought, if we were good enough, we'd be on an independent label, and people who followed those curators would find out about us. We'd have a place in the canon.

Local Bands

"I'eeeem sayyy-leeeeng ahh-waaaaayyyyyyy, set an open course, for the virgin seeeeaaaa" crooned Rick Didjit, loudly into the starry night. It was after Bandjam, an outside festival on the Quad, and I was in an entourage, walking through the scary, frat part of campus, where I'd once been ridiculed for wearing my Dr. Who scarf. Around his neck tonight, Rick Didjit had worn a feather boa. I had always marveled at his confidence, his lyrics, stage presence, and guitar playing, but at this point, I marveled at his voice. It was a perfect imitation of Dennis DeYoung, and more of the crystal-clear, deftly handled irony he'd had mastered, singing the antithesis of the punk rock he'd just performed on the Quad. Poster Children had also played, but I'd seen my personal dorm bully from the stage, and though I was on a stage with my cool punk rock bass, he'd still yelled "Geek" at me. I'd felt the terrible sting and onstage there was nowhere to hide. But now, I was part of the musicians and fans following the Didjits to an afterparty at Rock City, and Rick turned back and was smiling at all of us, and I was safely protected by punk rock and irony. ". . . To caaaaarrrryyyyy on. . . ."

By 1988, the Didjits had put out their second album, *Hey Judester*, on the great Chicago label Touch & Go Records. They played regularly in Champaign and were gods to us. Their stage show was amazing. Rick Didjit would strut onto the stage wearing a feather boa and circular mirrored sunglasses, holding his swear finger up high, like a cross, saluting an already overexcited audience. He'd chide loudly into the mic, "Hello Cleveland!" or "Who's ready to get high?" or some other sarcastic one-liner, "all credit to the disgusting right-wing dick Ted Nugent," he reports. "Oh yeah, I would purposely say the wrong town. People were so sensitive about that! I would also say the Ted Nugent line from the stage (trigger warning), 'the Champaign pussy is looking good tonight!'" Didjits songs were incredible, tight, classic rock mixing Jerry Lee Lewis with AC/DC, with hooks and wonderous guitar solos. Steve Albini spoke approvingly of their honest, base lyrics, songs about cars and girls and cars. It was the best rock 'n' roll you've ever experienced, and it was ours, it was Champaign's, even if they said they were from Mattoon.[6]

The first time I ever met Rick Didjit, I had gathered up all my nerve and gone up to him and announced, "Hello: Fuck you, Rick,"—from his crass stage presence, I figured that would be the proper way to greet him in person. He just looked at me and said, in a small, hurt voice, "Why are you swearing at me?" Messing with me. I realized then that there are stage personas and nonstage personas and both could be the "real" persona. I think Poster Children is similar in that we were very loud onstage and quiet afterward.

One evening, Rick Valentin and I decided to draw an ancestral tree of the bands in Champaign. We'd procured a three-foot-long scroll of paper and had begun setting down in mechanical pencil, around eight-point type, names of bands and their spinoffs. After filling up most of the sheet within an hour, we realized the task would be impossible and gave up, feeling proud of our scene. Just some other locally developing bands at the time were Lonely Trailer, Corndolly, Bowery Boys, badflannel, Hum, Mother/Menthol, Steakdaddy Six, Honcho Overload. Fliers from Mabel's, Trito's, and Chin's reflect the huge number of bands in the area.

Gurus

Who Booked the Venues

During the late 1980s, and onward, a number of people in Champaign were in charge of which bands played where. There were promoters who were trusted by local club owners to place bands in their clubs, and during our time, these people included Sasha Martens, who had booked Fugazi; Chris Corpora, who booked Trito's Uptown and Chin's; and Ward Gollings, who later booked the Blind Pig, Highdive, and Cowboy Monkey.

From our own time in the dorms, Chris Corpora became a promoter and our booking agent/manager. He got his start by "watching this high-school kid booking shows and learning from him," he says, speaking so reverently of late local legend Josh Gottheil that he wouldn't even use the name. Chris collected phone numbers from Rick Didjit and just started calling booking agents and bands and asking them to come down to Champaign and play.

Offering out-of-town bands shows gave local promoters the power of networking pre-internet. They had a collection of phone numbers and controlled who played where, and with whom. With their out-of-town connections, they could then book local bands outside of town, trading shows as favors. With this power came great responsibility, of course, because there was no way to know if a show would break even. Most larger bands wanted to play the bigger cities (like Chicago, three hours away) on weekends, so small-town promoters would likely have their chance for a show on a Sunday or Monday. The bigger traveling bands would also ask for guarantees, payments from $200 to $500 or more. Local openers who could draw audience became important in maintaining the scene.

Ward Gollings says, during these times, mailed press kits and demo cassette tapes were of utmost importance, the sole resumés of touring bands. Presenting a collection of positive reviews from certain writers or zines, signing to highly regarded labels, or being booked by a highly respected booking agency such as Go Ahead, Bug (Tom Windish), or Flower ensured your chances of Ward possibly listening to your cassette tape. Great reviews from respected zines like *Big Takeover* or *Flipside* were the equivalent of ten to twenty thousand "likes" on Facebook. Word-of-mouth was also big back then. An affirmation from a loose tie would make you consider checking out a band or artist.[7]

From the hard work of our local promoters, I landed a 1989 Nirvana press kit (from before they were famous)—eight single-sided black-and-white xeroxed pages held together by a staple in the corner. "It was kind of the standard Sub Pop kit," Ward recalls. "Tad's looked very similar, just a different bio." This particular press kit is interesting because the bio is a joke; they were pretending they were famous in 1989, but it came true. Does visualizing your future actually work this way?

> Although only together for seven months, Kurt, Chris, Chad, and Jason have blessed the world with a single, an LP entitled *Bleach*, and one cut on the Sub Pop 200 compilation, as well as attaining success, fame, and a following of millions. Selling their bottled sweat and locks of their hair has proved to be the biggest money maker so far. . . .
>
> . . . Nirvana sees the underground scene as becoming stagnant and more accessible to big league capitalist pig major record labels. But does NIRVANA fell [*sic*] a moral duty to fight this cancerous evil? NO WAY! We want to cash in and suck up to the big wigs. . . . Soon we will need groupie repellant.

Santanu/Holly—WEFT

I received a letter from Santanu Rahman, a local scenester, in the 1990s. He introduced himself though I'd already known him from the scene. He complimented me as a local musician and invited me to begin learning Choy Lay Fut kung fu with him in a new school he was starting. He knew I'd stopped Taekwondo a couple of years back, through our mutual friend and sound guy Jimmie Myers, who played in Santanu's band Marvin Nash. For many years, Santanu taught me and Jane (of the Poster Children song "Jane") the beautiful, circular forms of CLF kung fu in a studio in his parents' old house. We'd learn weapons forms along with twisting and turning forms with so much back and forth that when we'd completed one particular form for the first time, we'd each run to the bathroom to throw up! My arms were black and blue, and I loved it. Each bruise marked a contact from either Santanu or Jane.

Santanu was a townie, a UIUC student who grew up in Champaign (I was always jealous of those people). He was the martial arts instructor for various musicians but was more known for his love of the local scene, and involvement as a musician and radio DJ. He had a magical voice, and enrolled in the airshifter training class at WEFT, the community radio station, where he'd obtained his FCC license. Patiently waiting to immerse himself in the scene, he'd finally received a slot in 1992 for the live and local music show.

For years, Santanu and his friend Holly Rushakoff hosted a live performance and interview with a different band each week. Santanu's philosophy was to "provide a glimpse into everyone's creative process, and how they came to make their art, and also, what their journey was, once they put it out for us."[8] It was an amazing and generous show, and it seemed like Santanu and Holly would feature any and every band that played original music in town. It really showcased our scene, and where it possibly could have resulted in scene jealousy, it did the opposite. The two fostered such a sense of community so that if you listened to the show, you couldn't help but be incredibly proud of everyone involved in local music.

Trashcan Records

I slowly unwrapped a one-pound sack of soggy paper that had been placed into my hands. Warm gray juice oozed through my fingers as I bit into the first steak burrito I'd ever eaten in my life. It was beige-colored and as big as my head and had a meat texture that seemed more authentic than I was used to. We were taking a break from doing vocal overdubs on a four-track, and Chris Corpora, our friend and now booking agent, had brought food back from a new restaurant on campus, La Bamba, now a mainstay on Illinois campuses. Afterward, we continued overdubbing vocals in Chris's apartment, finishing *Toreador Squat*, our first commercial release, a cassette tape named after a type of plain brown paper bag: Rick finding beauty in everyday, utilitarian design.

In 1988, Chris Corpora and college DJ Jim Slusarek started a cassette-only label called Trashcan Records. This was not an effort to capitalize on nostalgia, it was because you could dub (duplicate) cassettes in your own house by attaching all your friends' cassette machines together. Trashcan released a couple of incredible compilation tapes of Champaign-Urbana bands, and many full-length cassettes by bands like the Bowery Boys with future Wilco member Leroy Bach, badflannel (future members of Hum, Menthol, Steakdaddy Six, and Honcho Overload), as well as our first Poster Children cassette.

Tapes were useful for a number of things—mailed to clubs and labels as part of a press kit, sold to fans for three dollars to help pay for gas money, attached to zines, and even played on some radio stations. Compilation tapes featuring the work of many bands helped spread the word to a wider audience, as each band had its own fans who would end up being a captive audience for all the other bands on the tape.

CHAPTER 7

Local

Recording enabled us to tour; touring enabled us to record. Our first out-of-town show in the Big City was at Phyllis' Musical Inn, the legendary club in Chicago's Wicker Park neighborhood, and we were able to book a show there because my dad was Phyllis's beloved dentist.

Dad had played at Phyllis' with a big jazz band many years ago. He told me that Phyllis used to sit on a platform in the window and play the accordion. "She was always so nice, always smiling at me." She's been his patient forever. Dad tells a story that just recently, Phyllis was sitting in his dental chair, both of them around ninety years old, and Dad says, "I was making her some kind of a partial [removable appliance] and I was hurting her because I had to make certain movements in her mouth to get it to fit, and with my hands in her mouth, she yelled, 'You son of a bitch!'—I wore it as a badge of honor, because I love Phyllis. Once I got through, I gave her a big kiss."

Playing Chicago

Dad somehow coerced Phyllis's son Clem into giving us a show at Phyllis' Musical Inn. Saturday, October 3, 1987, as we loaded in, the TV set in the bar aired the premiere of *Star Trek: The Next Generation*, broadcast on Channel 50, glitchy and snowy gray in my memory. I remember thinking sadly that I was making a choice now between geekdom and punk rock. It was also between a future livelihood of consumption or creation, the latter always seeming to be a scarier path. Though there were only five people in the audience and they leaned against the back walls watching, my memory sticks with a different metric from that night. The radius of our influence had expanded 150 miles as I played on that stage. That measurement compelled me to play my ass off that night, no matter the size of the crowd. $\pi*\Delta d^2$, the area of the land determined by the change in distance from the previous show is always in my mind, every show, and figures deeply into my stage practice.

We traveled the three hours back to Chicago numerous times, and I remember gleefully telling people that the first Phyllis' show had five people, and the next had twelve, and that, to me, this was a very promising mathematical progression. The standard payment for a show for us then was around fifty dollars, so we may have just recouped gas money, but each excursion was a celebration, a vacation, and a "learning experience." Yes, we played at Dreamerz in Chicago at three a.m., after the headliner, but how amazing was that, to be permitted to perform in that brightly painted upstairs space at a time when most people were meant to be asleep? After we played, we loaded our heavy equipment down the stairs, and outside on the desolate Chicago street were gifted with the vision of a car on fire, interior flaming, no top (or perhaps it had burned off) parked right along the curb! You could find magic in every experience if you simply looked for it.

Making a Record

Amid our little jaunts to Chicago and other cities within a five-hour radius, and while enjoying a constant succession of national acts coming through Champaign, Rick started talking about the possibility of Poster Children making an album. At this point, I couldn't fathom the idea of actually being on a record, but I just nodded to Rick and went along with it. I never expected to end up with him either, yet here I was.

A feasible indie route toward putting out a record was to pay for a recording session. With master tapes, we could look for a label or, if we couldn't find one, pay to press our own vinyl. A well-recorded demo would also help us get larger shows. Chris was already doing a great job booking shows for us all over the Midwest, so we wouldn't be waiting around for a label to approach us. We were self-sufficient. If a label did want these masters, we could sign, and we wouldn't owe the label money for recording. We'd be able to recoup faster.

The producer's name on the Didjits' *Hey Judester* record belonged to a real person who you could just call up and schedule time with, at CRC, Chicago Recording Company, which also was a real place, a scant 150 miles away from where we normally parked our van. That name, Iain Burgess, was on many of my favorite albums, namely the Naked Raygun and Big Black albums I loved for their sheer power.

A Naked Raygun show was my first ever mosh pit. It was the late 1980s, and Naked Raygun's music demanded audience participation: call and response as well as physicality. The mosh pit at the Cabaret Metro in Chicago consisted of a ring of audience members stomping around, moving in a counterclockwise direction, with smaller interactions where members of the pit slam into each other, creating a group motion and equilibrium speed that correlates rather surprisingly with a Maxwell-Boltzmann distribution of particles in a 2D classical gas.[1] It looked like controlled chaos to me, and an exciting place to practice my martial arts. Arriving at the show, I jumped straight into the middle of the pit and immediately tripped and fell on my face, sprawled under people's stomping legs.

When one person falls in the pit, it can cause a chain reaction. I was not only at risk of hurting myself, but of causing others harm as well. You had a lot of responsibility as a member of the pit; it was like riding a giant, community-shaped bicycle. A giant man standing guard on the perimeter, an audience participant, quickly pulled me up from the ground and crossed his arms protectively around me as the mosh pit raged. He held me for a while as I centered myself. "Are you OK?" he asked me, and I nodded "yes." "Do you want to go back?" he questioned. "Yes," I answered. When he felt I was stable, he uncrossed his arms and gave me a gentle nudge back in. I remembered that feeling forever, that hug from a stranger, the caring alongside the aggression in the pit.

By the summer of 1988, we'd saved up enough money and guts to call Iain Burgess and book CRC for a weekend. We lost a van in the process—my family's van that we'd inherited died in Gilman, Illinois, and Rick's dad drove ninety miles to pick up us and our equipment and deliver it all to the studio in time for us to record. I remember the recording session set up in the cool wood, glass, and leather spaceship rooms of CRC as being a lot of cigarette smoking and beer drinking on Iain's part with Chris acting as mediator, and the tension of trying to get the parts as correct possible, all recording together, worrying about the drummer's sanity (drummers have it the roughest, because all other parts could be fixed by overdubbing). We recorded and mixed fifteen songs over two days for $1,500.

Hugging Billy Corgan

After a show at one of the larger clubs in Chicago, Chris came backstage to introduce us to a man named Barry Waterman. I remember that Barry was dressed much nicer than the rest of us, in business black. I had a habit of wearing shorts with long underwear underneath them so I could look like Ward (the Champaign–Urbana promoter), who I considered one of my fashion mentors. Barry was putting out a compilation of Chicago bands and even though we were from Champaign, Chris had convinced him to include two of our songs from our recording session. The comp was called "Light into Dark," and featured ours—and Smashing Pumpkins'—first vinyl. We had a record release party in Chicago with us and the other bands opening for the Pumpkins, and another in Champaign where the Pumpkins opened for us.

Billy Corgan, lead singer of the Smashing Pumpkins, has a pretty contentious backstory in Champaign, with people insisting that the Pumpkins ripped off Poster Children songs. I'd heard that throughout the nineties Billy was constantly reminded about it by Chicago and Champaign scenesters. We never played into that story. Rick's theory is that every band is a sampler, a machine that regurgitates everything it has ever heard and seen. The songs you write are a conglomeration of your musical experience, and you try to emulate what you liked. The worst "samplers" make the best bands. Plus, personally, I think they ripped off Hum and Tar.

That said, I know there are similarities in some songs on *Flower Plower (like Wanna)* compared to "I Am One"— both are in the key of F-sharp, for example. But the truth is, there was a fabulous Champaign band called the Shakes who had even better F-sharp songs with more accidentals in them, and we thought F-sharp was a badass key, so we wrote songs in F-sharp. And I'm sure that the Shakes didn't invent F-sharp.

Rick also insists that bands don't "sell out" intentionally. Some just like music that more people enjoy listening to. I remember Mercy Rule's Heidi and Jon lamenting about writing music for a major label. Heidi told me she was completely aware that if she moved her hand one way, it would be more of a hit song, but if she moved it the other way, she'd like it more. You had to decide your path.

Over the years, I'd heard rumors that the Pumpkins considered me for a bass player. I would never have fit in with that scene. I don't equate that type of success with happiness, and in fact, it's very rare that I see a happy rock star. I'd met D'arcy Wretzky back at that Champaign show, and she was very sweet. Though unnecessary for both of us, she was giving me tips on how to dress in a way that would hide your tummy fat on a stage. I put it in my memory for later use. It was widely known that D'arcy and James Iha hadn't been allowed to play on their albums. If the guys didn't let me play on an album, I thought, I'd leave the band instantly. It's the opposite of DIY. I did hug Billy Corgan once, to comfort him. It was after a show we had played together, and he was crying, worried about his future. It seemed like a different level to me, and I felt bad for him. Our future never worried me. It seemed like an adventure, an experiment.

Mike Potential

The first time we recorded with Steve Albini, as mentioned, was at his house, where he had an eight-track, a live room in the basement, and a control room in a closet off the kitchen. We recorded and mixed five songs in six hours, for $250. It was soon after that we met Mike Potential, after one of our Chicago shows. Clad in a leather jacket and long hair, a young Roxy Music era Brian Eno (sans makeup), Mike offered to put out our first full-length vinyl, and this consisted of four songs from the Albini sessions and four from the Iain Burgess sessions. We graciously accepted. Rick and I did the cover art at Kinko's using Zipatone and color-copy machines to reverse the white and black. The original version of *Flower Plower* came out in fall 1989 and was vinyl only. Mike had charged up credit cards to the max, $5,000, to pay for the pressing. All the time, I was in disbelief that someone would be so generous as to do such a thing. Even having done it myself, it still amazes me that people spend their money putting out other people's records. It is the ultimate generosity and shows a belief in disseminating the arts and their healing power.

According to our one-page contract with Mike, he would have control of the masters for five years, after which it would revert to us. In 1989, my five-years-out mental picture of myself was a man in a business suit with a briefcase, an unknown number of kids, and a vegetable garden. I was part of Generation X and never expected to live past an imminent nuclear bomb, and thus had no ability to conceptualize my future. A half-year into our contract with Mike, he licensed our record to Frontier Records, out in California. Frontier Records housed Suicidal Tendencies, the band everyone knew from their song "Institutionalized" on the *Repo Man* soundtrack, and Thin White Rope, the Chico, California, band who was a Champaign-Urbana favorite. I'm pretty sure Lisa from Frontier had heard about us from her good friend ML, Thin White Rope's manager, who later became our manager.

Indie labels were still thriving, but some were becoming part of major distributors (Sub Pop sold 49 percent of its stake to Warner Music Group in 1995).[2] In late 1988, Sonic Youth put out *Daydream Nation* on Enigma Records, which was released by Capitol. We were bemused. Why did Sonic Youth want anything to do with a major label? It wasn't like music like theirs was going to sell the millions required for major label success!

CHAPTER 8

Regional

We get to play with House of Large Sizes tonight! They are fantastic—very soul, rootsy, and seventies-influenced rock from the Midwest, with some angst-ridden, screaming vocals. They are awfully nice people too. Barb, the bass player, is a complete rock-goddess, with two long braids and her blue mod dress. We traded some stories with them.

Iowa City, winter, two a.m. Bliss. We climb the tottering outdoor steel staircase up to the second-floor load-in at Gabe's Oasis. Melting snow flurries cake gray ice chunks into the jagged metal teeth that we hope grip our sneakers as we load refrigerator-sized cabinets out of the club. In the sleet below, the van blocks other cars in the alley and people honk. I smile and wave at them because we are *working* and need to be there. Inside the club glows, wood warm and gold. House of Large Sizes just finished and hangers-on in the audience are hugging everyone with words and arms. Barb Schilf and I stand around admiring each other, and the rest of the gentlemen in our bands have an after-show playdate. HOLS fans were so friendly. I think of my first experience at this club—by accident, we'd arrived a day early for

Barb Schilf, House of Large Sizes. Courtesy of Barb Schilf.

our show (a four-hour drive), had no place to stay, and the bartender, after telling me we weren't playing that day, charged me twenty-five cents for a tiny plastic cup of water. I cried in response. Also, the water was terrible. Repeated efforts at the town had yielded better results, and sometimes, on a good night, I didn't even have to pay for the water.

We'd begun traveling to other cities within a nine-hour radius of Champaign. Iowa City on Saturday night, then Minneapolis on Sunday night, was a regular route for us. We'd leave around one a.m. after the show, drive, stop home with time to shower and go straight to work programming flight simulators. It was invigorating to step off the stage, into the van, out of the van, and then dive straight into assembler code. Rick and I took great pride in our dual lives and thought of ourselves as two of the best in the small team of software programmers. We traveled a bit for work too—Rick spent an extended period in Indonesia to install the simulator he worked on. I loved my bosses and coworkers, and the fact that the company was family-owned and a bit old-school. At some point, they had hired drug consultants to determine whether or not their workers were on drugs. We found this amusing, as we fit all the "warning signs"—especially the "late to work," "wearing odd clothes," and "laughing uncontrollably during meetings," but we were not on drugs. There is no way we could have kept up the schedule of touring and coding had we been.

Nine hours to Minneapolis, beautiful dusty chandeliers in old wooden houses and stylishly dressed girls at the shows. I always loved the glamourous vibe I felt there and saw its relation to the Big Apple. Repeated trips for fifty dollars a show at either the 7th Street Entry or the Uptown Bar also paid off in other ways. Chris became friends with Ellen Stewart, a booking agent who worked in the Twin/Tone offices. Ellen liked us and talked us up to Twin/Tone, and soon, after a show with Babes in Toyland at the Uptown in Minneapolis, Twin/Tone approached us, offering to release our records. Twin/Tone was famous to us, one of the three best known independent labels at the time, home of Soul Asylum, Babes in Toyland, and the Replacements. We were thrilled—we hadn't been shopping any demos around or waiting for our big break, we'd simply been practicing, writing songs, and performing as much as we could.

How Do You Get a Nun Pregnant?

Now we had new songs, a new drummer, $2,000, and a three-record contract with Twin/Tone.

We booked two weekends at Chicago Recording Company with Steve Albini, and again recorded everything live and added vocals later. Working with Steve was entertaining because if you were bored or stressed, you could always press the encyclopedia button on him and he'd just start talking about some subject or, at least, giving opinions. Rick remembers some studio shenanigans—one involving a lemur call from a nature video ending up in the song "Space Gun," our first sampler experience; an hour fixing a single snare drum hit on "Pointed Stick"; Jeff's guitar being put through something called the "Van Halenizer"; and leaving board mixing settings exactly as they were from mixing our song "Freedom Rock" to the mixing of the next song, "Carvers of New York City."

There was an exciting moment when Aerosmith arrived at the studio to record *Rockline*, the live radio call-in show, in the room upstairs. Steve furiously began fiddling with the phone system trying to get a tap into the show until someone came down and put a big X of white tape over the flashing button on the phone. "DO NOT TOUCH." Bob went hunting around the studio for Aerosmith to tell them his current favorite joke: "What's brown and sounds like a bell? Dung. Dung," he'd sing. He'd returned to our studio beaming. He'd delivered the joke and Brad Whitford, deadpan, had quickly replied, "How do you get a nun pregnant? Fuck her."

CHAPTER 9

National

First Tour East

"I gave a guy a free *Flower Plower* tape," said Jeff Dimpsey (later of the band Hum, but our second guitarist at this time) after the show, climbing into the van outside Woody's. "WHAT?!" Rick and I yelled. That was five dollars we could have used for gas money to get back to Champaign from Manhattan! We were in no actual danger of running out of "job" money to cover the gas, nor in any danger of recouping this first tour, but it was the Principle of the Matter. "He said he worked for *Rolling Stone*," Jeff shrugged. "Everyone is going to tell you they work for *Rolling Stone*, this is New York City!" we yelled back at him. A couple of months later, a blurb about us appeared in *Rolling Stone* magazine, in print. I hope we apologized to Jeff at some point.

The Pitfalls of Being on an Independent Label

While indie labels afforded bands support via budget and people to help press, distribute, and promote records, along with the curatorial aspect of "label," there were many infuriating aspects of being on one. For one, we actually didn't have complete artistic control. Twin/Tone hired an artist to do our *Daisychain Reaction* cover art, and that was the only cover in our history of albums, major-label and otherwise, that we did not create ourselves. For another, the funding model for a record label needs built-in lag time, along with being a crapshoot. Imagine: you press 2,000 of a new album at a cost of around five dollars per unit. The distributors shop it to record stores and ship out orders. Then you wait for people around the country to walk into their local record stores and decide to buy your record. Hopefully your band has gone on tour, was reviewed in one of the three national, monthly rock magazines, or can be heard on a local college radio station. Pre-internet, why else would someone purchase said album?

The money comes back from record stores to pay the distributors, delayed. The distributors will pay the label back months after that, and may also ship unsold copies back. Here's the catch—if the label sold out of your record quickly, and wanted to press more, they had to do it before recouping from the first batch of sales.

We knew about these things because at this time, we were running our own label, 12 Inch Records. We'd put out a few singles and some full-length albums, and though we'd sold plenty of records for Hum, our distributor Cargo had decided not to pay us. We couldn't press up more, and we couldn't pay Hum. We could sue, but the only winners would be the lawyers, at $250 an hour.

So independent distributors were a key part of the indie scene. As we finished *Daisychain Reaction*, distributor Rough Trade USA, which also helped finance Twin/Tone (and a lot of other indie labels), went bankrupt. All of a sudden *Daisychain Reaction* wasn't coming out in the fall of 1990 as planned but was on hold indefinitely until Twin/Tone could put together new sources of money and distribution.

We were consoled by Sub Pop asking us for a single of the month, and we gave them two songs from the DCR sessions with a cheeky design-nod to our Chicago friends Tar, but touring is what advances and sustains your band, and it is hard to tour when you are between albums. You cannot play your new songs, because that would ruin the surprise, and people would be tired of them when the album finally came out. You can't tour on old songs because audiences would get sick of you. So you had to wait. *Daisychain Reaction* finally did come out in 1991 and we started touring on the East Coast. We'd play shows in Boston, New York City, would stop in record stores on the way and find out there were no copies of the record. Now we were starting to get some good press, but it was still very hard to find the album in stores around the country. Extremely frustrated, but still reeking of "indie cred," we started wondering how much worse life could get if we did indeed "sell out" to a major label.

CBGB

Enter CBGB and you're entering a cave. The last bit of sun-filled New York street vertilinearly transitions to nothing as the heavy door closes behind you. You find yourself in a dark, wet atmosphere, at the far end of a long, narrow room with gleaming beer lights along the walls. A mirrored oval shines from the floor in front of you, a puddle of dog piss, silver, reflecting. It has been peed by a thin, gentle, black-and-white dog with red eyes. This is a Holy Water Font, and you are entering a church. There is a Buddhist meditation you can perform where you consider that the air you breathe is the same air that has been inside and outside all other bodies. You are only a temporary shell for all things natural. I always thought this as I entered this holy space and reverently circumambulated the dog pee, which I believed was part of all nature.

Beautiful Louise Parnassa, sweet goddess manager and talent buyer of CBGB, sits at the business desk next to the door. At the other end of the narrow hall is the stage, made of shiny, beaten-down wood, compressed by ages of rock. The sound system is incredible; it is impossible to sound bad in that room. The air molecules feel permanently oriented toward perfection. The bathrooms are behind the band, so you make your way to the thigh-high stage, pass on the left of the band, and then descend the steps behind the stage. In the women's bathroom, all surfaces—including mirrors—are covered with stickers and lipstick. Thick ropes across the top or sides of the stalls are threaded with communal toilet paper. I return to soundcheck and lie on my back on the wooden stage, contemplating the sweat and heroin that dripped off Blondie, Talking Heads, and the Ramones soaked into that wood. I'm lying on a forest floor atop decomposed punk rock earth.

"Rose, Kim Gordon is here!" a voice behind me said, excitedly. *The* Kim Gordon? And Thurston Moore, too! How amazing to be in New York City, having just purchased a third copy of the *Daydream Nation* album (this time on CD!) and then have the gods themselves manifest inside the Temple! They certainly wouldn't be there to see us, I figured, but there was always the slight chance that they'd stay to watch our soundcheck and be so impressed that they'd then ask us to tour with them. In Japan. Do famous people understand how exciting it is when they have made themselves available to us "little people"? I needed to make contact with them, to reward them for appearing, and to inform them that yet another person on earth loves them.

I ran back to the van to get my new *Daydream Nation* CD, an icebreaker, hoping I'd be able to work in the fact that we also had two vinyl copies of the record back at home. Made my way to the Font, where they were standing, haloed, with Louise and the Dog. "Look, Thurston! I just bought your record on CD!" Thurston nodded his approval. I hoped he didn't think I was just a new fan. There is currency to being among the first to know about the music in this scene. I was hoping that being an early adopter of new technologies also counted for something.

Kim Gordon stood apart. I'd have to ascend to her, deliberately. Would she even talk to me? Would I be creeping on her? Would she acknowledge me as a bass sister? Extrapolating from the mythological narrative of how female bass players are born, borne of every male (redundant) rock critic, I envisioned her seated upon her Rock Goddess throne this morning, sipping her special fancy tea brought by faeries whose job it is to inform her of new developments in the Sisterhood of Rock. They'd brought her news of a newborn Female Bass Player, Rose Marshack of Poster Children, playing CBGB tonight. I shook the fantasy from my head. As she had no hand in my bass-playing inception, this would be a tribute I did not deserve. I even remember the time when, holding a bass, I was asked about her, and did not know who she was. Now I was aware and grateful, so I walked up to her to introduce myself and thank her for her art.

"Hello, Kim Gordon! I am Rose from Poster Children! I play bass. I love you. You are the most amazing, most incredible, most inspirational, and beautiful rock goddess of all time."

Kim's response:

"Hello, Rose. How is your tour going?

Where did you play yesterday?

How many days have you been on tour?

Has it been weeks?

Are you all getting along?

Are you writing new music?

How many new songs have you written?

Who are you recording with next?
What label are you on?
Do you like your label?
Where are you going next?
How long is the tour?
Who are you playing with on this tour?
When are you recording your next album?"

It was a barrage of questions, one fired right after the other, without regard as to whether or not I finished the previous question, delivered staring straight at me, so fast that I couldn't keep up, like an interview, an audition into punk rock's canon. It made me think that I had better prepare for next time, but also, I was floored at the generosity. What a way to interact with fans and upcoming bands, to just ask a multitude of questions about them, deflecting the attention from yourself! This way I didn't have to explain the inexplicable things, like how it's important that her voice sounds so honest and imperfect on her records, why it's significant that she is on a stage with and married to Thurston (at the time), why her presence exudes such strength and femininity, and why there should be a connection between us because we're female, all things that really shouldn't matter, and that I don't really have the vocabulary to discuss.

So often fans don't know what to say around stage musicians—and so we have an opportunity to either distance ourselves or be there, off the pedestal, approachable, to help people learn about themselves. That's what Kim did for me, and it changed my life. It's the kind of generosity you learn from practicing the way of tea or martial arts, where it's necessary to acknowledge the person in front of you.

And then we drove back to Illinois and went back to work programming flight simulators.

Nevermind

Sometimes the flight simulators at work just crash. It might be twenty minutes in, or fourteen hours, but you can tell it's crashed because it's unresponsive. You flip a switch and a light doesn't go on, or pull on the helicopter collective and the dials don't move. The tens of thousands of lines of 80386 code all run through four registers, like four nucleotides or eight notes, creating a system so complex that it's hard to debug. To locate the errant code,

I left a breadcrumb trail of print statements through each section, so the monitor screen would bleep a letter as it finished munching on a section of code. The last letter left on the screen was a clue to where the error might be.

I was going to miss all this. Our request for a six-week leave from our jobs at the flight simulator factory had been denied, so we'd given our two-week notice. There was no question in our minds that we needed to go on tour. We needed to promote *Daisychain Reaction*, and we wanted to make another album. On our last day of work, a Friday night, Rick and I stayed extra late, commenting our code for posterity, to make sure we did not leave our coworkers lost. The boss of the company stood watch over us. I had no idea what was going through his mind, but I hoped he knew we were doing everything we could to make a comfortable transition for the next hires. When I walked out the door, I was not scared. Maybe it was because we'd spent the last hours so genuinely immersed in good deed. Leaving, I actually felt a huge load lift off my chest and shoulders. Our full US tour would begin in a couple of weeks. When we came home, if necessary, we could get other jobs.

Ellen Stewart, Poster Children's booking agent at the time, was very well respected and would go on to represent Afghan Whigs, Stereolab, and Elliot Smith. We had money saved up and a van. We'd become accustomed to asking for a floor to sleep on from the stage after the show, and had lots of t-shirts with us to sell, and because of this, usually returned from touring with money. Ellen was well connected, so if a promoter stiffed us, her network of booking agents with bigger bands would punish them. In addition to this, because of some great press (like the *Rolling Stone* blurb), we had a bit of major label interest, from Sire, Columbia, and Atlantic Records.

We found major label interest in ourselves pretty amusing because it was a path we never envisioned for ourselves. It went against being "indie" and having any sort of DIY credibility, and also, we were a pretty weird-sounding band and didn't have any plans to normalize ourselves for better commercial value. However, we were very frustrated by Twin/Tone's inability to get our records into stores, and we also weren't too thrilled that even on an independent label, we still didn't get to design our own cover art. National distribution meant a lot to us, and that was a given on a major. And by contract, we owed two more records to Twin/Tone, so to leave the label, we'd need to be bought out by an entity with a lot of money.

We were torn. Having grown up indie, we wanted our control and our credibility, and through word of mouth, we knew the pitfalls of signing to a major. But more and more odd bands were starting to sign to majors. Sonic Youth had signed to Geffen subsidiary DGC halfway through 1990, which we thought was pretty brave on all parts, since Sonic Youth sometimes sounded like an airplane landing from the outside (in a good way). They seemed OK on their major, but another band we loved, Hüsker Dü, had signed to Warner Bros., released two records that didn't sound heavenly punk like their earlier ones on the SST Record label, and then had broken up.

So, Rick came up with a test, using the latest odd release. If DGC could do a good job promoting Nirvana's new *Nevermind* record, then perhaps we should consider signing to a major.

We now had a new drummer, Bob Rising, and Rick's younger (by two years) brother Jim as our new second guitarist, which made me really happy. There had been fighting and turmoil for a while in the band, usually stemming from people wanting to do things differently. We were pretty set in our ideologies, so variance would cause conflict. I'd known Jim for years now as the mild-mannered, brilliant, superhero brother of Rick, smart and creative, and more laid-back, and I figured another one of them certainly wouldn't hurt. I'd never seen them fight—their whole family was lovely, respectful, scholarly, and cultured—and much quieter than my own. I thought Jim would make a good companion for Rick, and in all the years of touring, I'd only seen one grumpy exchange. To this day (and he's still in the band), I've never seen Jim mad.

We began our tour the week after *Nevermind* had been released, and we were listening to a tape of it on the van's cassette system on the first day, driving west. We all liked it. I liked how many odd chords it had, very minor but still energetic in my opinion. The tour took us counterclockwise around the perimeter of the United States, starting at a Days Inn, in Rapid City, South Dakota—funny, because I figured punk bands did not usually play at hotels. But this was one of the best audiences we ever had, a bunch of junior high school kids.

I sat in the passenger seat of the van, eyes peeled, looking for any signs of magic. I love road trips. At the sight of a huge green statue of the Jolly Green Giant along I-90 in Blue Earth, Minnesota, it occurred to me that the treasures that we'd find weren't even going to be subtle. We would not have to hunt at all if, here in the middle of nowhere, we had already fallen on a fifty-foot-tall monument to a cartoon character that I only encountered on my beans, with free admission. On the road, I decided, it wasn't going to be hard to live in a state of constant total amazement.

Thursday (and Friday), September 18, 19, 1997

SEATTLE, WA, BRUCE LEE'S GRAVE

We visited Bruce and Brandon Lee's grave, which is located in Seattle. Rick was reticent to go to a cemetery that we didn't have any dead people in, but I think I convinced him it was OK because Walt Mink had sent out Christmas cards with them standing around Bruce Lee's grave, so it had to be open to the public. Just to make sure, I called the cemetery and asked, and they said, "Oh YES, it's open to the public." It's weird to visit someone who isn't related to you in a cemetery. I've never done it before.

So there we sat on the bench facing Bruce and Brandon Lee's grave. I don't know a lot about Bruce Lee at all, and don't know which conspiracy theory to believe. But I sat there and thought about Bruce and Brandon practicing martial arts and I thought about how practicing martial arts makes me feel; it's probably the most enriching thing I've ever done in my life. Practicing martial arts is kind of like playing silent music with your whole body. Then I thought about how I wished Bruce and Brandon were still alive.

But when we went back to the car, Jimmy Soundguy (who also practices) said something I'd never thought of. He said that being at his grave was sort of like spending a bit of time with Bruce Lee. It was the only way we could meet him or be near him. I thought that was really neat; we were alone there for about fifteen minutes near Bruce and Brandon in a way.

More magical things happened during this tour. We stayed at the house of a former Champaign resident whose son came to our show in Missoula, Montana, and heard tales of the local sixties scene with REO Speedwagon and Irving Azoff. The van was repaired in a Seattle parking lot by a mysterious itinerant mechanic. A fellow musician playing across the street from the San Jose show not only offered us a floor to sleep on but also got us a show for our day off, a couple of weeks down the road in Pensacola. In Texas, after our show, in the bar, we watched our "If You See Kay" video appear on MTV for the first time while the patrons—who'd only just met us—cheered. We played Chapel Hill with the original lineup of Seam, no one knowing that within a year, Bob (who had unfortunately quit our band early on tour but agreed to stay until the end) would be their drummer. We drove for what seemed like hours through a dark, swampy forest to Kill Devil Hills, North Carolina, and played for an unexpectedly large and enthusiastic crowd of Fort Raleigh National Historic Site workers.[1]

Monday, April 17, 1995

NATIONAL ATOMIC MUSEUM IN ALBUQUERQUE, CO/NM BORDER

I love sightseeing.

Today is a day off, so we did some sightseeing. We went to the National Atomic Museum in Albuquerque, which I enjoyed immensely. The museum is better than the Sigmund Freud Museum in Vienna, but not by much. We saw a terrible documentary called "10 Seconds that Shook the World" that made the everyone in the band very angry, and then walked around a Marie Curie exhibit and saw lots of pictures of bombers and scientists. The most amazing thing I saw was a large American flag, with about a quarter of the stripes end of it completely missing, tattered and dusty, in a glass case. The flag had been flying ten miles away from Ground Zero during the Trinity explosion. The winds had ripped it to shreds.

I am intrigued by and terrified of nukes, so you can imagine how excited I am to be driving around NM, northeast of the Trinity Site, where the first atomic bomb was tested. The site is open two days a year now, the first Sunday of April and the first Sunday of October. Apparently it is not radioactive anymore, but I am not convinced. I pore over the New Mexico map while we are in this area of the country, and sometimes even when we aren't. Areas of our map are marked "Road not open to the public" and "Inquire locally before driving on marked roads." Last tour we slept at a rest area thirty miles west of the Trinity site, and I stayed up all night trying to figure out which way the wind was blowing.

I have two new books, *The Making of the Atomic Bomb* and *Genius* by James Gleick (writer of a great book about chaos theory), about Richard Feynman, a punk-rock physicist. Jim has a Freeman Dyson book called *Infinite in All Directions* or something like that. Rick just ate a Dolly Madison blueberry muffin cake that expired on April 4th. Joe has been silent for almost half an hour, and Howie is hungry.

It is nice to have a day off.

As we circled counterclockwise around the country, there were hints about Nirvana's progress. In Seattle, with our Sub Pop connections, we ended up at a warehouse where a lone guy was pressing up Nirvana shirts, black ones with a yellow face with Xs for the eyes. He was kind of surprised at the number that had been ordered and was worried about fulfilling all the orders. (I asked for a misprint shirt and got one with a dimmed-out X). At college radio interviews, we'd been requesting "Smells Like Teen Spirit," until a week into the tour, in San Francisco, where the DJ replied, "You're kidding, right?" "Why?" I asked, defending it. "It's a great song!" "'Smells Like Teen Spirit' is playing on commercial stations now," he informed us. "We won't play it on this station anymore." Nirvana had "broken." Normal people were listening now; indie rock was now sanctioned by Miller Lite, local car dealerships, and Wendy's. By the time we started heading up the East Coast, we had seventeen different major and boutique labels wanting to talk to us.

During this tour, the Buzzcocks, high school idols of mine, invited us to open for them in the Midwest. It was mid-November, so two more weeks were tacked on the end of the tour. Thankfully, Bob agreed to continue with us. We have video footage of the Buzzcocks bowling with us in Nebraska. They were really funny guys, so smart, and so nice to us. They worried about our safety, with me asking for places to sleep each night from the stage, and I had to assure them that the United States—especially the Midwest—wasn't as dangerous as it seemed from abroad. It felt kind of neat teaching the Buzzcocks a bit about my country. Still impressed with my "bravery," Pete Shelley paid me the highest compliment ever, calling me "a real punk." Watching them from in front of the stage each night was an affirmation of the anger and angst that helped me through high school.

Saturday, November 11, 1995, San Francisco
WHY CAN'T I TOUCH IT

The Buzzcocks were in town tonight, getting ready to record with the guy who produced the Green Day record (which seemed blasphemous to me), and they came to our show, so I took the opportunity to tell Steve Diggle that a week ago, we were driving through Montana and I had a "perfect moment"—I was listening to one of their records and staring at a deep blue sky, watching a single star, between two cloud masses, with the moon shining down on mountains all around, and I was listening on nine-dollar headphones to them scream, "There Is No Love in This World Any MORE!!," then "Why Can't I Touch It." I had asked him once what the words meant, did they mean a penis, and he'd responded no, it could be anything; it was about things you can feel but cannot actually see, like religion or maybe God. Then they all had a good chuckle. They have such beautiful lyrics. I got really, really happy, as happy as I can get depressed sometimes.

On December 7, 1991, *Nevermind* was number 40 on *Billboard*'s Hot 100 and it would peak at number 6 in six weeks. Being on a major label certainly had not ended Nirvana's career (yet), and now, every A&R representative in the business was on a quest for the next Nirvana. We came home from around eighty-eight days on tour (and no hotels) with even more major label interest and a bidding war.

We took a month off to find another drummer to replace Bob. A fellow named Johnny Machine, recommended by Steve Albini, was next in line, and we then added another month-long tour with the awesome Swervedriver, shoe-gazer band extraordinaire, and absolutely sweetest guys on the planet. Now there was really what the industry calls "a buzz" about us. We were interviewed by CNN for a report on "grunge rock." Our Boston show was raided by the fire marshal, who decided the club was overcrowded and wouldn't let any bands play until 100 people left. We hung outside the club and ecstatic fans of ours were exclaiming, "I just got paid to leave after your show!"

We weren't the only band with drummer problems. Apparently while crossing the border into Canada, Swervedriver's drummer had walked off the bus, never to return. Danny from the band Run Westy Run appeared on the drums in Toronto for Swervedriver's soundcheck, intently listening to a tape of the band. He played the next couple of shows until another Danny (Ingram) was found to finish that tour. This furthered my belief that all drummers are magical, mystical beings.

Now was the time of punk rock's "breaking," and everyone was looking for the next scrappy college band. Amid all the buzz, at our San Francisco show, Dave Kendall came to interview us for *120 Minutes* in anticipation of our possible move to a major label, and Rick was asked if we would ever change our sound. Much to his later chagrin, Rick utters for posterity, "Grunge? All we know is grunge." But even with all this national attention, our Twin/Tone record was impossible to find in stores. Still owing that indie two more records, we resigned ourselves to make the jump to a major. Now we only had to decide which one.

PART THREE

1993–1996
Major Label Life

Friday, September 23, 1995, Elvis, Memphis, Hooters

WHY GUYS LIKE BREASTS, AND WHY IT'S OK

For those who don't know, Hooters is a chain of restaurant that features waitresses with large breasts, dressed in tank tops and shorts, serving your meatburgers. It is billed as a Family Place; one that "you take Dad out to, for a little fun." I was appalled at hearing this from Rick, and a lively discussion ensued, with the guys explaining to me Why Guys Like Breasts, and Why It's OK. I should explain that I am in a band with the nicest, gentlest, most progressive-thinking, pro-feminist guys in the world. Even calling them that is an insult; they treat women as equals to men, and there is no question or discussion about it. They also like a good debate, and especially Rick loves to be a devil's advocate, so they took it upon themselves to defend the mustache-sporting, shotguns-and-pickup-owning men walking guiltily around the premises of Hooters.

According to Jim and Howie, the Reason Men Like to See Breasts and Why It's OK harkens back to our Primitive Days (Tennessee by the way, the state we're in, is where in 1925, John Scopes was found guilty of teaching evolution to children, in the Scopes Monkey Trial), when the breeding/survival instinct in men made them especially aware of women's breast sizes. (And women still look for a man who would be good as the Leader of the Tribe.) So it's a Breeding Thing. The guys know I can't argue with Darwin. I asked why the place wasn't called "Thighs" then, since men should also focus on the size of a women's thighs for childbearing reasons, and then we got into another discussion that I think I won't write about here. . . .

CHAPTER 10

Mashed Potatoes

David Kahne, head of A&R for Columbia Records, sits in Maxwell's, in the restaurant part of the venue, in Hoboken, New Jersey, sizing us up over his two orders of mashed potatoes. I look away from him, ashamed of my own homeliness, wondering if he's ever been out to dinner with a woman who wasn't wearing makeup. Could we be the Next Nirvana, But with a Girl Bass Player? Would a female Kurt Cobain have to wear eyeshadow?

This guy was so important, I thought to myself, a famous record producer, and he was Peter Shershin's boss. This was our first meeting with someone this high up at a label. I could have at least put on blush or lipstick. Shershin was A&R at Columbia and loved us and needed to show us off to the higher-ups to move ahead with courting us. I'll bet Laura Ballance (bass player of the Chapel Hill, North Carolina, band Superchunk) wears lipstick when she plays at Maxwell's, I thought, unhappily. But part of the rebellion of indie rock was shunning dressing up, posing, costuming. Being anti, anti-fashion, until I could achieve anti-anti-fashion. But at this point, I owned no makeup, because I was completely opposed to portraying any type of sexuality onstage. It wasn't part of my dialogue, and I would have described it as "cheap."

For the most part, my fellow midwestern bass sisters weren't spending too much time or money on preening, either. Heidi Ore (Mercy Rule) says, "[On stage], I wore what I wore every day—jeans, tee shirts, skirts—mostly from the thrift store. We wanted to look like we just rolled up and jumped onto the stage."[1] Candice Belanoff (Walt Mink) says, "Once in a while I'd dress up on stage and 'be a girl' but it was like a costume. I really felt I'm here to play the bass, to play it well, to get the notes right. I rarely felt like 'I'm a woman up here playing the bass.'" Barb Schilf (House of Large Sizes) says, "Subconsciously we were definitely thinking I wanna be thought of as a good musician and not the cute girl. And that's sort of number one in your head and I probably dressed more girly as I felt more confident as a musician." There was focus on musicianship, and some either self-induced or peer pressure to not dress up.

But David Kahne now sat here across from me, in this fancy Hoboken restaurant/venue, "across the street" from NYC, with his mashed potatoes, at one of the gated entrances to Corporate Rock World, where I ostensibly wished to enter, and where there existed very few female archetypes. On stage, men of rock were able to represent everything from their intelligence level to their political leanings via scarves on mic stands, low canvas tennis shoes, sweater, glasses, or beard. Women really only got to choose sexy rock star or anti–sexy rock star. Just like we got to choose Wonder Woman.

Courtney Love versus Kim Deal

For most of my career thus far, I'd purposely ignored any performers who acknowledged their gender onstage, but had recently seen something that really intrigued me. Courtney Love, onstage at CBGB a few months before the mashed potatoes, had been dressed elegantly, like a bride, onstage, but her lipstick had been smeared, and she'd been screaming. Watching her, I was transfixed. She'd even yelled at the monitor guy during the show, which was the bravest thing I'd ever seen anyone do, ever, because a sound guy can deafen you by feeding back your microphone into your monitors, and then pretend it was an accident. Babes in Toyland, who I'd seen a couple months before, also had worn torn baby-doll dresses and runny makeup while screaming. The reclamation of strength while wearing feminine disheveled clothing fascinated me.

Marion Leonard writes that the messaging inherent in performative aspects (screaming vocals, vintage baby-doll dresses) of female indie rock musicians is understood on different levels depending on the audience, and that which is meant to be subversive may also just be read as the conventional style of the genre.[2] Being a perfect target audience, though, I read screaming while dressed as a battered baby doll as innocence stolen and anger morphing weakness into strength. Courtney's onstage power scared and thrilled me. I much preferred this combined spectacle to overtly sexual dressing, which I thought could be misunderstood as an invitation to be objectified, and also a distraction from one's performance of musical prowess. This was not so much an invitation as a threat, and it felt safely readable to me. Lest one tries to subvert sexism through blatant overcompensation, Leonard provides another warning, quoted from her conversation with John Peel: "If ever there is any area of human activity which is liable to be misunderstood, it is by someone trying to deflate, or remove, the menace from sexism by being grotesquely sexy. You are really playing with fire there and there are not many people, including Madonna, who managed to pull it off."[3]

Kim Deal, of Pixies and Breeders fame, another midwesterner on a major label, later provided a counterirritant for me. Her choice of dress on stage—rumpled, loose dark clothing—seemed asexual and not a part of the conversation. When we toured with the Breeders in 2002, girls in the audiences were still screaming and crying at her, "I LOVE YOU KIM DEAL" and some actually had hand-scrawled papers taped to their backs saying "Kim—Make Out With Me!" From the stage, she'd yell back, "I LOVE YOU TOO" or just laugh. "Kim [Deal] stood out as representing an alternative model of rock-girl desirability. She was a crush object counterpoint to the status quo cute indie bassist in a miniskirt and vintage go-go boots, a look inhabited with empowered grace by many of her contemporaries (then and now), but also easily co-opted by Urban Outfitters and reduced to a cliché of non-threatening sexiness."[4] With the inception now of "non-threatening" sexiness, there is nowhere to turn. No matter what you do, anything can be read as "sexiness." For me, it was a message I never wanted to convey.

A note on Kim Gordon's (Sonic Youth) stage clothes—since she was married to her guitarist and was already a goddess, I had decided she could wear whatever she wanted. Goddess accoutrement, to me, had transcended sexuality and her boobs would be, at this time, the property of Thurston Moore and unavailable to others, thus not applicable in my critique.

Even if sex and body objectification didn't play a role in how one chose to portray oneself on the stage, one still needed to pay close attention. Barb Schilf remembers, "Someone had a photo [of me] and because of the sweat and the material and the stage [lighting], it looked like I had a see-through shirt on, and I thought, 'OH NO! Oh my god! I have to be concerned about the material when I'm up there!'"

I peeked back at David Kahne. Being signed to a major label meant being thrust into a bigger public sphere, so I was thinking about the extent of code-switching that our group would consider. I even wondered if there were actual methods available to a producer like that to make me into a star. Whatever they were, I probably wouldn't agree to them. "Complete artistic control" was going to be the deciding factor in who we signed with. Still, I thought, "with great power comes great responsibility." I knew we'd be getting a huge amount of money to represent a label, and I hoped we'd figure out a way to respect that. I dug into my Maxwell's East Coast Creamy Meal (all meals on the East Coast are creamy) and hoped Mr. Kahne found Rick, Jim, and Johnny pretty enough to compensate.

Led Zeppelin Box Set

Al Smith, A&R from Atlantic Records (who we are friends with to this day), flies us out to New York City upon our request, conveniently on the same weekend as a Jesus Lizard show at CBGB. From him Rick scores a prized Led Zeppelin box set and hometown love in Cheap Trick CDs. Al seems the most outwardly enthusiastic about our band, and it's a joy to spend time with him, but Rick has reservations—we really don't think we have potential to sell a huge number of records, so major enthusiasm is a red flag. We do not want to get anyone fired! Al Smith would have to settle with signing the Melvins and Walt Mink.

During this time we also met Seymour Stein, the president of Sire Records. He ordered a protein shake from his secretary while we were in his office. Rick remembers, "He compared us to the Ramones instead of Talking Heads, which bummed me out even though it was obvious that was something he said to all the bands whether it was true or not." He'd probably not heard us, but others at Warner Bros. had been to our shows and had been very supportive.

We were also courted by a good number of newer, boutique, unproven labels. By the time we got to meet famous producer and head of the brand new Interscope Records label Jimmy Iovine, I found myself really wishing I could put on a bit more airs. If we seemed more exclusive, more enigmatic, more pretentious, people could feel like they were really getting something special out of meeting us, but it just wasn't our way. Jimmy was very sweet and enthusiastic but his favorite song from *Daisychain Reaction* was "Freedom Rock," which, to me, is a very commercial-sounding song. Although we liked it, we didn't really intend to write more songs like that, so it wouldn't have made sense to follow up on Interscope.

All in all, it was thrilling to be flown out to New York and Los Angeles and meet representatives from the different labels, and the best part was the feeling of not really caring what happened to us, that this decision would not make or break us. We were going to make music no matter what and would find jobs to fall back on if we needed to support ourselves. There was no worry of becoming rich and famous. This was just all an amusement park visit to me.

In the end, we decide to sign with Sire. We'd been in talks with them before the whole Nirvana thing happened, and at this time, they had a history of being an artist-friendly label. Our Sire A&R guy, Joe McEwen, was a quiet, older gentleman, who had signed Uncle Tupelo and always loved talking to Johnny our drummer about James Brown. Joe wondered why we didn't do more electronic stuff since we were so technical. Rick remembers that Joe had the original gatefold artwork for *Their Satanic Majesty's Request* in a frame on his wall in his office. Joe's background was music and critique, not business. He seemed to be a "cool" A&R guy as opposed to a cheesy hit-maker. And now we would be on the same label as the Ramones, Talking Heads, and fellow midwesterners the Replacements.

Livin' the Dream

Friday, April 17, 1992, Chicago, IL
SIGNING TO SIRE

We are in Room 2007, Le Meridien Hotel in Chicago, looking out the windows. It feels gray and important here, the beginning of a dystopian film. I'm dressed in all black, to signify mourning. We don't want to "sell-out" but with an indie contract with two records left, on an indie that cannot press up or distribute our records, we have little choice.

A Music Lawyer has flown in from New York to go over the contract, and he seems to match the desk. You can hire a lawyer to shop your music around to labels (for bands more commercially viable than us) or you can just hire one to help you go over the contract. It is suggested that the lawyer be from NY or LA as per contracts and discrepancies with record labels need to be handled in courts in those states. There are two lawyers who are handling all of the recent indie-to-major signings, and we have the second one, because he has agreed to work for a flat fee of $10,000 instead of percentage points from our future albums. This works toward our advantage because he will have no future interest (or meddling) in our creativity.

The Lawyer reads aloud through the ninety-page contract and explains every detail to us. All our own contracts (like show booking contracts) have been stolen from those of the Replacements/ Hüsker Dü with names changed, since they're coming from the same offices, and I'm sure they didn't originate there. This contract has to be the same one presented to every Sire band, but our lawyer still crosses out phrases here and there, in front of us, to earn his 10K.

"Here it says that we will only be paid for 90% of our records sold," he explains, because in the past, records made from shellac would have a 10% breakage during shipment. "We'll cross that out," he says confidently, since our records will not be made of shellac. "Here they want to give a bunch of free records to record stores and radio stations and charge it back to us," he says, crossing that out too. He must say this to every dumb midwestern band. When the contract comes back from Sire, they have crossed out all our crosses out. We have no power.

We do have $75,000 coming straight to us in the next couple of months, as a signing bonus, however; the money that drummers use to buy cars when they "get signed." Then another $125,000 for the first album, and more for the second. When we split up the advance, we (and ML, our manager) will each put $15,000 in our bank accounts for that year, a one-time deal. Yes, as Steve Albini says, less than you'd make at McDonald's. But we also have a two-firm deal, which means Sire must put out two of our albums. There are five option periods and a total of seven records owed. This describes their power over us. In the off chance that we become famous and worth more than these sums of money per option period, we are still tethered to them. It is more advantageous for the band to have fewer option periods and fewer records owed.

A small part of me is excited, because I could be across the street in a mauve-burlap, fluo-rescently lit cubicle, programming an insurance database right now, waiting to wait in line for a hamburger-hour lunch. But I'd already quit my flight simulator job. To me this label is that bigger plane that you have to take in the middle of your journey from your home to the exotic, remote place where there are the same amounts of people as your small hometown. It's a utilitarian placeholder, a necessary evil to buy out our Twin/Tone contract (around $70K), and we will still be able to press up records. Through our midwestern humility and practical choices, we'll attempt to stay on the major label as long as possible, fly under the radar, let them help us develop like they've done with so many other bands. When they drop us, we'll continue making music. We'll use label resources to build ourselves up for longevity. Though Rick and I are straightedge, we sip the champagne, looking out high over gray Chicago. I sign with an ordinary Bic pen. We are serious, sober as death.

CHAPTER 11

Recording

GDUNGE, GDUNGE, GDUNGE goes the bass part, lowest string dropped to a D. My new heavy metal pedal provides a new, deeper, louder place to prevail under the rest of the band while stuck in the key of D. Across the country from the Seattle grunge scene where Nirvana and Mudhoney happened, a new math rock contingent of Bitch Magnet, Codeine, and Slint swept westward from Ohio, New York, and Kentucky, and throughout the Midwest. Bands swapped heroin for science and passive aggressiveness, and now everyone had a couple of slower songs with quiet, angst-ridden poetic talking in them. We marveled at Mike McMackin's production of clear fuzz on the Codeine record, and everybody worshipped Bitch Magnet's drummer Orestes, who, it was said, could switch time signatures many times within the same measure.

Tool of the Man

Now that we're on a major label, not only do I still dislike recording, I even have a reason to feel guilty about disliking it, like looking a gift horse in the mouth. Rick, however, like any normal musician, was excited, for it would be at a different studio, with a new producer, and with a larger budget and more time. We had certainly chosen the right label. We had complete control over recording, songs, producer, studio (suggested by producer), cover art, choice of videographer, and budget. It seemed Sire agreed with us that we should prove we hadn't sold out. So we chose Mike McMackin, genius of the math rock genre, and wrote a bunch of non-selling-out songs, just the way we liked them, no compromise, and with no suggestion of a radio hit.

Authenticity was of utmost importance to many bands who jumped to majors at this time. No one wanted to be labeled "a sellout" even though there wasn't much you could do about it. Nirvana pursued Steve Albini in 1993 to recapture their "rawness" for the album that came after their blockbuster *Nevermind*. Steve had warned them, "I'm only interested in working on records that legitimately reflect the band's own perception of their music and existence."[1] He'd asked for a flat fee of $100,000 and, as was his custom, he'd insisted on no royalties from sales. Unfortunately, the major label machine wasn't ready for that much authenticity, and some songs ended up being remixed by R.E.M. producer Scott Litt.[2] Steve says that clients dried up for a while after *In Utero* was released, as groups now either considered him unavailable due to his new stardom or didn't want to jump on the next Nirvana bandwagon. And at least one major label actually blacklisted him.[3]

To remain sustainably independent, Poster Children spent great energy charting our own course through major label territory. Rick did our cover art on our home computer; Bill Ward, who did our "If You See Kay" video for the previous record, did our "Clock Street" video for this record. We retained Ellen Stewart, our same booking agent. We even figured out a way to buy our own records from the major label in order to sell them on tour. We did not take tour support, which is money the label fronts you to help pay for your tour. How would we be able to continue after the label dropped us if we became reliant on them?

We did make the classic major-label mistake (for us, anyway), which was to go far from home to Destination Record, "so we could concentrate on making a record without any distractions." This didn't work out too well. We began by recording basic tracks in a large empty church in upstate New York. Then, overdubs in a house our producer rented on East Hampton (in the era before Airbnb). We discovered the owners were living in an Airstream in the backyard, which seemed creepy to me. They had decorated the house for us, but expected our arrival two weeks before we actually showed up, so there were dead flowers in vases all over the house.

At some point, the owner came into the house to grab something from her bedroom, and I ran up to try to clean it before she went in—I may have scared her, and she ended up knocking over a large screen, which cut her cheek open. She said she was fine and left quickly, a trickle of blood dripping down her face, and I didn't see her again. Johnny, freaked out about the threat of recording with a click track, was up all night in the next bedroom, silently twirling sticks, and you'd hear the faint sound of a stick accidentally hitting another in the middle of the night. Rick was painfully aware of how upset he was. Out in the town, I experienced the strange coldness of East Coasters. And in upstate New York, a land foreign to me, the temperature never exceeded my favorite, 90. For me, it was the year that summer never came.

I know plenty of people who heard *Tool of the Man* as their first Poster Children album, and they love it, and that makes me very happy. The first song, "Dynamite Chair," is probably on my top-five list of Poster Children songs, because it is really fun to play. I feel as if I'm prancing off cliffs when I go from the C-sharp, B, then to the low, open E string and bounce up and down on the Es. The song also contains some of my favorite of Rick's lyrics, which, to my understanding, emerged from a story about Dennis Hopper trying to cure himself of mental anguish by blowing himself up in a dynamite chair. Rick is most brilliant when he draws from his love of film and narratives about actors and directors. I say "emerged from" because I think Rick sometimes uses incidents as metaphors, so if this song fits what you're feeling, you can wear it.

> Loaded up on dynamite
> Hey brother can you spare a light
> I'm going to scrape the sky tonight
> And shake down all the stars

Friday, April 28, 1995, En Route to Athens, GA

MAJOR LABEL, SHMAJOR LABEL

We spent time in Atlanta with our Reprise Records reps. Reprise reps must be the greatest label reps in the world. We haven't met any that aren't kind. They all have their own special personalities, too. There is Bruce McGuire up in Minnesota who is our King of Style, very urban and sleek. There is Tim Hurst of Cleveland, one of the less-"alternative-looking" reps we've met, who we love very much; he is always at our shows in the area and is so supportive. There is Patrick up in Michigan who got us a snowboarding show who snowboards and the last show he had put on before ours was a Minor Threat show. There is Joe Janecek, our man in the Los Angeles area, who is way into the internet, is from Nebraska, and thinks our van is blue. There are so many great label reps and one of the best things about touring is meeting friends you haven't seen in a while; these are just more friends. (Plus they buy us dinner.)

This week, the gold star goes to Warren, our radio guy in Atlanta. Not only was he there to help set up shows for us on the radio and interviews, but he also came to our shows and took us out to lunch and dinner and went extra out of his way to help us figure out a way to sell CDs at our shows. Most major-label bands cannot get hold of their own CDs to sell, but we are on our way to being able to do that now, thanks to Warren.

Since we are a very small band on this label, we do not expect all the label people to come out to support us, but when some do, it is very nice. It helps them understand what we're all about, too. Tonight Warren gets to hang out with the Throwing Muses, another Reprise band, who are also playing nearby.

Our marketing team, led by Jo Lenardi, met with us to ask how we wanted our records to be promoted. The marketing team at Sire was a team of indie graduates—Jo had begun her career working at a suburban Chicago record store, and she was very nice, easy to talk with. Bruce McGuire and the others really were all cool kids who made it to the majors; they were like us and you could tell they really wanted us to succeed. The problem was always the higher-ups, and the amount of resources (like time, or perhaps, spots on radio playlists) that could be spent on a noncommercial band.

I remember waiting in Howie Klein's (president of Reprise, and one of our champions at the label) office with the rest of the band—he hadn't come in yet. We were seated facing his desk and I noticed he had a long brick of demo cassette tapes lined up like dominoes across his desk. I saw in middle of the line of tapes a cassette by the band Hum that Rick and I had released on our own 12 Inch Records label, one we must have sent him. I glanced at the door to make sure no one was coming, snuck up to his desk, and extracted the Hum tape from the middle of the line and placed it first in line, so he'd be listening to it next. I ran back to my seat as his assistant entered the room. She walked in to lay a stack of folders on his desk, and as she left, the weight of the paper she'd placed down set off a chain reaction, dominoing the cassettes across the desk. The Hum cassette, now first in line, comically fell off the desk and plopped right into his trashcan. I ran up, grabbed the cassette out of the trash, placed it back on the desk, and jumped back to my seat before he walked in.

It seems reductive to hate on all major label people. In all meetings, whether they were young or old, hipster or not, all were genuinely excited to talk to us.

Friday, September 13, 1996, Cincinnati, OH, Sudsy Malone's

TIM HURST

Tim Hurst, our wacky local Reprise representative, was at our show. He's such a character! He's so completely straightforward about music with us in a way that no other label rep is. I think the other people who work at the label are way too polite to act the way Tim does with us. We absolutely love Tim for how honest he is with us (boy, have we learned a LOT from him)—so tonight I wrote him a special set list and asked him if he'd rate the new songs and he DID! I just think that's the most awesome thing in the world!

Tim's Set List—with Ratings

Black Dog	★★★★½
Attack	★★★
Junior Citizen	Not rated (old song)
Bulletproof	★★★½
He's My Star	★★½ (old song)
Good Cop Bad Cop	★★★
Speed of Light	★★½
Music of America	★★★½
Persimmon	★★★
Ferris Wheel	★★★★
If You See Kay	★★★★ (old song)
Ankh	★★★½
Pink	★★★★½
Wide Awake/King 4aDay	★★★½ (old songs)
Rock and Roll	★★★★
Dynamite Chair	★★½ (old song)
Everything Must Go	★★½
Happens Every Day	★★★

Tim likes ROCK music. There's a couple of new songs we've written that I think he will like a lot, but Rick doesn't have words for them yet. Tim says the song "Black Dog" sticks out like a sore thumb. I can't imagine why everyone likes that song. I like it, but it doesn't sound very commercial to me.

Everything Steve Albini says is true about the music industry, but there is also another way to look at it. It's a building full of people who are making money from music, and yes, I know it was Madonna's music, and they were making it because they were selling a CD that cost them twenty-five cents to make to twelve-year-old girls for twenty-five dollars, and only 13 percent of that money went back to Madonna, and label execs are very rich, but $250,000+ of that money was bestowed upon us for our own music. Of course the people who work at labels are enthusiastic and exuberant, and happy to meet us. They're giving us money for our art. They were authorized to redistribute Madonna's money and we were enabled to have it for a short time. They were figuring out how to sell pop music and channeling some of the money back to smaller bands. And it's dangerous; A&R people are constantly thrown out of their jobs. But it's all in the endeavor of making music. Think, for a moment, about the Buddhist concept of Right Livelihood. At least they are not making bombs.

That one should be making money at all playing music was a questionable affair to some of our idols. Fugazi refused to make t-shirts or play for higher than five-dollar ticket price. There was a prevailing attitude that once you spent your main hours on your music "job" or made a living from it, you were a "sell-out." In America, anyway. In Europe, there was government money for that sort of thing.

March 16–April 2, 1995, Europe

WEA, PARIS, FRANCE

This was one of the highlights of the tour: A person named Didier (I hope I spelled this right), who works for WEA, our record label in France, took us out after the show. We saw the Eiffel Tower at midnight, unbelievably awesome and HUGE. Apparently, it is being painted dark green right now—it gets a new paint job every seven years. The lighting is astounding. Rick remarked that it is one of the few buildings that incorporates its infrastructure with its artwork. We walked around underneath the tower for a while, in the gravel, marveling at its hugeness. It's so great to see it at midnight, when there isn't a huge amount of people around. Didier told us that there is a restaurant on the bottom floor that is booked three years in advance, and already booked for New Year's Eve 1999.

Didier took us out to a restaurant—it was around one a.m. now, and we knew we would be driving all night to the next show, but heck, we weren't gonna be at the wheel. We had wonderful conversations with Didier, about the future of the internet, and Americans ripping off French movies and redoing them worse. Didier seemed worried about what would happen to record labels in the future if everyone could just self-publish on the internet. We decided that even though there will be lots of self-uploaded music on the internet, record labels will still be needed to be able to lend some credibility. And Warner Bros. will probably have to fight Microsoft for a band like Girls vs. Boys.

I felt pretty smart with this big label exec asking us questions about the internet, until I ordered a shrimp cocktail and when I got it, I noticed that there were little eggs stuck in it so I cleaned them off in the water-filled finger bowl. I wondered in my silly, midwestern way (we don't have shrimp in Champaign) why such a nice, fancy restaurant would forget to clean the eggs off the shrimp. The last time I had seen something like this was in science class when we were dissecting crawfish. Later I found out what I began to suspect after the fourth egg-laden shrimp, that the eggs are a delicacy. Someone in England later remarked, "The French will eat anything that moves."

Our Own Team

On our own side, we were mostly self-managed. We wanted to make all our own decisions but were not really "phone" people. At the very beginning, Chris Corpora, our friend in the Champaign scene, helped us get shows and was our mouthpiece. Later in our career, when we were getting ready to sign with Twin/Tone, Ellen Stewart became our booking agent. ML Compton, who managed Thin White Rope, became our manager after Chris Corpora, and helped us navigate our jump to the major label. From playing on Lollapalooza, we moved to the Lollapalooza management company, and Kristin from Larrikin became our manager for a while. Management is more important when you are on a major label because the people who work there are not always comfortable communicating with "the talent"—they want to coddle and complement them, and then send them out of the room while they tell the adults what is really going on; sales not up to par, don't hear a hit, etc. There were a few times when I was aware that we were being told "the truth" and thus, treated a bit differently than other bands. Rick and I always enjoyed knowing what was going on.

• • •

Sunday, April 25, 1999, DAY OFF!!!!!! Summerville, GA

HOWARD FINSTER WILL MAKE ME AN EINSTEIN

We went to Summerville, GA, to visit Howard Finster, an awesome folk artist. You may recognize his artwork from Talking Heads record covers. He has built this incredible place called "Paradise Gardens" in Summerville, which is in the top left-hand corner of Georgia. There are piles of junk, huge signs with biblical sayings on them, and drawings and mosaics everywhere. You can visit all this any day of the week, but if you happen to come on a Sunday, Howard himself is there! There's a picture of me standing with him. He's not feeling too good today, so he wasn't very talkative. I told him my ear hurt, and he showed me that he had a rash on his head. He said that the pollen was very bad today, and I said maybe it's the pollen that caused the rash on his head. He snapped back, "Maybe the pollen is in your ear, too!"

He told us that the doctor had told him that maybe it was the fluorescent light in his bedroom that was causing the rash. I didn't want to disagree with him, but then hoped he'd elaborate, but he had set out to finding an Einstein drawing for me. I was there because I wanted to meet him, but also I wanted to buy an Einstein cutout. Howard Finster does paintings of famous people like Elvis, Marilyn Monroe, Reagan, and Jesus, and one of his lesser-known figures is Einstein. Today, all the Einsteins were gone, so I'm going to get a fresh one—and it's gonna be personalized!! I'm very excited about this. I even requested glitter on it—I never saw an Einstein with glitter, but maybe if I'm lucky, mine will have it. I hope it does.

CHAPTER 12

Touring

Wake up at the crack of noon and head out on the road
Get lost for an hour while we're looking for the show
Tear the roof off every night and load back in the van
Find a place to sleep before the whole thing starts again
—Rick Valentin, "Zero Stars"

Thursday, June 22, 1995, Lawrence, KS

A DESCRIPTION OF OUR VAN

I'm sitting in our touring vehicle—it's a fifteen-passenger, white, Chevy Sport with a blue plastic interior—amid clothes caked with body-salt, once sopping with sweat; pillows; books; shoes; and wheat. We're in Iowa now, on our way to Kansas, and the wheat must have gotten tracked into the van when we were stopped on the road. It is at least 100 degrees in here; the outside air temperature is in the high 90s, and our air conditioning doesn't work; we don't have time to stop and fix it. Water in bottles laying in here heats up to whirlpool-temperatures and is undrinkable; a little hotter and all our deodorants will probably melt. There is a topper on the van, purchased in Decatur, IL, which looks frighteningly like an upside-down fiberglass rowboat glued on to the top of our van. Most of the original top of the van has been removed, except for an area above the driver's and passenger's front seat, where three huge boxes of t-shirts, a tent, and other "hard" things (objects you don't want to get hit with) can be stored.

The first passenger bench of the van has been torn out, leaving enough room to sleep two on the floor. I am sitting in its place on the floor now, which is covered in egg-carton rubber foam, typing on our very warm laptop. The computer probably shouldn't even be on; it's way too hot in here.

The remaining bench seat sleeps Howie or Jim usually. The very back of the van has a wooden loft, elevated by metal bars. Under the loft fits all the band equipment, amps and cabinets and drums, held back by the bench seat. Above in the loft we can stick soft things like our sleeping bags and sweaty show clothes. If a really fast stop is made, everything from the back loft falls on top of whoever's sitting in the back seat. There is no one else traveling with us right now; just the four of us in the van, and everyone is sharing driving duty, but Jim has been doing most of it lately. The van can sleep four, and uncomfortably five if it needs to.

We have no tape player or CD player, just a radio.

For us, touring on the major label was no different. Ellen continued to book shows for us, and we mostly played the same venues; there was no push from the record label to get us on bigger shows. We still drove our own van, and we had no roadies, although we did enlist a soundperson on later tours. We were usually fed at night by the venue and took ten-dollar per diems each day from our band fund. We never took tour support from the label, because we didn't want to rely on something that could be revoked. We never had any days off, because those days had no income, and mostly just generated fights. We always slept on people's floors.

I coerced a local t-shirt printer, Ed, owner of Weiskamp, to have his workers teach me to screen shirts so I could screen ours and get a discount. One day while working on Poster Children shirts, I saw Mosaic (the first graphical web browser, developed down the street at UIUC's NCSA) shirts on the press next to mine. I begged to be allowed to screen one of those shirts and I still have my own Mosaic shirt, to this day. On tour, we sold tons of t-shirts, and that sustained us more than anything. Playing shows for around $250–$500 a night, we came back from each tour with thousands of t-shirt dollars to split. We came back to Champaign, where it was cheap to live, and were able to live as musicians for almost a decade. If you housed us, bought a t-shirt, or fed us, it went straight into touring, and we are grateful to you.

Wednesday, October 8, 1997

THE COVERED DISH, GAINESVILLE, FL—CRAPPING

We played again with the Swingin' Neckbreakers, a retro rock band from New Jersey. We encountered them on the West Coast somewhere and also in Minneapolis, back weeks ago. They are SO New York/New Jersey, too, they have the accent and everything. They are funny, funny guys. We asked them how their tour had gone so far and it sounded like it was kind of like ours.

I asked them what they talked about in the van, and their t-shirt/tour manager guy said they had a fight in the van about which would win in a fight, an alligator or a gorilla. Can you imagine a bunch of New Yorkers sitting in a van screaming at each other about whether or not a gorilla would maul an alligator? The last interesting discussion we had that I remember was we talked about why it was good to eat dirt and whether or not antibacterial soap was going to destroy our race as we know it by creating new strains of immune bacteria. Both our bands found common ground, though, of course, in the one topic that every band discusses thoroughly each day, and that is Crapping. "Oh Yeeah," says Westy Neckbreaker. "Where to do it, how it looked, the shape, smell, and what was in there before you did it. . . ."

Same as It Ever Was

The best part of touring was circling the country and running into old and new friends. From the stage after the show, we'd ask if anyone had a floor we could sleep on, and there would always be offers. Staying at people's houses made touring a very rich and educational experience. We'd get a feeling of how people lived in each city and state, the media they consumed, work schedules, similarities and differences, touching people's lives in a new city every day. I became very comfortable sleeping on a wood floor with my sleeping bag and pillow, and being able to sleep like this made me feel strong and independent. When at home, we'd house traveling bands and feed them, believing that the "tour karma" would return to us when we were on the road.

Mercy Rule has great stories about landing at houses with parties; funny because they were not "party people," and sometimes Heidi and Jon would, in the midst of a raucous after-hours party, unroll their sleeping bags in the middle of the floor, and Heidi would state, "Your Mom and Dad are here now." Somehow, Poster Children normally ended up with like-minded geeks, possibly because I would also request a home with an internet (dialup) connection. After-show parties for us consisted of watching movies (like *Real Genius*, *Buckaroo Banzai*), eating "snack salads" (a combination of gas station foods featuring all the different food groups: salt, sugar, chocolate, and something spicy), and being invited to places like SRI and shown VR experiments, way back in 1993.

WEIRD AL YANKOVIC WAS AT OUR SHOW! CLUB SODA, KALAMAZOO!

Ok, check this out—WEIRD AL YANKOVIC was at our show!! I didn't see him; only Howie saw him! After the show people just kept coming up to me and telling me Weird Al was at our show—I guess he watched the whole thing and stayed until the end! I couldn't believe it. I can't believe I didn't get his autograph. I was so busy doing merchandise after the show. Rats!! But people came up with our posters, they had signatures of all four of us and Weird Al Yankovic's signature right in the middle of ours! Man, that is SO Great!!

And a very special person had us all sign his zip drive. That is the first zip drive I've ever autographed.

We slept on other bands' floors from time to time—I was once sleeping on the North Carolina band Polvo's floor next to a couch, and beside my sleeping bag, under the couch, I found a guitar. I wrestled it from under the couch, cradled and strummed it and it sounded like I was playing a Polvo song. The Polvo tunings? I smiled happily, replaced the guitar and went back to asleep. We slept at Six Finger Satellite's house and I remember never feeling more comfortable in my life than sitting on their floor.

When we could, we attempted to bring Champaign bands with us on tour. We had decided to start a record label (12 Inch Records) to help out other Champaign bands, and we'd paid to press the first two Hum records. We were able to bring Hum, Steakdaddy Six, and Lovecup on tour with us, all amazing Champaign bands.

We met our wonderful friends Walt Mink, Mercy Rule, and House of Large Sizes on tour during this time. We played with Jawbox, Superchunk, and Seam, among other notables. We also toured with some larger bands and learned a lot about the industry from them—the Fluid, a wonderful band from Boulder, Colorado, who could descend from their mountain and play in the flatlanders' extra oxygen for hours like supermen, had a road crew that were going hungry on tour—their major label had decided to just not give them their already-promised tour support. (This was why we never took money from the label for touring.) On tour supporting the lovely Screaming Trees, we were surprised to learn that after their tour, they would go home and have to go back to work. We came up with the phrase "the Golden Nugget" after hearing successful rock stars comparing themselves to others, not being happy enough with what they had already achieved. You could always strive for the Golden Nugget, we decided, something consistently out of reach, but maybe not what it seemed. Perhaps the Golden Nugget really was a piece of shit.

Three Learning Opportunities

During these years, there were many opportunities to play with larger, more famous bands. Sometimes this was because the larger band's management, or the venue, could be convinced that our record label would pay for advertisements, or pay for some tickets to give away, and therefore, our presence on the bill would help bring audience. Poster Children didn't always accept the offers, because the billing had to make sense. Around this time, singer-songwriter Sinead O'Connor, known for her courage and outspoken ideas, was booed off the stage while performing at a Bob Dylan thirtieth-anniversary concert at Madison Square Garden, because she tore up a picture of Pope John Paul II a few weeks earlier, on *Saturday Night Live*. She had been protesting child abuse in the Catholic Church. Apparently Bob Dylan and his audience's anti-establishment sentiments stopped just short of the Catholic Church and a woman with a shaven head.[1]

Another phrase that came out of touring with larger bands was "a Learning Experience." This occurred when something went horribly wrong.

Friday, June 12, 1992, Detroit, MI, between Prong and the Smithereens

This show was going to be the biggest we'd ever played so far, a radio festival in Detroit in a 3,000-capacity semi-covered amphitheater. While Rick was leery of opening for the Smithereens, whose audience probably liked softer music than ours, I was more worried about playing after Prong, who was harder rock than us. Still, we had heavy metal songs to play for their fans, and soft ones to help the transition to the Smithereens, and I decided that if Prong's audience saw that there was a girl on the stage, they'd assume she'd forced the men to play softer music, and, with some of them possibly being acquainted with women, I figured they might give us a pass and not beat us up.

I also planned on being very nice to the swarms of roadies on the stage, and in doing so, I assumed, they would be very respectful back; they were probably so used to mean, assholey big bands, and we would be a breath of fresh air. This is not what happened. When we were finally allowed on-stage, I had to ask a roadie where I could plug in my amp. "Where might I find power?" I asked politely, and the man looked me up and down and then replied loudly, "I'll take No-Name bands for fifty dollars," and walked away. Everyone in the vicinity wearing a black tank top laughed. I angrily unplugged someone else's amp and plugged in my own, attached my cable to my bass, and strode haughtily toward the front of the stage, only to be YOINKED midway, because my cable wasn't long enough to reach the front. Then we all had to move our amps forward.

It got so much worse. The show started. Leather-clad Prong began by playing a bunch of minor chords rather quickly. I can only imagine how angry they may have been to have to open the show—and in the afternoon! CHUGGA CHUGGA CHUGGA. Three songs in, their audience finally rose out of their assigned seats and ran toward the front of the amphitheater, fists pumping in the air. The music was very powerful. The stage manager was horrified at the sight of the dancing! "We can't have people out of their seats during the music!" he yelled. He motioned frantically to the security men—"CUT THE POWER! CUT THE POWER!"

"DJUNG DJUNG DJUNGITY DJUNG . . . foont."

The stage lights and sound went dead. Poor Prong, now devoid of electricity, consisted only of black leather, drums, and daylight. Angry fans climbed onto the stage. I watched from the side of the stage with great amusement. The management was horrified, yelling into giant walkie-talkies. What seemed like only a few moments later, a line of Detroit riot police paraded onto the scene in helmets and shields and began herding the fans off the stage! I was now entirely delighted—this was way more entertaining than I thought it would be! But as the crowd left the stage, chanting "PRONG! PRONG! PRONG! PRONG!" my glee turned to horror as I realized what was supposed to happen next.

It was now our turn to play. The Detroit riot police formed a protective semi-circle in front of the stage as the roadies carried Prong's equipment backstage. Our tiny amps were trotted into the foreground. The stage manager came up to me and threatened, "THE SAME WILL HAPPEN TO YOU IF THE AUDIENCE GETS OUT OF THEIR SEATS!" "PRONG, PRONG, PRONG!" added the audience angrily at us over the heads of the riot police. Tiny amps set up and turned on, I stood in front of the mic, looked at the other members of my band, then back at the audience and stammered, "THIS SET IS DEDICATED . . . TO PRONG!!!"

We began playing a Loud Song. "Prong! Prong! Prong," the audience murmured as it began filtering dejectedly out of the amphitheater. I'd never even met Prong, but man, did I feel bad for them. So we played ferociously and self-righteously, to show the Detroit riot police, the Smithereens, and the waning crowd just how punk rock we were. Then Rick lobbed his beloved Musicmaster guitar over the riot police's head, straight into the audience, and a lucky crowd member ran off with it. The riot police, watching the guitar get carried off, stood valiantly still, protecting us from the crowd who was leaving in droves by this time.

This is what we decided to call a Learning Experience. I learned that a crowd is more than the sum of its parts, and that exposure to a crowd doesn't necessarily mean exposure to its parts. A crowd, whether it's Prong fans, Detroit riot police, or a corporation, thinks as one.

And Rick learned not to throw his guitar into the audience.

Sunday, September 20, 1992, Lawrence, KS, Public Enemy

Sonic Youth played with Public Enemy in Chicago, and the audiences meshed perfectly. Never mind that there was some sort of riot afterward, we were at the show and we didn't get involved, and it was Chicago, so we assumed the police started the riot. So when we were asked to play with Public Enemy in Lawrence, Kansas, a college town, we figured it would be OK. The brainy college kids, of course savvy enough to love Public Enemy, would also appreciate our witticisms, our computer and film-nerd references. Afterward we'd set a spell with Public Enemy and talk shop and politics.

Which is not what happened. When we got on the stage, the audience, a thousand white college kids in backwards baseball caps began to boo loudly. "Get off the STAGE," they screamed. Some even held up their tickets with their middle fingers crossing-out the name "Poster Children" as support act. "We are supposed to play for forty-five minutes before Public Enemy takes the stage," I explained into the mic. We played another song. The crowd continued booing. I know there were Poster Children fans in the crowd too, but it's hard to focus on the happy people when there are others booing.

After another song, I polled the crowd. "How many of you just want to sit here in silence for forty-five minutes before Public Enemy plays?"—which was a mistake. To ask a question that can only beget an enthusiastic and POSITIVE response is something important to learn for both rock stars and politicians. But somehow as the shouting and cheering diminished, I mustered up the guts to answer "Too bad! We're gonna play anyway!" and we started "If You See Kay," a song that starts with Rick screaming.

Both we and the audience survived the opening act. We were very excited to see Public Enemy, and their S1Ws came up and complimented us after our performance. Chuck D started the main show and performed for a while by himself. Flavor Flav arrived very late to the show, and when he got on the stage, he'd apologized and said it was because he'd lost his clock, which was funny because he normally wore a large clock around his neck. He then implored the audience not to vote, which was sad, because it was right before an election, and there were voter registration booths set up all around the perimeter of the show. Perhaps he knew what he was talking about, however. It *was* a thousand white kids in the middle of Kansas.

Saturday, August 28, 1993, Kansas City, MO, Memorial Hall Supporting Fugazi

Being asked to play with Fugazi is the pinnacle of existence for me. I can think of no greater honor. This show would be affordable, inclusive (all-ages), and there would be no extravagant light show, only white lights. No beer cozies, no t-shirt sales, and no stage barrier. Where we might have been performing in malls and participating in pyramid schemes for every other show, gorging ourselves in gluttony, we will now be attending church. Or a library. It is a detox.

Fugazi kindly grandfathered us in to play even though we were now on a major label—since we already had a machine behind us to promote us, Fugazi would be wasting that spot on us, where they could be helping promote a more indie band. Only one other band had had this honor, Ian MacKaye tells me, Jawbox, a month afterward, and then no more. "We were already friends," Ian explained to me, and said that he respected our energy on the stage. Later, after our major label years, we'd once again have this honor.

This show in particular, was one of the most vivid experiences of my life, and Ian seems to find this show of note too, so I will write about it.

Conversations backstage with Fugazi reside at the highest levels of hierarchical thought: think creation and evaluation. There is an exchange of ideas and then appraisal and critique, a playful riffing back-and-forth. The content could be anything from recent books read on tour (a book on crowd theory, for example) to why Bob (our drummer) was panhandling outside a show (is he poor? If not, please explain the action). You have to concentrate really hard when you talk to Ian because everything is a question to him, and everything needs to be explored.

Today's show presented many problems for Fugazi. The management had slapped on an additional one-dollar service fee, making the ticket price six dollars. Fugazi had constructed a sign explaining this, which made the management very unhappy. During the set, audience members had been restrained from moving and standing where they wanted, which had also upset the band. To keep an eye on the proceedings, Ian had asked for all the lights to be turned on in the gymnasium as they played. This upset people, who did not want the house lights on in the room. They yelled at Fugazi in between songs. Ian replied, "I'll turn off the lights if I get a petition of 100 names." Soon after, I watched questioningly from the balcony as the side of a cardboard box was tossed around the crowd. A couple of songs later, the box was pushed onto the stage, and Ian picked it up. The box had handwritten names of audience members, and Ian announced that his request had been fulfilled and that the house lights would now be turned off. "Turn them ALL off!" yelled someone in the audience, and Ian replied, "Ok, turn them all off, I'll show you how democracy works!"

It was pitch black in the room. The audience was silent. The band began a slow strumming, "Blueprint." When the loud part of the song kicked in, whoever was in control of the lights blasted them on again. I cried. Rick said it was one of the most profound moments he'd ever experienced at a show. It was performative and participatory; the audience was part of the show. The absence of light had made the light grow more significant, and more dear to the show.

Later on, there were more problems with the management. A fan's camcorder had been smashed to the ground, and a gun had been pulled on the band! Somehow, we were in the van and missed most of this. A Fugazi show is always a profound experience. Twenty years later, Ian was visiting my class, and I asked him to tell us a tour story, and this is the one he recounted. Does he have stories like this for each day of tour, for every opening band's classroom?

Junior Citizen

After a good amount of touring and learning, it was time to settle down and write another record. This time, we weren't going to worry about selling out, and to me, it seemed like we almost embraced the idea. This meant adding a keyboard to a song.

Our second record for Sire was *Junior Citizen*. Determined to record in a more familiar setting, we settled in Madison, Wisconsin, in April 1994, recording with Brian Anderson, second in control at Smart Studios. A combination college town and state capital with an amazing assortment of restaurants and hippies gave us plenty of distractions and made the recording process much easier this time. Rick remembered that the Clash had made a fort out of guitar cases while they were recording, so one of the items in our Reprise recording budget was a tent, which Rick set up as a chill-out space. Another line item was a Mac Quadra 650, which we set up in the control room, where we could work on interactive programming and cover art—and also spend hours playing *Sim City*.

Recording in Madison was a blast. I had many favorite foods and restaurants, sampling Tibetan, Afghani, and Nepali food for the first time. We again lived in a small, rented, plain apartment during recording, but there seemed less pressure to Not Sell Out this time. We had fun experimenting with poppier techniques. Jim decorated the wall of the apartment by hanging a fork, knife, and spoon on it. During the recording sessions, I found out that Urge Overkill was going to perform nearby and got ourselves added to the show. They forced us to play before the doors opened, unfortunately, so it wasn't that much fun.

Smart Studios was owned by Butch Vig, who had recorded the widely successful Nirvana record *Nevermind*, which we'd used as our litmus test to help us decide whether or not to sign to a major label. It was during our time at Smart that Kurt Cobain shot himself in the head in his house in Seattle. My parents called to make sure I was OK, which really surprised me, because this proved that Kurt was a household name. Reporters arrived and were pounding at the door. They were looking for a statement from Butch, but he wasn't at the studio, he was traveling, in the process of assembling the band Garbage. (I remember he'd played a demo for us in the downstairs studio and it had sounded very disco to me.)

We sat in the second-floor kitchen watching goth teens in Nirvana shirts crying on the TV and waited for the pounding to cease. No one wanted to talk to anyone. Although Kurt was one of the few people I'd not met in person, I remember being really frustrated that someone with such a powerful voice would have wasted it this way. Having recovered from being suicidal earlier in life, I felt I had earned enough credibility to be upset with him. I was now trained to believe that suicide or thoughts about hating oneself was egotistical, selfish, and unskillful.

In literature, the death of the leader could be foreshadowing, but in my book, it's the Zen koan "if you meet the Buddha, kill him." We would have to make our own path now.

Thursday, June 22, 1995, Lawrence, KS
TRUE DREAMS OF WICHITA; DRIVING THROUGH KANSAS CITY

A brown haze hangs over the surprisingly urban Kansas City skyline as we cruise through on a deserted I-70. The fresh cat-pee and cow-dung smell of fertilizer that greeted us at the Kansas border now gives way to a potpourri of chemical smells as we drive through a restaurant row of chemical factories; first we smell melting rubber, then burning sugar, a couple of miles later, acetate, then freshly mown hay, then *nothing*, which I find strangely ominous, and then metal cleaner. The highway system running through the city looks more like an airport runway system, four lanes each direction that I have never seen full. The sun is still blaring down, high in the sky at 7:30 p.m.; today we are one day past the solstice. I love this part of the US. I have crystal-clear memories of driving through Kansas City around dusk, pink sky and towering, ice-blue halogen lamps shining down on an empty, sandstone-colored superhighway. This is what I picture, shivering, listening to Soul Coughing's "True Dreams of Wichita."

Lollapalooza 1995

Thursday, June 29, 1995, Cross Country:
Live from I-88, West of Schenectady
BOSTON TO CHICAGO TO CHAMPAIGN TO MADISON TO SEATTLE . . .

Now we are on our way to Lollapalooza. This is a REAL cross-country drive. You can't get much easter than Boston, or much wester than Seattle. We are taking I-88 through NY now, avoiding the Roy Rogers hamburger restaurants on Highway 90 at all costs, because we had a bad experience there once. We drive through rolling green hills—a couple of years ago, I would have called these green hills "mountains" but compared to the Alps I saw in Switzerland and Los Angeles, they are just foothills. I see little SUNYs (State U of NY) sporadically placed all throughout upstate NY, but mostly there's just green trees, willows, ponds, firs, and deciduous forest everywhere, except for a clearing we just passed where a couple of bulldozers frantically construct the gray, red, and blue concrete skeleton of a Wal-Mart as if they are building a bomb shelter.

In 1991, Perry Farrell, lead singer of the band Jane's Addiction, along with a few other manager and lawyer types, founded Lollapalooza, a music festival that would highlight "alternative" music and, originally, traveled across the country. We were fortunate enough to perform on six of the 1995 shows: Seattle, Vancouver, BC, Denver, Kansas City, St. Louis, and Indianapolis, on the Second Stage. We may have worried for a minute about the possibility of selling out to play this show, and fears were allayed by the fact that Pavement, Hole, Beck, and the Jesus Lizard were also playing the show. The Jesus Lizard, especially, made the tour legitimate. Capture one legitimate band, and you've got credibility for the rest. This worked for major labels as well; A&R people would be allowed to sign a "pet" art project band to attract other, bigger bands, and make the band feel like it was OK to sign.

The Lollapalooza tour was set up at outside arenas, with record-store tents and other types of sales booths. Management on the first couple of nights was wonderful—they made a concerted effort to make even the smaller bands feel welcome. We had brought hundreds of t-shirts with us, though, and were able to sell them ourselves with no overhead charge taken by Lollapalooza (normally unheard-of in corporate concerts), and this helped us feed ourselves. I had printed up a bunch of shirts with an oval that said "Fucker" in them—no Poster Children logo or verbiage. I figured we could still sell those shirts, even to non–Poster Children fans, and I was right.

I was already writing "tour reports" in html, and each night on tour in 1995 we'd fight to find a dialup connection—a phone where I could disconnect the cable and plug it into my laptop so I could upload the html to the Champaign Freenet, prairienet.org. My writing about Lollapalooza came right after a really rough Canadian tour, then a drive to Boston to make a video for "He's My Star," a drive from Boston to Champaign to pick up eleven boxes of t-shirts from Weiskamp and Joe the Soundguy, and then straight to Madison to play with Mercy Rule. Tore ourselves away from visiting with them, then drove thirty-five hours and fifty minutes. We had estimated a thirty-six-hour trip, and had been that close even having run out of gas and stopped for four hours on the side of the road. We obviously didn't need a tour manager.

We finally arrived at the Gorge, in George, Washington, and I was amazed at the beauty. I was also amazed at the friendliness and cordiality of all the people running the Lollapalooza.

Monday July 3, 1995

THE GORGE, GEORGE, WA

My jaw drops because I've never seen anything as beautiful as the Gorge. I see a huge, bright green lawn with stone-cut seats, stretching out to the huge black metal-frame stage. As big as my thumb are the tiny figures of Pavement, but I can hear their voices like they are standing next to me.

Just as clear as Pavement, I can hear Possum Dixon playing on the other stage, but for some reason I can hear and understand both songs at once. I attribute it to the fact that I am staring out at the backdrop of the Main Stage, which spreads out as far as I can see, red, gold, and brown striped rock, with a huge gorge cut through it by the (Columbia?) river at the bottom, shining blue. I can see the white wake trails of tiny boats speeding along the river. If I felt nervous about playing before because it is Lollapalooza, now I sort of feel overwhelmed by the beauty of this place, like I will be playing in the presence of the Creator. It's almost blasphemy, to be playing before Sonic Youth, Jesus Lizard, Pavement, and the Gorge. Wow.

Do you want to eat dinner? We walk behind the Main Stage to the catering, which is set up in a yurt. The dinner is skewered meats, hummus, rice, tabouli, spinach, assorted cooked vegetables, a couple of salads, a banana-y chocolate cake, pita breads, and most any soft drink you'd want. And it is really, really good. You go back and sit down near a fountain set up in the middle of the eating tent, with white quartz rocks set up all around it. The tables all have a huge slab of granite on them with a bunch of grapes on top. Someone really went to a lot of trouble to make this whole meal very, very fancy. We eat right overlooking the Gorge.

Eating, we saw our friends the Jesus Lizard and their illustrious booking agent, Boche. David Yow, the lead singer of Jesus Lizard, looked pretty healthy. He always starts out looking pink and healthy and then by the end of the tour, he's black and blue. A topic of discussion among us was deciding which bands had tour busses—we were relieved to see J. Lizard going back to a VAN to get some beer. They sure know how to tour right.

Reviewing my writing from Lollapalooza, I find common themes. I would always report on the kindness of any more famous group, and was constantly in awe of Pavement, Sonic Youth, Beck, and the Jesus Lizard. I wrote a bunch about Sonic Youth's baby, whose cries sounded to me like a Sonic Youth song. I was euphoric for the first couple of shows, commenting on the audience and the sweet and humble alternative rock stars. By Denver, though, it started getting hot and the grounds weren't as nice.

Saturday, July 8, 1995, Denver Lollapalooza

I DON'T THINK DAVID YOW LOOKS VERY HAPPY

Fiddler's Green is a crappy place to have a show like this. It is DEFINITELY NOT the Gorge. Instead of Grand Canyon—like scenery surrounding us, we are sort of in the middle of an office park, in an Edge City. When we arrived at the Second Stage today to load our gear, we found the trailer-stage set up on the side of a little street. Lollapalooza Street Party. In front of the stage was the two-lane street (closed off), and behind that, a spit of lawn, and then a huge metal fence. Beyond that was the rest of the grounds, the vendors, and the entrance to the main stage. It was about 100 degrees outside, and the crowd seemed to move around like they had somewhere to go after the show.

Eating. I yelled in pretend fright as David Yow (singer from the Jesus Lizard) slunk past us with a plate of food. He looked terrible. He looked at me sideways, then glared at all of us (we sat with Yo La Tengo), then grimaced at Rick, shook his head, and sort of crawled into the corner. Rick had watched part of their set today and returned depressed; he said the Main Stage had CHAIRS set up in front of it, and you couldn't even GET to the chairs unless you had special tickets. Can you imagine SITTING and watching the Jesus Lizard? What's the POINT? Anyway, I'll bet the area in front of Jesus Lizard was empty—I heard that David spent part of a song sitting in a chair in the front row.

"I don't think David Yow looks very happy," Rick said. I stared worriedly at Yow slumped in the corner with his back turned away from everyone while one of the movie-star-looking Possum Dixon guys (who were as nice as they were pretty), sitting next to Georgia, talked at us for a half an hour about David Yow throwing beer bottles at him during an interview today (making me feel even worse for Yow), something about Yow yelling during the interview that he wanted to "Fuck Sinead O' Connor" (we laughed about this), and the interviewer deciding to end the interview prematurely. (I never saw any press today, so I don't know what all the fuss is about.) Mac from Jesus Lizard stopped by to say hi to all of us, and he seemed a little healthier in attitude and appearance.

I worry about these bands, playing these huge amphitheaters. I hear Courtney Love stories all the time: she punched Kathleen Hanna; she was verbally assaulting Beck. I have to start hanging out backstage more often, because I still haven't even seen her. I am sure Courtney can work a crowd like this, but the other bands like Sonic Youth and Pavement and Jesus Lizard do not thrive on that sort of hype. They are music, first and foremost. I hope they can survive this tour—it seems like a completely different audience than any of us are used to. A terrible tour can break a band's spirit, and cause tons of friction between the members; sometimes even break a band up. I feel bad when I hear people say that "the steam seems to have gone out of Lollapalooza"—and other people are even saying it's a "sell-out thing now; its integrity is gone." I can't believe it—this is the only Lollapalooza I'd ever even think of going to. I probably would have paid to see this one, and that is saying an AWFUL lot, since I haven't paid to see a show for a very long time.

Hasselhoff

OK. Tomorrow, David Hasselhoff is going to be at a mall, approximately two miles away from where we are staying tonight, signing autographs. I don't know how many people actually know this, but, well, "He's My Star," the song we are currently "pushing," was partially inspired by David Hasselhoff. It's sort of a joke but not. Rick and Jim went to high school at Lyons Township, in Western Springs, IL, where David Hasselhoff went to school. We have a mission tomorrow; we HAVE to meet him. We have to bring him a CD, tell him about his song, and possibly get him to sign something. At least, he's got to know about us! Isn't this exciting!

Sunday, July 9, 1995, Drive to Kansas City

BOOBS, AND OTHER THINGS I FORGOT, IN DENVER

Last night while Courtney Love was probably eating dinner, or finishing a book, or dressing her sore arm, I was standing in our t-shirt booth, watching the pre-Coolio Second Stage Extravaganza, emceed by Foley. This consisted of a Hickey Contest, an impromptu woman rapper who had jumped on the stage from the crowd (who was pretty good), and a Spanking Contest. These are things that never happen at our shows. Meanwhile, I was chiding Ira from Yo La Tengo for only playing two songs for their entire set because he was complaining that Pavement had tuned for ten minutes during their set. Rick was on his side, but I tore away from the conversation because I wanted to see what the crowd had suddenly gone wild about.

The Second Stage crowd was screaming and applauding now, not because the woman rapper had finished, but because two nubile young bikini-clad women had jumped on the stage, wanting to be spanked by "Trigger," a member of one of the rap bands. Howie had the pleasure of standing backstage, watching members of Cypress Hill videotaping the women and screaming "SHOW US YOUR TITS! SHOW US YOUR FUCKING TITS!!" and watching the drunken girls eagerly comply. Howie was horrified at this humiliating and vulgar display, but in true Poster Children cynical form, I asked him how the tits were and he said that they were OK. All this going on out at the Second Stage, probably while Thurston Moore watched his baby take her first steps across a dressing room, and while Pavement put together jigsaw puzzles in their trailer.

He's Our Star!

No lesser man than DAVID HASSELHOFF descends the escalator of the Denver Mall into a crowd of dozens, tan, gorgeous, and forty-five, shirt open, chest hair exposed. MIX95.1 (or some similar station) responsible for this spectacle blasts his song and the crowd screams. He sings along for a few lines, and the music dies down. He addresses the crowd. "Hey EVERYONE! How're you doing today?" The crowd squeals. The next thing he says is "This is MY Song!! How many of you have heard this song on the radio?!" The crowd goes silent, and someone blurts out a sheepish "hurray," and then he screams, "Well, That's because THESE PEOPLE ARE NOT PLAYING MY RECORD!" I gasp.

He continues, semi-playfully, "HOW MANY TIMES HAVE YOU GUYS PLAYED THIS SONG?" and the radio DJ says, "Well, we played it that day last week that we interviewed you!" "AH, SO YOU ONLY PLAYED IT ONCE?" David screamed, when Rick and I, on the outskirts of the crowd, looked at each other, realizing that we were IN THE SAME BOAT AS DAVID HASSELHOFF, and we felt compassion.

David continues "I'LL TELL YOU PEOPLE WHAT THIS IS ALL ABOUT. YOU SEE, IN GERMANY, I AM A HUGE STAR! I SELL HUNDREDS OF THOUSANDS OF RECORDS IN GERMANY!! PEOPLE THERE LOVE ME! BUT HERE, I don't get played on the radio! I am SICK OF HAVING TO FLY ALL THE WAY TO GERMANY TO GO ON TOUR!!" Laughter from the crowd. "I'LL TELL YOU WHAT I WANT YOU ALL TO DO," he cried, "PLEASE CALL UP THIS RADIO STATION AND REQUEST MY SONG! CAN YOU DO THAT?"

At this point, I felt weak in the knees. Now I KNEW I had to get our CD to him. Our paths were inextricably entwined, from our humble beginnings in Western Springs, IL (Rick and Jim's, anyway) to this mall here in Denver, CO, all wishing for the same thing, for the radio to love us. Knowing our story, and that we'd written a song about him would provide a salve for his tender and exposed heart.

The seed idea for our song "He's My Star," incidentally the song we were pushing to radio at this time, was David Hasselhoff. It came from both David and Rick being Lyons Township High alum, Rick walking through the same halls as David past and seeing him on TV. The idea that you can have a relationship with a famous person even though they don't know you. Using David H as a seed also protects Rick, part of Generation X, from writing sappy lyrics. When Joe McEwen, our A&R guy (a bit older than us), found out about the Hasselhoff factor, he was disconcerted. He had loved the song but now it seemed cheap to him. He didn't understand both sides of the irony. The song is very meaningful, Hasselhoff or no, and to discount it upon reveal of its DNA is a mistake.

The Golden Nugget exists on all levels—everyone wants to be more! Even David Hasselhoff wasn't happy, and was complaining about the same things as we were! Just the next day, I'd mentioned in the tour report that our fans had actually been threatened by Q101 to stop calling and requesting "He's My Star." Reprise was at this time pushing the band Filter, not us. Filter posters were everywhere in the Lollapalooza record tents, even though Filter wasn't on the tour. When we could actually find our records, we had noticed that our EPs were mistakenly priced as LPs. We were disappointed at the lack of label support, feeling that Lollapalooza was a good opportunity for exposure. Still, the president of Reprise Records had carried my bass off the stage for me in Canada. It was such a sweet gesture, and I guess it didn't cost the label any money. I often wondered how upset the label people actually felt that they had to choose which bands to push, and which to leave behind. With California people, you never really know.

By the end of Lollapalooza, I had plenty more to complain about. At one of the shows, we were somehow mislabeled, and people came up to me after the show with Yo La Tengo shirts, begging me to sign them. Yo La Tengo is and always will be much cooler than our band. When I insisted that I wasn't in Yo La Tengo, I was told, "You are the BASS PLAYER! I SAW YOU ON STAGE!"—"No, I am in Poster Children." The answer was "But I thought Poster Children SUCKED! I liked YOUR band!"

In addition, shod in my new, free, Doc Martens (given away to the bands at one of the shows), I had to put myself on our own guest list in order to be able to watch the Jesus Lizard in front of the stage. Even with an official Lollapalooza laminate with my picture on it, I wasn't allowed in the seats in front of the stage. People had paid for those particular seats, but they were vacant during the opening acts, like the Jesus Lizard and Pavement. I wondered if these bands understood this was the reason why the front of the stage was empty when they played. The rules at the midwestern amphitheaters were for more corporate rock bands. Maybe Perry hadn't continued on into flyover territory and had already abdicated his management throne. By St. Louis, I was remembering the local stage management company that I'd run into on earlier tours, a bouncer with a bald head standing right in front of my stage area, protecting me, with a bright shiny new greasy tattoo of Hitler's face on top of his head. Would he be there?

Wednesday, July 12, 1995, WAAAAAAAHHHHH!!!!!
(Our Last Lollapalooza Show—Indianapolis)
I SAID GOODBYE TO BECK

Before we went on the stage today, I noticed parts of Jesus Lizard, parts of Pavement, and their entire booking agent standing around the stage, and all of a sudden, I felt a huge load of responsibility on my shoulders. You WANT these bands to like you! But knowing that these bands are standing around watching us, what I did to stop myself from worrying was to just turn off my surroundings, like I'm playing in a white room, and absolutely nothing matters except whether I'm in tune. That's pretty much what it's like for me anyway most of the time; it's just sometimes I try to remember to pay attention to the audience, because the audience likes that,

I think. Sometimes when I actually look out into the crowd, though, I can either have a paranoia attack, or I sometimes get really, really angry for no reason, just looking at someone's face; like they transferred all their anger into me or something. This is pretty weird, isn't it? Well, anyway. Can you believe it? Some of the members of Jesus Lizard stuck around afterward to tell us they enjoyed our set! WOW!

I'll tell you, the Rock Star with the Most Charisma Backstage is definitely Beck. He just seems to wander around backstage all the time, and talk to EVERYONE! He'll just stop and listen to whatever you have to say. Tonight I was saying goodbye to him because it was our last day of the tour. I told him there is a girl on AOL who I met yesterday who's named "Beck Gerl" and that she wanted to say "hi" to him, and he said, "Wow. Beck Gerl?" and then he thought for a minute, and he was holding this little purple flower and he smelled it, and said thoughtfully, "Well, tell her I said hi, and that I just smelled this flower for her." That's pretty damn nice.

Better Than Nothing?

After Lollapalooza, we learned we'd been picked up for another record for Reprise, so we'd started writing new songs (for *RTFM*) and went on to open for another couple of pop bands doing well on major labels, Better Than Ezra, and then Sponge, and then some dates with the great Archers of Loaf. I'd never listened to the two pop bands, but we had agreed to support them, because it's really fun to play in front of people who have never heard you before. We thought some of those people might like us, and we were really enjoying touring.

Sunday, October 1, 1995, Sponge Tour Day 1

WHAT THE LITTLE "E" MEANS ON THE GAS GAUGE

We are starting to see a pattern with our van. Each time the little gas-gauge needle stays on the little "E" (in the red area on the left of the gauge), the van stops working after a while. It starts working again after we put gas in it.

Yes, we ran out of gas today. Twice. And both times, about a block away from a gas station. The first time, Jim and Howie pushed the van down the ramp and we all pushed it to the gas station, with Rick steering. It's pretty easy to push, actually. The second time, it ran out of gas but miraculously started again to drive us the next block to the gas station. Incredible. Are we a bunch of idiots or what? Doofuses? There is nothing wrong with the gas gauge, just us.

So we were late for the first Sponge date. And we were so proud of not having a tour manager or a bus, but we were late. As we drove over the Cuyahoga River, which is the river that caught on fire [in 1969] because it was so polluted, Rick came up with the phrase "Tinder for the Cuyahoga."

We were talking about killing people again, and instead of the old "kill 'em and eat 'em" slogan we had before, now we have, "Make Them Tinder for the Cuyahoga." I think we were starting to feel like Tinder for the Cuyahoga tonight.

Discussions in the Van Today

What Does It Mean When the Cows Are Sitting?
It's going to rain
It's going to rain fire
There is extra gravity in the area
Aphids will come down from the sky
Did you ever stop to think about the actual name "Burger King"?

"The Crocodile," by Dostoevsky

Rick and Jim were watching the public TV overnight, which is the greatest thing ever invented in the history of the world—educational TV, all night long! A couple of nights ago they had short plays and one was a play called *The Crocodile*. The story was about a man who gets trapped inside a crocodile and wants to stay there, but his friends want to rescue him. There is a German guy in charge of the crocodile who says that the man is on his property now, and wants to charge admission to the crocodile.

The friends do not want to go along with this; they want to save the man, but the man wants to stay inside the crocodile. So once again, the four of us were trapped in the van without a way to get the information we needed; this particular time, we needed info about Russian history so we could figure out what this story was an allegory for.

The Inevitable "OJ: The TV Movie Cast"

Susan Sarandon as Marsha Clark
Noriyuki "Pat" Morita as Judge Lance Ito
Ralph Macchio guest appearance as the bailiff
O.J. Simpson as himself (of course)

Entertaining the Audience with Your Spit

We could spit
We could spit at each other
We could spit and catch it
We could spit at each other and catch it
We could spit at each other; pass it all around the whole band, and then spit it out into the audience to share it with them

Monday, October 2, 1995, Sponge Tour Day 2

We went to visit the memorial to the protesters shot in Kent, which happened back in 1970 (info source: Jim). We wondered if the national guardsmen who shot them still lived in the area. There were policemen at the show last night, with guns. I thought it was weird since we were in a college gymnasium; I don't connect college gymnasiums and guns.

The monument is near the middle of the campus, and made out of a gray granite. There are four big boxes at one end, and a bench and a granite patio with inscribed words: "inquire, learn, reflect." There was a woman sitting on the bench, dressed in black, staring at the trees off in the distance while we walked around the monument. The names of the four people who died are on a plaque set into the ground, along with the others who were injured. Howie sang a little of "4 Dead in Ohio," the Neil Young song, in remembrance.

After a while, the larger shows started to wear on us. The members of the headlining acts were sweet when you'd run into them, but their soundchecks would go on forever and we'd not be able to test our own gear. Our playing time and volume would be limited, we'd be forced to sell our shirts at the same price as the headliners, and because nobody wanted to move the headliner's equipment, we'd have to perform in the tiny space in front of the main act without drum risers. (Although Sponge was *very* cordial to us, moved their gear, and treated us wonderfully.) Mostly, though, as openers, we'd be mistreated by club and stage management companies. In addition, audiences were made up of what I began to term "Music Haters," people who just came out to the shows because they had nothing better to do, or wanted to get laid. Not because they loved the music and the bands. It was very impersonal.

Saturday, October 7, 1995, Driving to Omaha

AUTUMN

The sun is blaring down on us like a bright orange laser beam, more brilliant than I ever remember it, like it's the reason all the cornfields we're passing are empty or filled with standing skeletons of burnt, dried cornhusks. Leaves are beginning to turn brown; they're all a dull grayish green color. Everything is waiting to die. I don't like autumn unless it's nighttime.

Wednesday, October 11, 1995, Good Audience Comments Tonight

Audience member: "SPONGE!"

Audience member (after show): "My roommate says you guys aren't very good."

My retort: "Well, he's probably right."

By the time we got to Washington, DC, with Better Than Ezra, which I have nothing good or bad to say about, I was very surprised to see my old friend and mentor, Ian Mackaye, who had a message for us.

Wednesday, September 13, 1995, Washington, DC

THE BETTER THAN EZRA TOUR PART III

Fugazi! I could go on for days about how much I respect this band, and how honored I feel each time I see Ian and Joe at our shows. They make me feel so special by showing up and talking to us, and I know we are NOT the only ones who they do this for; I think they make everyone who comes into contact with them feel special. This is a great gift; I would like to be able to do this one day. Ian sat up in our dressing room and told stories—he has incredible stories about every aspect of the music business—especially touring—he has been through so much. He should write a book.

The place we played in was a huge, scary disco-venue. The area that the club is in is a total dump. Off in the distance you can see the Lincoln Memorial, right over a KFC. Laying in the dirt outside the club, Rick found the front panel of an 80286 computer!

I'm looking at the bright side of things, like the techno-garbage, but Ian isn't. He wants to talk about respect. He brings to my attention the ways we are being disrespected on this tour, shakes his head at me, and I feel dumb. He wants to know how I can agree to go on tour with a band I've never heard the music of. He finds it absurd. He wonders if it's the label's doing, and I assure him it isn't, which makes me feel better, but doesn't seem to make him feel any better. He is correct; in a perfect world, we'd only tour with bands we knew, and loved, and that is the way we've worked it up until now.

But now we don't seem to be getting asked to tour with the bands we love, so it is time for us to meet new bands. Maybe we tour too much. We just want to play in front of people and we can't keep going on our own tours, or people will get sick of us. We have to build a new audience.

Sometimes talking to Ian is really scary; it's like being in the presence of the pope or something; it really makes you question everything you do. He always seems so perfect, and he always asks you the right questions to make you wonder about your decisions and motives. I know it's good to be thinking about this kind of stuff. I always wonder if he's ever made a mistake. It is too bad that more bands do not or cannot follow the Fugazi way. In the religion of the music industry, Fugazi are prophets, or saints. No—better: the Buddha.

Europe with Steel Pole Bath Tub—A Lovely Tour

I'd first seen Steel Pole Bath Tub when they blew Nirvana off the stage at Tritos, in Champaign. There wasn't really anything Nirvana could have done (including be on time), because Steel Pole Bath Tub is one of the best live bands on the planet. (A band must be seen on a small stage with minimal lighting to determine this.)

Then, May 20, 1995, we played with them and Faith No More at Nautica Stage, in Cleveland, Ohio, in between rushing from one state to another. I was excited to talk to them, but this was a radio show, and my tour report reflects that we were mistreated and exhausted and ended up missing SPBT's set. We only were able to talk with them for a moment. "They were really nice. One of them seems to know a good amount about computers—I had the geekiest chat with him," I wrote. Angrily, we drove back home. What a waste of an eight-hour drive, there and back, I thought.

Just to prove that no positive action goes unrewarded, a few months later, SPBT called us up and asked us to tour Europe with them for six weeks. We were thrilled and said yes immediately!

Friday, February 23, 1996

EUROPEAN TOUR SUPPORTING STEEL POLE BATH TUB, FEBRUARY–APRIL 1996

The TOUR BUS, YES, THE TOUR BUS picked us up in front of my sister's apartment in London. We are on a TOUR BUS. It is Steel Pole Bath Tub's tour bus, they are paying for it; it is much cheaper than getting hotels each night. For us, it makes it possible for us to tour with them; if we would have had to pay for hotels for all of us, there is no way we could tour here. So a tour bus is the best and cheapest option! Steel Pole had never been on a tour bus before, either; I've been sitting in here for about two hours now and have decided that it's pretty damn neat.

This tour bus has twelve bunks in it, and there are thirteen people total on this tour. Right now the opening band Surrogat isn't with us yet, so we're pretty comfortable. The bunks are very, very small, very coffin-like; they are probably six feet by three feet by four feet, I'd guess. You have to slide yourself in exactly the way you want to sleep because you can't really twist around inside the bunk. You are also supposed to sleep with your head facing the back, in case the driver hits something! There are other rules we were told, which I'll talk about later. The bunks are very comfortable; I went in one for a couple of minutes and fell right asleep. There are windows looking out of the bunk and shades if you don't want to see outside. Right now I'm typing and everyone is asleep in their bunks, and we're on our way to Leicester. In the back of the bus is a sitting area that would probably seat eight people, and a little TV and VCR and CD player! In the front are two tables for eating, and seating for eight. The very front sits the tour manager and obviously, the bus driver. There is also a bathroom that it is very hard to sit down in, and no toilet paper, because you're not allowed to crap in the toilet. I guess there aren't usually girls on the tour busses, so there's no toilet paper in sight. There are two girls so far on this bus: me and Amy, the t-shirt-selling person. She seems very, very cool. The Steel Pole Bath Tub guys are very nice, too. I want to make sure we never crowd them. The best part about the tour bus for me right now is looking at the people outside; they stare in and don't know what rock stars are inside! It could be the Rolling Stones, for all they know! Rick says, "They know it can't be the Rolling Stones because there's no life-support systems in back."

There is a month and a half's worth of writing about how much I love Steel Pole Bath Tub's music and how nice and sweet the band members are.

Thursday, March 21, 1996

I find these guys really quiet and really sweet, the sweetest people, really, that I've ever known. I love to watch them walk on the stage and become these shy monsters of rock. I find myself even wanting to imitate their speech patterns; I love to listen to them talk. I guess we fit great with them because we are pretty quiet off the stage too, and then when we get on the stage I think we transform, also. I also find that I like to listen to their CD after the show when I'm lying in my bunk trying to go to sleep. I can't get enough of them.

This is interspersed with some angry moments—by this time in our career, I had taken to intense critique of my performance at shows and would often come off the stage crying and trying to destroy my hands. Even the late Mark Lanegan wrote so generously about me as we toured with Screaming Trees, "The female bass player in tears every other day for some reason."[2] I looked toward performance mentors and found one when we played with the Cows.

Saturday, March 9, 1996
ZURICH, SWITZERLAND—THE COWS AND SHANNON'S TEACHING

The Cows

Tonight we all played with the Cows, an awesomely noisy band from Minneapolis, and I must say that this whole day has been sort of a religious experience. The last time I saw the Cows I felt the same way, like I'd attended a Punk Rock Inspirational Teaching. The lead singer, Shannon, is so full of charisma that it's a band I would consider following around like a Grateful Dead fan.

What Do You Care What Other People Think?

The great thing about Shannon that I know from watching him and the Cows play is that Shannon doesn't care what the audience thinks. This is an important lesson to learn. In fact, I don't think the band cares at all what the audience thinks. Patrick from Surrogat (the opening band, from Germany) and I had a little talk the other day, sitting in the back of the tour bus, about whether or not to care about what the audience thinks—he says that Steel Pole Bath Tub says they don't care about the audience reaction. Patrick says that although he thinks that is a valid way to go through a show, he tried it and cannot go through with it. I'm the same way.

Other Teachings

By the time I got off the stage today I was raging mad. Rick told the audience we were 0 for 2 here at Rote Fabrik, the beautiful and famous Zurich club we were playing at. We had already had two crappy shows there. Then I went up to the mic and said, "Well, if you're gonna suck, make sure you suck HARD." I don't know what the audience thought. I know they were clapping sometimes; it couldn't have been such a terrible show, but by the time I got off the stage I was screaming at everyone. I was electric, powered, enraged. I went backstage and dared bewildered members of the Cows and Steel Pole Bath Tub, "Just TRY to go on stage and SUCK as badly as WE did." I had pulled my cable out of my bass amp about five times this show, sang out of tune, and everything seemed too fast again. The stage sound was unbelievably quiet, adding to the feeling of "suckage."

Afterward, in a vast backstage dressing room filled with vegetable trays, breads, cheese plates, and Swiss chocolates (in Europe, bands are treated like royalty), crying, I got a lecture and pep talk from Shannon Cow (lead singer) himself. He explained to me that I had to go on the stage and "find that special place where I would just have to not give a fuck what anyone thinks." Then he went on to tell me more; he talked on and on about going on the stage each night and cutting out a piece of your heart (during this part, he also gestured, to illustrate exactly what he was talking about) and placing it out on a platter for the audience and they could do with it what they want. "Your goal is to leave the stage with your dignity intact." That's what he said. Stunned and thoughtful, tears clearing from my eyes, I told Shannon that he was a Teacher. He replied, "Fuck That. Fuck You."

Then I watched them prepare for their show. Some bands do physical warmups before they play. Some bands have a group prayer. Today, the Cows' preshow prep consisted of Kevin, the bass player, drawing a bra on Shannon's chest with a thick, black marker, finishing up the fallen bra strap around his shoulder, with a fair amount of wordplay between them—it always seems like the noisiest bands are the wittiest, and then Shannon disappears into the bathroom with a banana and two pieces of duct tape. He must have been hungry. I left the backstage dressing room to join the audience.

By the time they went on the stage, with no soundcheck, I was out in front. Shannon looks like a movie star, a prettier Brad Pitt, but the music sounds like the apocalypse (which I love). Two songs into the show his motions become more deliberate. He begins to strut back and forth on the stage, silent, pacing to the music. At one point, he stops, facing the audience, and dramatically pulls down the zipper to his pants, and pauses for a minute, staring out at the audience. Then struts more. Music continues. Stops again, and reaches into the zipper opening of his pants. You're not sure why he's reaching in there now; what good could come of this? Struts a bit more, and then you can see he's pulling something out, and of course it's the banana. It's been in his pants this whole time during the show.

He struts around some more holding the banana vertically at his crotch, and then finally turns straight, facing the audience again, starts peeling it, very seriously. This action seems to take another three or four minutes. I was almost on my knees in hysterics. Another bit of strutting, staring straight at the audience the whole time, and then he starts breaking off pieces of the banana and eating them. Four strokes to peel the banana perfectly into fourths. Then he breaks off a series of four chunks, eating two and giving two to the audience. He carries off this pageantry with the pomp and sobriety of someone giving a lecture to a college class or to a political rally. Or maybe to a church congregation. It's an absurd comedy, some sort of burlesque + food sustenance commentary. There are so many signals and references and potential meanings inherent that you just have to laugh, because maybe none of them are actually being represented here. He's just trying to leave the stage with his dignity intact.

The Accomplishments of Others

The rest of the night I think I spent listening to Mike from Steel Pole Bath Tub talk, three bands cramped in the tour bus in the middle of Zurich, Switzerland, next to a pier. By the end of the night when he is about ready to drop, Mike starts explaining to everyone how the universe operates. There was a whole discussion in the back of the bus involving three bands, about everything from physics unification theories to a one-sided debate on how purification of water and milk (and everything else) has led to the absence of certain elements (like lithium) that are necessary to balance people's brain chemistry, resulting in people becoming more and more off-balance emotionally as the decades pass.

By the end of the night everyone had fallen asleep, and Howie had woken up—it was just dawn and I discovered Mike half-asleep in the front of the bus listening to a Pogues tape that was blaring over the bus speakers. How is everyone else asleep with this noise? I think he got up to try to turn it off once but couldn't figure out how to do it so he was just listening to it over and over. I was staring out over the water dreaming of when I saw swans last year (same place, crying despondently) and the sky was lavender blue.

HOWIE: (appears from nowhere, trying to act annoyed.) "Could you turn that tape down?"

Mike fumbles around in the front, turns the tape down to about 110 decibels

ROSE: (still carrying on the conversation from hours ago, which involved mutual compliments from both bands).

HOWIE: "It's getting light out."

Pause. . . .

ROSE: "This reminds me of Madison, Wisconsin . . ."

HOWIE: "Yeah."

Pause while we stare out at the water and boats.

ROSE: ". . . except it's Switzerland."

HOWIE: "Yeah."

MIKE: "I'll never admit to my own accomplishments. But I'll always celebrate with much joy the accomplishments of others."

Then he passes out.

Failure Tour

The great Los Angeles band Failure asked us to tour with them near the end of our major label tenure. "Their music is slow and dreamy and really pretty. Their singer's voice is beautiful. Also, their fans seem really intelligent. They must be pretty happy," I wrote. The opening band was called Summercamp and they were a new hot band being pushed by their label. For whatever reason, there were some famous people at these shows. Hilarity ensued.

Wednesday, April 30, 1997, Portland, OR, on Tour with Failure and Summercamp Supporting

RYAN O'NEAL AND BEN STILLER WERE AT THE SHOW!

The other night we were driving through Idaho or something like that, and it was pitch black, mountains all around us, and there was a tiny city off in the distance, with sparkling orange and yellow lights, and the comet was hanging down directly ahead of us, like it was falling toward the earth, about to destroy it. It was really beautiful.

We got lost coming into Portland again, missed the bookstore [Powell's], and when we arrived at the club we found a review for the show, talking about how underappreciated Failure is, and how they should be huge rock stars. And then about us it said something like "Sarcastic keyboard-pop music you'd expect from a ten-year old jaded indie rock band." Keyboard-pop?

Failure cancelled their show tonight. From what I hear, their drummer has hurt his hand! I hope he gets better soon! He missed a really fun time!

This show was great! It was a really nice little club, and on top of it, Ryan O'Neal and Ben Stiller were at the show! Rick was beside himself; he is giddy around anyone who he's seen on a TV set. I think Ben Stiller is a friend of Summercamp. I wish I had gotten up the nerve to go talk to Ryan O'Neal, but I don't really know too much about either one of them. I should've gotten their autographs or something. I kept thinking, "Gee, I hope they stick around for our show," but I don't know if they did. Jimmie said Ryan was completely plowed. He was rocking out for Summercamp! Ben Stiller slunk around the club, either trying not to be noticed or trying to be noticed. Both Rick and I almost ran over him on our way onto the stage, he was in the way. But can a movie star ever really be in the way?

It's hard to play when famous people are in the audience, because you want them to like you, but then you got to wonder how good their taste actually is. And why would I want Ryan O'Neal to like our music? What's he going to do, ask us to be in a movie with him?

Monday, June 9, 1997, Whisky a Go Go, Los Angeles, CA, on tour with Failure

PATRICIA ARQUETTE?

Greg from Failure came into the dressing room and talked with us for about a half-hour. It was the most animated I'd ever seen him. It was wonderful. He is twenty-five years old. He was talking about authors—he must read a lot. HE FINISHED GRAVITY'S RAINBOW. Rick has finished it too; Greg was impressed and said that Rick is the only other person he'd ever met who has finished it. For those of you who don't know, *Gravity's Rainbow* is a big fat book written by Thomas Pynchon, and it's about math and people getting stiffies before a bomb drops, in WWII. And an adenoid, and a guy going through a toilet (I'm sure that *Trainspotting* scene is a reference) and Gaussian distributions. Each time I try, I read further, but up to now I've never really gotten past page 200. I have the beginning memorized, because each time I start at the beginning. Rick read it when he was working in Indonesia. Greg read it on vacation with his family in Hawaii. I think you have to be trapped somewhere in order to finish it.

OK. We played our show at the Whisky. Howie wouldn't shut up about how great it is that he's getting to play the Whisky, where Jim Morrison from the Doors was Discovered. It's a nice club; the stage is really high so people can see you mostly from wherever they are. It was PACKED tonight, a Monday night! Amazing!

The last time I was at the Whisky we opened for Swervedriver, about five years ago. And Keanu Reeves was at the show. That's what I kept telling Howie, in order to irritate him every time he mentioned the Doors, since I don't care about the Doors. But tonight, tonight, after the show, I was walking away from the stage and a woman grabbed me sort of shyly and said, "I really loved your show" or something like that. I looked down at the floor and shyly said "thank you" and blushed like I usually do but then I looked up into her face and I SWEAR I was staring into the face of someone who looked EXACTLY like Patricia Arquette. She was EXQUISITE. I walked away half-stunned and then watched her for about fifteen minutes from the t-shirt booth. Then I told Rick, "Rick, go over there and tell me if that's Patricia Arquette." I explained to him that she had touched me and had complimented me on our show. Could it have been Patricia Arquette? He asked me if her teeth were pointy. "She has those two pointy teeth in front, you know." I pushed him down the aisle. When he came back, he said, "Well, it kinda looks like her," but he wasn't sure.

So I just stared at her a little longer. My cousin and a guy who I knew from high school were there too, sitting with us at the t-shirt booth. I kind of wanted to watch Failure but the place was so jam-packed and there was that possible Patricia Arquette standing right on the side of my field of vision, so I watched her some more. She had beautiful long whitish-yellow hair, which she sort of flopped over when she got tired. No one was standing very close to her; she had a little field around her.

So then I got the bright idea of since I couldn't go back and politely ask her to show me her teeth, I realized I'd seen her breasts a lot in that David Lynch movie. So I decided to go walk back and see if they were the right size and shape. So I walked back down the aisle and nonchalantly gazed at her breasts. They kinda looked smallish, where I thought she had big ones. But she was wearing a halter, I think, so maybe she had to go braless. I noticed a lot of women having to go braless in LA. And maybe in the movie, they could have been stunt-breasts. I walked back up to the guys at the table and asked Rick, does she have small breasts or big ones? Rick thought big ones. So I guess maybe it wasn't Patricia Arquette, but by god, this woman was gorgeous. I should really have just walked back up to her and said, "Is that YOU?"

Tuesday, June 10, 1997, San Diego, CA—More

I'm still thinking about Patricia Arquette. I finally asked ML, our ex-manager (who we're staying with) what he thought and he said that Patricia Arquette comes into his record store that he manages ALL THE TIME. She lives here! It could have been her! The other guys seem to think it was possible, too. Halter tops can make your breasts look much smaller than they really are, you know. If this woman wasn't her, she should have been, anyway. I could KICK myself for not just coming up and asking her. When I did look into her eyes (and they were gorgeous), I sort of looked questioningly and alarmingly at her like, OH MY GOD ARE YOU . . . ??? and she sort of just looked back, like maybe she was saying, Yes, it's OK if you recognize me. I mean, would you hide in a club if you were Patricia Arquette? Would you have to? I give up. I just don't know anymore.

God. The woman was Richard Feynman's wife! In the movie [*Infinity*]. OK, maybe Matthew Broderick's, but STILL.

CHAPTER 13

Radio Sucks

Remember how angry David Hasselhoff was? Radio in the late 1990s was still the most efficient method of selling CDs, and he wasn't on it. Did he know that being played on commercial radio (like Q101, KROQ, or DC101) meant paying an independent radio promoter to push the song to the radio stations with whom they "had relationship"? For my entire career in rock and afterward, it cost thousands of dollars per month to pay a third party whose "relationships" with the radio station program director involved gifts of golf clubs, free show tickets, contests to fly to performances, etc., to add your song to their weekly playlist. There were three tiers of playlist: Heavy Rotation (six–eight times per day), Medium (four–six), and Light (two–three). There was also a "back-announce"—when the DJ would say "You just heard the new BANDNAME on the radio"—which also cost money. Now remember, payola, or payment for commercial airplay of a song without mentioning the payment, is illegal. These were all ways to get around that.

Consider how many records a label releases per week, how many labels there were at the time, and how many spots exist on a Heavy Rotation list (which were identical throughout the country), and you'll realize that the radio promotion department at Reprise could only push one or two songs onto that list per week. There wasn't enough time in the day to play everyone's song, and one Reprise rep begging a radio station to play more than one or two songs that week seemed just pathetic. If you were not the number-one priority album release that week, you weren't going to get on the radio. It had nothing to do with who liked anything. It was all about the money and whether or not a song was something to take a chance on. If the Reprise rep—or the independent promoter—pushed the wrong song, they'd lose their credibility. As more stations consolidated over the years, there were even fewer people to take chances.

Friday, June 16, 1995, Toronto Area
RADIO, RADIO, WHEREFORE ART THOU, RADIO?

I guess our single for "He's My Star" has been out for over a week now, and from what I hear, there are two radio stations across the US playing it. This is beyond our comprehension, and it's driving us mad. We *know* that this song is radio-playable.

Radio was especially elusive to us. We didn't really do much to ensure we had radio-friendly hits, and we obtusely did not select the most radio-friendly songs as our singles—stubbornly "refusing to sell out"—and Reprise basically let us do whatever we wanted. There were "call in to request your favorite band" contests, like on Q101 for example, and our fans would tell us, "We tried to call but the radio station said they didn't have access to your song" or "The DJ said they really liked it but they weren't allowed to play it." Just like Hasselhoff.

Thursday, June 12, 1997
ROCK BUSINESS, LOS ANGELES, CA

Today we spent all day doing Rock Business stuff, and I'm going to write about it here. . . . We went to Reprise/Warner Bros. and had a nice talk with the radio guys there. Basically, we talked about how we're going on tour in the fall, and we have an "add" date, which means that on August 19, someone from Reprise will (possibly) start mentioning our name when they call radio stations—they'll try to get our song added to those lightning-bolt stations. The radio guys are less than enthusiastic about our song; they don't think it's a radio hit, and they tell us that. "It's a hard thing to hear," they say, and they're right. At some point, I just sort of wanted to think, well, what the hell are we doing here, why don't we just give up and make another record. This one isn't any good.

The meeting went on. I wanted to get them to try to at least get radio stations to MENTION our SHOWS in the fall even if they won't play our song. It's weird to know in advance that very little confidence from the radio dept. is in our song. They say that if a DJ at a station loves it enough to bring it to their program director and get it added, then they will feel a little different. They need to see someone else having faith in us, basically, before they will. Unfortunately, Rick tries to tell them it's very hard to get someone else to have faith in us if our record label radio dept. doesn't believe in the song. Radio only wants to play the biggest hits.

After a while the radio people were excused, and we went to meet with the reason we're still on the label, Howie Klein, the president, who still seems to love us. We try to figure out ways to help ourselves without getting radio airplay.

Summercamp was being pushed to radio, though, and the following is a tour report describing the process.

Monday, May 12, 1997, Grand Rapids, MI, on Tour Supporting Failure, with Summercamp Opening

HITSVILLE HITS, MI

Get This.

Tonight, I noticed about fifty people hanging around, all wearing radio station t-shirts. I thought, "Uh oh, radio show." One came up to us and interrupted our soundcheck, carrying a huge banner. "Excuse me, would you mind if I hung this up behind you tonight?" I said, "Does your station play our record?" (knowing full well they don't) and she said, "Well, I am not sure" and I said "Well, you should find out. You wouldn't want to hang your banner behind a band you do not support, would you? You'd probably feel really silly." She went away, and then came back and asked if we'd like to be interviewed on the air. I said, "OK."

Later on, I went over to the radio booth and said, "Hello, I'm Rose from Poster Children." The guy sitting at the booth just sort of laughed at me. Then I found the woman who said we could be on the air and the night DJ; he wanted to interview us right in the room there while Summercamp was soundchecking. That seemed weird, but whatever.

After we interviewed (and it was one of those really scary quick professional DJ interviews), I went over to the t-shirt booth to find Hector, the Summercamp tour manager. He told me that the radio station had been chasing Summercamp around to get an interview and THEY CAN'T interview because he doesn't have CLEARANCE from the label yet. (That's why the radio station agreed to interview us during Summercamp's soundcheck, in the same room!) Then he said there are two radio stations and they are both having a sort of war over Summercamp; one added it last week and the other added it today. The one that added it last week said that if they interview with the other, they will drop the song off their playlist. So the Reprise rep has to come fix the situation. Of course they need *both* radio stations to be happy!

I set up our t-shirts and stared out at the huge radio booth across from me in the tiny venue and after about a half-hour, I realized that it was really TWO radio station booths. I hadn't even noticed they were two different stations! Meanwhile the radio station number one had been chasing all members of Summercamp and they had to evade. I guess the Reprise rep finally came and fixed the situation; they will do two interviews but neither will be tonight. They will do them tomorrow.

When it was about time for us to play, I was hoping some of the radio station people might stick around and see what we were all about. As I walked up to the bar, I heard some huge guy going, "Poster Children! Hahaha!! Hey, buddy! Look! I smell TUNA!" poking his friend. "I smell TUNA! Get it!!" I don't know what that was all about. I hope it wasn't about me.

After the show, a DJ came up to us from the not-so-aggressive radio station, and told us he wished he could play us. He's seen us five times, he loves us, he loves the new album. I told him I would give him a CD if he needed it. No, his hands are tied. He can't play it. He was almost in tears. He doesn't want to be fired. I told him then to talk to the Reprise rep. He said he already had.

Then the Reprise rep came up to us, and introduced herself. She was really nice. I told her that there was a radio DJ here who wanted to play our record so badly, he seemed despondent. "I know, I know," she said; "He's already come up and talked to me! He really, really loves you guys. He wanted to play '0 For 1' so badly." Then she said this: "I told him, 'HEY, if you REALLY want to support this band, buy one of their t-shirts!'" Rick and I just looked at each other. I started crying later.

Everyone feels sorry for us.

You hear bands complaining about this kind of stuff all the time. I want you all reading this to know that we are not complaining. I am telling you a story about what the world is like. To be fair, I should also tell you that when we played "Music of America" tonight (our obvious diatribe against commercial radio), Rick told the audience it was about the biggest sin of all, "Prostitution." We're not really doing anything to make it easier for ourselves.

The Summercamp guys know what happened, and everyone feels sorry for us. Everyone's wearing our t-shirts, telling us we put on a good show. We don't want sympathy. We are a happy band, none of this is really getting in the way of our performance. It's just the feeling that we are a resource that is being wasted. But *we're* using ourselves to our fullest potential. We have run out of our new record now, too. We are selling a lot of stuff. All things nonradio point to the fact that people like us.

Later on, a guy from Radio Station number one told me that Radio Station number two was sliding their little paper questionnaires on TOP of radio station number one's little stickers, on the table, obscuring them so no one could see their stickers. Meanwhile the other radio station's stickers were in plain view. He told me that radio station number two had actually put a banner on top of the radio station number one's van. "THEY BANNERED OUR VAN!" he said. Can you believe it?

I couldn't stop laughing. I hope he didn't take it personally.

So this is what it was like being on a major label, but not really playing along with the game. Our job was now our creative output, and there was a mismatch between our own message and the rules of the machine that supported us. Only a few bands had been able to transcend the system while griping about it, and when they did (like Rage Against the Machine) they were still called out. We definitely weren't going to "win" at the job by being ourselves, but also probably wouldn't win even if we tried to play the game. I'm glad we stayed true to our ideologies.

CHAPTER 14

Computer Experiments

Monday, June 16, 1997, North on State Route 95, San Francisco to Boise

PINE-SCENTED PLEDGE, SOUTHEAST OREGON

The sky is the color of a sky-blue crayon and the air smells like someone sprayed pine-scented Pledge all over the grasslands, an odor just hanging in the air above the ground, so potent you should be able to see it. It's beautiful outside, driving north along SR 95 in Nevada. The sun must have baked the scent out of the shrubs covering the land. Off in the distance, the sun sets gold behind the mountains. The drive to Boise from San Francisco involves driving through Reno, feeling the temperature rise from about 65 degrees in San Francisco to 85 degrees inland. Then you get onto State Route 95 through Oregon, which starts in Winnemucca, Nevada, pretty much the last town you see until Boise, five hours later. Once out of Winnemucca, you drive through more grasslands, more perfumed air, and on the map, there are no towns at all. Just a little red line that forks somewhere in southeast Oregon. I was actually fearing for our lives later on that thin red line. There really was NOTHING along the road for hours, except the pine-scented bushes.

Boise, ID, is really a wonderful town. We all went thrift-shopping today and I bought new six-inch tall sandals and new shades. I'm starting to have real problems with the web page ever since I moved it off AOL. People on AOL don't see the changes. This is terrible. Plus, I spent almost the entire hour before we went on stage sitting in the back of the promoter's store trying to upload and install the working version of Apple CD-ROM driver on his Performa 6116. It finally worked and then I discovered that he didn't have enough RAM to run our e-CD *RTFM* anyway. ARRGGH.

Website—Anticorporate Media

Tarik is a six-foot-six, handsome goth/geek who is in the part of our band that stands in front of the stage, facing us as we play, and can feed the words to Rick if he forgets them. He's also the reason we started our web page; he offered to help, and control freaks that we were, we politely declined and did it ourselves. An email from November 1994 details our discussion about gaining access to a UIUC lab through the "real" internet (not a dialup) so I can see pictures. The National Center for Supercomputing Applications (NCSA)/UIUC was making images available to people via MOSAIC browser right at this time. I was creating an interactive floppy disk for the press kit for *Junior Citizen* and had all the graphics we'd made for the disk, so it was easy to plop those into html. So, thanks to Tarik, in 1995, the first Poster Children website was uploaded.

Http://www.prairienet.org/posterkids/ was served on prairienet.org, a Freenet connected with the University of Illinois. I had asked permission to be allowed onto Prairienet before it was released to the general public in Champaign–Urbana, and we had an official band email address (posterkids@ prairienet.org) and some space on the server for a website. I was so proud of still having some ties to the UIUC and made every attempt to help connect town to gown. Prairienet was a perfect opportunity for us; it was initially funded by UIUC and community organizations, including the NCSA, Illinois Cooperative Extension, Parkland Community College, and the *News-Gazette* and open to the public; anyone who lived in Illinois could get a free login.[1] On his personal website, cofounder Greg Newby has Prairienet listed under "Anti-Corporate Media."[2]

The earliest evidence of a Poster Children website is a screenshot that I found in the online archive of *CMJ* magazine from June 1995, in an article I wrote about how to create a website and how we maintain ours.

> We try to update our information at least twice a week and redesign our entire page every other week. There are plenty of dead sites on the Web, and it's a challenge to keep ours interesting. . . . Right now the Web provides us with something akin to running our own pirate television station; we

can publish anything we want for free, and anyone with a computer and modem can access it. It's nice to know that a network originally designed for military use now contains everything from band info to current statistics about how many Dr. Peppers are left in cola machines in university labs. Let's hope the freedom continues.[3]

At this time, most band sites were designed by companies that did a one-time collection of info and displayed it on a page and went onto the next client. I was keenly aware of how stagnant this would be, and figured, if I kept a diary, that would be an easy way to add new information every day. I formatted the html in short sections with headlines so people could skip to the next section if that looked more interesting. In retrospect, I realize this was to mimic my experience watching MTV. If the current video wasn't of interest, I always knew there would be another coming up, so I'd give it a chance for the next couple of songs. A person could sit for hours like that, in front of the TV. I wanted my audience to do the same for my writing.

On tour, it was a struggle to get online; we had to try to find a floor to sleep on where the people also had a landline (there were no cell phones) that they—and their roommates—would allow me to use to upload the latest tour reports onto our website. Some people had to pay per minute to use their phone line, and many times the call to Urbana's Prairienet would be a long-distance call. Sometimes we would have to stay in motels and we'd hope we could disconnect the phone line from the phone and plug it into our computer.

I continued my tour reports until 2002, when we went on baby hiatus. After a while I noticed that we'd come home from tour and everyone around us would already know everything that had happened to us. In fact, during the tour, in each city, people already knew what had happened to us the night before. They also knew a lot more about us, our likes and dislikes, our temperament, our politics and culture, and not because they read about us in *Rolling Stone* or *SPIN* (because we were nowhere near popular enough to sell paper with writing about us on it), but because we were self-publishing and creating an internet community back in 1995.

At the time of this writing, prairienet.org is gone, and there are no archives of its early days—Jill Howk Gengler (Graduate School of Library and Information Science, UIUC) informs me that Martin Wolske, who had been saving all of Prairienet on a commercial server, was in a bike accident, hit a pothole, and almost lost his life. During his recovery, the monthly bill for the server had been due. It had been paid late and the server had deleted the entire archive.[4]

The Mission of Prairienet

- Strengthen community organizations by helping them provide and retrieve networked information;
- Empower individuals by providing access to networked information and by teaching the skills necessary to access and use this information;
- Facilitate information and resource sharing in support of community development efforts;
- Promote equity of access to computer resources for everyone in the community.[5]

E-CDs

Tuesday, November 14, 1995, Archers of Loaf Tour

UCLA—THE COOPERAGE CAFETERIA IN THE UNIVERSITY

We had a great time again at Warner Bros. compound. We got to walk around the studio lot—we didn't see any stars up close, though, but the food was amazing. After we ate, we talked to one of our A&R people about what our plans were for the future, when we wanted to start recording and PROGRAMMING (!) our new album. Then we tried to get everyone in the office to call up our label-mates the Flaming Lips and ask them to take us on tour with them in Japan. That didn't work out so well.

Then we met a guy from Apple and grilled him about QTVR, what we'll be using on our CD+. I'm kind of scared to think that we're going to be doing this all alone, but other people are doing it already, so if I need help, I guess I can just call them up and ask them. If it's already being done, we can do it too. Just like a rollercoaster. No need to be afraid because others have already been on it, and they didn't die. So jump on. Even if you do die, it'll be a fabulous death!

In 1994, the Residents had released their *Freak Show* CD-ROM, an experimental multimedia disk containing an animated, interactive 3D world, which Rick bought, and we marveled at it for a while. Laurie Anderson had a CD-ROM in 1995 also.[6] This was the future, Rick had decided, and we would make one of these also. In a meeting with Sire, Howie Klein was perfectly happy to support Poster Children interactive content, as long as we did it ourselves. "You are computer scientists, right? You know how to do this sort of thing."

Now, we knew how to write operating systems and program search algorithms, were fluent in x86 Assembler, and by god could we calculate code optimizations. But I'd never actually made a *color* appear on a screen. Rick had taken the one computer graphics course offered in the 1980s and could code an algorithm to display a gradient. So between the two of us, we had well beyond no idea how to make a CD-ROM.

"Make interactive disks? Of course we can do that, yes, we are Computer Programmers," I answered. "We'll get right to work on that when we get home. Meanwhile, can I talk to the person here who creates the ones for the other bands, just to make sure I do it the same way that you do it here? You know; for compatibility issues."

Our interactive output began with a little floppy disk sampler for *Junior Citizen* with graphics and sound clips from the album. The graphics were developed by me and Rick, who acted as lead idea person and quality control. I programmed it in Macromedia Director, an authoring tool that allowed me to "spreadsheet" out pictures and sounds on a timeline and create buttons and other programming that would allow users to jump back and forth between screens.

This floppy disk was packaged in a cardboard envelope with a two-color (magenta and cyan) label and was sent out as free swag to record stores and other interested parties. Sire also entered it into a design competition, and it won an award and was part of the traveling exhibition for "The 100 Show: The Eighteenth Annual of the American Center for Design." At the time I was being such a punk, I was not in the slightest bit interested in an award for making art. This is something I regret. I am grateful that in the end, someone sent me the book that commemorates the exhibition.

The Poster Children interactive press kit was designed to be a companion piece to the band's fifth album, "Junior Citizen." The graphics were inspired by Japanese anime and the CD was designed in the spirit of a fireworks package. Our goal was to make a demo that people would look at more than once. We believe that there is more to the concept of "interactivity" than pressing a button and watching a QuickTime movie. To us, the only true interactivity nowadays occurs in computer games, in which random elements force audience-generated outcome. We believe that the first step to the next level of interactive multimedia begins with the employment of random events.

We are a techno-peasant outfit (our only computer is a Macintosh Quadra 650), and this is our first excursion into the world of multimedia. Working with our limited resources, we decided to make a statement equating interactivity with television, since presently, the most interactive of all small demos still doesn't hold attention quite as well as a television set. (our "entrants' comments")

What is written here still stands, in my mind, except condoning the use of random events in artwork, which I now feel is a crutch. This missive on random events here feels as outdated now as Rick's proclamation that we'll never stray from grunge rock.

From the judge:

> The label alone for this piece is so warm and fuzzy that it deserved a prize. We looked at a number of interactive disks in this competition, and frankly, they were disappointing. Then, I stumbled upon this disk. "Wow, this is the best interactive thing we've looked at in the whole show . . ." It breaks the boring constraints of print work that most interactive work still falls into.—Marlene McCarty

This was mine and Rick's first foray into interactive media, which would become a career, and then something we would teach. Now that people were starting to rip songs off their CDs, the end of label control was becoming obvious to Reprise, and they were already experimenting with digital tech. What came next was embedding multimedia into music CDs.

RTFM

RTFM came out in April 1997, an enhanced CD, with an interactive program in one session and music tracks in the other. It's hard for me to believe that we actually created this and burned it in our house and sent the burned CD ourselves to Reprise to be replicated, and I remember being terrified at the time, scared of screwing up something that would be duplicated so many times. It all worked out fine, though.

The part I didn't like and was scared of, was creating the subject matter. But Rick is my muse, and my coach in creativity. I was very lazy, artistically; I would have copied other logos, used stars (when in doubt), and he never allowed this. I'd show him a design and he'd say, "It's not finished yet," and then I'd get angry, go cry for a while, and then work longer. At some point he was able to convince me:

1. The longer you work on something, the better it gets
2. Do not do something someone else did
3. Don't be afraid of the future, embrace it

Adhering to Rule number two, Rick decided that our e-CD would not have a normal menu system as a navigational metaphor. Some of the first e-CDs, like websites, had a screen with a list of clickable labels, "Play Movie," "About Us," and "Discography." Rick wanted to create something that no one else had ever done before. I remember being terrified when he stated this, because usually, if something hasn't been created before, it's not terribly easy for me to conceive of what it is. I was scared. But I also had rules. I wanted to create an interactive space that engaged people for more than five minutes. Therefore, my goal was to embed an insane amount of content in the 150 megs that weren't taken up by music.

We solved the problem of navigational metaphor by creating a 3D model of a building reminiscent of Frank Lloyd Wright's Larkin Building, which I fell in love with from a Champaign library book. Living on the Illinois prairie, you're shuttled around Frank Lloyd Wright homes and taught about fitting into your natural surroundings and Japanese design principles, and at the time we were probably joking a lot about Ayn Rand and the *Fountainhead* movie, so a building manifested. When you'd open *RTFM* on a computer, you wouldn't land on a basic menu page. You'd find yourself in the atrium of the Music of America building, and you'd have to move around in that 3D space to enjoy some "new media." We created environments using real and computer-generated 3D objects (using Strata Studio Pro and QuickTime VR) and items that could spin when dragged, and added hotspots with narratives and links attached. I hated recording, but man, I did love programming.

Juxtaposing photorealism and computer-generated 3D models into an interactive QTVR movie was something I enjoyed most, loving that I could create a landscape of modified truth. Scrolling around and clicking on the rooms, you'd find twelve different "learning experiences," real 3D images of our instruments against a backdrop of CGI, "technical readouts" of our van in 3D, information about previous records, a postage-stamp-sized video of recording (and the basement) at Pogo Studio in Champaign, a gorgeous gray metallic video maze game that Rick created at rat's-eye view, some glitchy-looking (on purpose) puzzles and games, information about the Situationist International, and, my favorite, an html-tutorial. I'm told this inspired many listeners to create their own web pages. To me, that was the most successful aspect of *RTFM*.

CHAPTER 15

Expectations

Monday, June 10, 1996, Washington, DC—Black Cat

WHAT LABEL ARE YOU ON, ANYWAY?

We had a good show tonight. Afterward, a kid came up to me and said, "I thought the Poster Children were a crappy, terrible band who got signed to a major label a long time ago! I mistook them for you guys, I'm sorry! You guys were great! What label are you on, anyway?" "Reprise," I answered. "Oh, cool," he responds. Then, like a moron, I tell him that it's a major label, because I don't like to leave people with incorrect information, and I go through the whole spiel, explaining our very wonderful experiences on our major label, and our horrid ones on the indies. I think he left re-questioning our music. I guess I ought to learn to keep my mouth shut sometimes.

Being on a major label was sometimes no different than being on an indie, except I sometimes felt guilt. We played with Mike Watt in the middle of our Sponge tour, and I spent days afterward talking about how nice Sponge was compared to Watt. Watt seemed to have a bug up his ass about our being on a major. Sponge, a hard-working band from Detroit who'd paid their dues for years, was all about equality for all the bands on the bill. They'd moved their drums for us each night, made sure we had soundcheck time. No rock-star attitudes at all.

Saturday, June 14, 1997, Sacramento, CA, Where We've Never Played

TOURING BEFORE THE INTERNET

So I looked for our sheet in our tour clipboard, our info on the show for today, and I don't have it. I don't have the phone number of the club. I don't have the directions to the club, and I don't have the NAME of the club. On top of it, there are CDs being shipped to the club, via Saturday Special FedEx. So there will probably be a little yellow sticker on the door saying, "we'll try to deliver your package again on Monday." When we'll be driving to Boise.

We called our manager and our booking agent over and over again to find out where we're playing tonight, but neither is home. When we finally pulled into town, we got a hotel room and began the hunt for the club. I started calling record stores first. Here was the funniest conversation:

ME: "Hello, I am from out of town, and I know there is a band called 'Poster Children' playing tonight at some club in town, but I don't know where. Would you happen to know where they would be playing?"

RECORD STORE: "Never heard of them."

ME: "I realize that, but maybe you can help me anyway. Where would an indie rock band play in this town?"

RECORD STORE: (silence)

ME: (deciding to use examples) "OK. Have you heard of Superchunk? The band Superchunk? Where would that band play if they had a show here?"

RECORD STORE: "Super, Chunk?"

ME: *sigh* . . . "Have you heard of Bis????"

RECORD STORE: "Yeah!!! Of course!!!"

ME: "Great!! Where would Bis play if they were playing a show here?"

RECORD STORE: ". . ." (I can hear them asking each other for a couple of minutes) " . . . nobody here knows. Sorry."

It was like that for about ten indie record stores. Nobody had heard of us (of course) and nobody knew any names of any venues where an "indie" rock band would play. It wasn't surprising that only ten people showed up for the show. And I think the promoter was embellishing the truth a bit when he said ten people paid. I only saw two people there who weren't in the other bands. (Oh—we found out where we were playing by grabbing a copy of the *News & Review* zine in Tower Records.)

1997: Being Screwed

There are plenty of stories about the drawbacks of signing to a major label. Here are a few from our midwestern neighbors, with the first in the context of the tour.

Mercy Rule

Tuesday, May 6, 1997, Omaha, Nebraska—
We Will See Mercy Rule Tonight!

A MUCH HAPPIER DAY!

Defying gravity: A bird flew into the van yesterday and crapped on the windshield!! Rick went to wipe it off and we were all screaming EEWWWW!! How can a bird crap upside-down, defying gravity?! On top of it, it sticks, upside-down!!

We're all laughing in the van now listening to an interview on NPR with the guy who compiled a book of suicide notes, called <u>Or Not to Be</u>. His favorite, and the one that gets the most publicity, is "Dear Betty, I hate you. Love, George." The "hate" ones are the scariest ones. Some people destroy their own suicide notes, ripping them up. Fewer than one in five people leave notes, the author says. Many notes contain petty instructions, like "don't forget to change the oil in my car." It's a pretty fascinating subject, but I don't think I'd like to own that book!

I had the weirdest dream the other night, that Billy Corgan was chasing me up and down the corridors of America Online, wanting to kiss me, and I was screaming and crying, running away from him. I had long, curly brown hair, and he was bald and had a huge, gaping red mouth and big hands. It was a terrible nightmare.

Apparently there was a writeup of the show in the local paper saying it was in Lincoln, at the Hanger, instead of in Omaha at the Ranch Bowl. What an absurd tour this is!

Tuesday, May 6, 1997, Ranch Bowl, Omaha, NE

A REVIEW OF THE NEW MERCY RULE BABY!

Heidi from Mercy Rule appears at the Ranch Bowl with the most gorgeous baby I've ever seen in my life. Zoie Taylore, Heidi and Jon's baby, looks exactly as you'd expect of a child of a god and goddess, huge blue eyes the color of the sky in summer, big cheeks, golden hair, very, very aware, and VERY calm. Heidi's baby.

Jon marches into the club with a guitar case under each arm and announces "Where are Jim and Rick? I need to talk to them." Jon has built two matching guitars for our band, one right-handed for Rick and one left-handed for Jim. They are like the bass he built for Heidi in that they have no knobs on them. Who needs a volume knob? They sound amazing and look gorgeous.

Heidi tells me that they finished their record for MCA. I had heard stories about her singing (Heidi is the singer of Mercy Rule) eight and a half months pregnant. When Heidi screams it is hardcore (HEIDICORE actually!) and she thrashes on the bass. She is fantastic; I learned how to rock from her. I can't even imagine what an incredible, beautiful record they must have made, with little Zoie in Heidi's belly, belting out songs at the top of her lungs. And now guess what. MCA has dropped them. Has decided not to put out the record. MCA has also decided that the record needs to be BOUGHT FROM them, so Mercy Rule cannot even put it out themselves. Get this: I ask if they can just come rerecord it in Rick's studio. No. THEY CANNOT EVEN RECORD THE SONGS AGAIN. MCA has the rights to THE SONGS FOR TWO YEARS.

I have nothing more to say about anything. Jon talked to Rick about how he would feel silly taking out a loan to buy their record back. Rick said he'd hunt him down and shoot him if he did that. This is the worst major-label fuckover story I've ever heard in my life. I can't believe I was complaining about not getting an "add" date from Reprise. Fuck. I'm surprised MCA let them keep their baby.

Menthol

During the post-Nirvana gold rush, bands in towns were being screwed by major labels and other bands in the same towns were hating them for "being signed." One of the many other fantastic bands in Champaign, Mother, who later changed their name to Menthol, received a call from "outta nowhere" from an A&R guy at Capitol Records, who called them from a restaurant payphone in the lobby of a restaurant in Beverly Hills where he was dining with his parents for the High Holidays (charming!)—he had a box full of tapes from a guy who was soliciting music from Chicago, and, upon hearing the Menthol tape in his car, he just had to call the number on the cassette. Balthazar De Ley, bandleader, felt that Menthol's discovery was distinct, something out of a showbiz movie from the thirties.

Their major-label story was similar to every other story I've heard (including ours)—the label didn't know how to market the album, weren't going to jeopardize their relationship with radio program directors by asking them to play a unique-sounding band, arranged opening slots for other larger bands on the label (which doesn't necessarily help a smaller band), and it was time to move on to the next album. This Menthol record, *Danger Rock*

Science!, was a prescient eighties revival science-meets-rock themed album, and at the time, it would have been a huge hit.

The record was fully finished and delivered to the label, photoshoots were done and bios were written, but no release date was set. Capitol ended up refusing to put out the record, stating, "There is no way that an eighties revival is ever going to happen." They also wouldn't release the record to the band and wouldn't give them more money to record again. They held the record hostage, waiting to sell it to another label, for an exorbitant price. At some point Menthol begged to be let go from the label and were able to rerecord the entire album, which was then released on Hidden Agenda, a subsidiary of the Champaign Parasol label. Happily, Balthazar De Ley is still working in the music industry, now making his own amplifiers.[1]

Die Kreuzen

The great Milwaukee band Die Kreuzen, who recorded a couple of albums with Butch Vig (before Nirvana) was courted with demo money by the MCA heavy-metal sublabel Mechanic Records. Bassist Keith Brammer states nonchalantly, "Whatever; I can go in the studio, and I like being in the studio. It was all up-front, we told Corey (who ran their current label, Touch & Go). We said, 'This guy is giving us money to do this,' and Corey's like 'Yeah, whatever,' he had laid it out for us why he thought it was a bad idea for us to sign to a major label." Corey, part of the same scene as Steve Albini, would have prepped Keith just as Steve did us. Die Kreuzen never signed to a major, but in a later band, Carnival Strippers, Keith did sign with Fox Records, a subsidiary of 20th Century Fox distributed by Arista. "I found out that goddamn, he [Corey] was absolutely right, it was unbelievable how accurately he had described it. . . . It wasn't like I thought I was gonna . . . be a hit, [I was] just in it for the ride; great, let's see where this takes me—it took me just straight down, a rollercoaster where you go down, you get up to the top and you go off and there's no rest of the rollercoaster, it just goes straight down into the ground (laughs)." Keith had decided that the endeavor was some sort of giant tax write-off for the label, because they didn't promote the band at all. "We're gonna throw all this money at you and . . . we're just gonna take it and let it die." He wasn't destroyed over it. "I didn't have any expectations, myself and our guitar player Mike Hoffmann had been through this multiple times with major labels. I had enough knowledge of how the music business works, looking up from the bottom, it didn't crush me when it crashed and burned."[2]

Thursday, June 12, 1997

AT THE WARNER SKI LODGE, LOS ANGELES

It seems that the view of people at the record label is that *RTFM* isn't good. I also get a lot of people complaining that we forced it to come out at a bad time, but I still think that if we'd delayed it, they still wouldn't like it. I hope I'm not wrong, and they're not just playing with our lives because they're holding a grudge because we were stubborn and forced it to come out in April. On top of it, it's still hard for me to believe that they don't like it. It seems like such a better album than *Junior Citizen*. Our email is all over the map though; it seems to me that most people writing like *RTFM* the best, but there is a small percent who like the others better. And it's not all *Junior Citizen* fans, either. Many of them like *Tool of the Man*, and still others say *Flower Plower* is the best. The *Daisychain Reaction*–favoring contingent seem to be lost during this album, or to not have email.

The worst part about it all is what I realized as I was tossing and turning on ML's hardwood floor last night, trying to fall asleep. We're talking about a twelve-dollar album here, trying to get people to spend twelve dollars. The cost of six beers. Two movies. A small percentage of the cost of a new shirt. And each one we sell counts as part of our career, as part of our lives. What a strange world we live in.

THE MUSIC OF AMERICA, TWO DAYS AGO—SAN DIEGO, CA, WITH MARCY PLAYGROUND SUPPORTING

A 91X jagged-yellow-lightning-bold-clad minivan (do you ever notice how all commercial alternative stations have the same stupid yellow lightning bolt on their minivans?) pulls up, radio station of the minute playing the Music of America, and asks if they can hang their banner outside the club. I casually ask if they're playing Poster Children. This guy doesn't mess around. "No. But we're playing 'Marcys Playground,'" he says. I just smile. I can see in radio in four dimensions now, the beginning, middle, and end of all radio play for all bands, and the beginning, middle, and ending of this guy's career at 91X. If they ever do play our song, this guy probably won't even be working there, and the month after they play it, they won't play it anymore. So what? Big deal.

CHAPTER 16

Big Changes

DOUBTS. WHO WILL COME TO THIS SHOW?

It's nighttime outside the 7th Street Entry, in the heart of Minneapolis, the North Star City. I'm standing on the edge of the largest parking lot you've ever seen. Like, after the bomb hit, they just turned the crater into a huge parking lot, a full city-block perimeter, empty, gray, bounded by a pen of brick buildings.

The night air above the lot is exactly the color of static, and all around the edges of the giant lot, faraway neon signs of restaurants cut through the gray air. It's lightly misting outside and about 45 degrees. The ground shines pebbly with the rain and colored light. The Target Center, tallest, and boasting the most gratuitous amounts of neon, stands at one edge of the giant city parking lot like a racecar cathedral. I'm looking for signs of life; for people who might come to the show, but there is NO ONE in sight—are there still people on earth?—only acres of cars bordered by restaurants and huge billboards. The air is perfectly still except you can hear Vivaldi's "Spring" from *The Four Seasons*, eerily blaring through the mist, descending from the sky, at a perfect volume to be heard throughout the entire parking lot, bouncing off the black-painted cinderblocks holding up the punk rock 7th Street Entry club, the only club where I've ever seen a person do coke. Once in twenty years of touring. The classical music is actually being broadcast from the largest billboard on the edge of the parking lot. After "Spring" they played "Jesu, Joy of

Man's Desiring" and after that, loud and clear, the Pachelbel Canon. I went in during the Canon. Still no signs of life. I couldn't take it anymore.

Being on a major skews your focus regardless of how knowledgeable and indie-driven you are. Somehow, knowing the major label terminology for our band's music—"product"—and ourselves—"talent"—even though we were totally cognizant of the parabolic bomb-path of the signing and, inevitably, being dropped from our major label, we couldn't help but participate in the theater. *A screaming came across the sky indeed. It had happened before, but we had nothing to compare it to now. You complained about having to learn Poisson distributions in literature and/or math classes? I'll never use these, you thought. But you could have predicted who would have the next hit, had you only listened.*

At Reprise, big changes were happening. It was the end of artist-focused development, with the label moving toward a bigger emphasis on budgetary gains. Mo Ostin and Lenny Waronker had left to cochair DreamWorks, our team of alternative marketing people had moved up in the label, and our champion Howie Klein had left. Taking his place as president of Reprise was my old friend, David Kahne of the Mashed Potatoes. Feeling lucky with our time and our three records on Sire, we submitted a proposal for our next option, asked for a quick response, and were politely declined. We were free.

The obvious advantages of being signed to a major label are the "consistent" money, resources, people. The disadvantages are the fact that you are constantly competing to get those advantages. Moreover, the army of people in the higher tiers who work at the label don't care too much about the smaller bands. The story everyone likes to worry about is that the label is going to interfere with their newer bands, but for most bands, that's not true. The real story is that the label won't care unless you start selling lots of records.

I always had a little guilt about signing, and the thing I hated most was convincing fans we hadn't "sold out"—something bands are accused of regardless of what label they are on. That, and having to explain the situation of being trapped in an earlier indie label contract, the "good guy" holding you hostage. It appears I'm not the only one who felt this way. Michael Azzerad writes about Nirvana's decision to move to a major in *Rolling Stone*:

> Sub Pop had begun talking to major labels about a distribution deal.
> Figuring that if they had to be on a major label, they might as well choose

it themselves, the members of Nirvana began shopping the Vig demos. Only a major could afford to buy Nirvana out of their Sub Pop contract, and major distribution would get their punk to the people. "That's pretty much my excuse for not feeling guilty about why I'm on a major label," says Cobain. "I should feel really guilty about it; I should be living out the old punk-rock threat and denying everything commercial and sticking in my own little world and not really making an impact on anyone other than the people who are already aware of what I'm complaining about. It's preaching to the converted."[1]

Although we basically had no choice, I'm still happy we did it.

Thursday, May 4, 2000
LOS ANGELES, THE SPECTACLE

So we woke up this morning to the sound of banging. The housekeeper and others are banging on the door two rooms down from us. BANG BANG BANG!! A man with a walkie-talkie says something about "a suicide" and "the mother called, she's worried." More banging. We are peeking out the window. Nothing happens for a while, and then finally a policeman comes and breaks into the room. Then we hear the sound of slapping, and a person yelling, "GUY! GUY! Wake UP!"

Two firetrucks pull into the parking lot, and then about fifteen minutes later, an ambulance and a limo show up. A man is carried down the Motel 6 steps in a large, blue tarp. A paramedic tells me, "He's still breathing." The limo driver pauses for me to take his picture. I have no idea why there's a limo driver here.

A kid comes up to me to talk, during all this. "What label are you on," he asks. I tell him the labels we've been on. "I have a band too," he states. "We're up and coming." I want to pour my record industry knowledge into this poor soul. He has already used the word "boku" to mean "a lot." He has already told me about his management. It's like listening to someone talk about how he is going to win the lottery. "I'm not going to sign any contract that is not totally pro-artist," he says. Fool. You can't even get the labels to change their policy for shellac breakage. Is this guy going to ask for his 12 percent of 100 percent of the CDs pressed when they're waving a big $50K check in front of him? If there are no pens in the room at that time, he'll bite off one of his own fingers to use as a pen, and sign with the blood. "What do you sound like?" I asked. "Pearl-Jamish" was the answer. Good luck, guy.

Today I had a US$14 salad, and then we went to the Museum of Geffen to see the 100 Years of Architecture exhibit. It was nice, except too many blueprints and not enough photographs, said Rick. The show tonight started with a band whose lead singer looked like Marcia from *The Brady Bunch*. They were dressed as Catholic school students. The girl looked really normal and nice in a preteen way, but she got these crazed looks in her face sometimes and she'd scream, and in between songs she had a silver flask that she drank out of. They had an entourage, and it was a huge industry spectacle. I liked them a lot!

I went to talk to the girl after the show, but she was shaking so badly and wasn't making any sense. She must have gotten overexcited from their show. We talked a little about how she wanted a record deal. The guy she was with was really intense, too.

Later I went in the girls' bathroom and everyone was babbling about how there was coke all over the back of the toilet seat. It took me a minute to realize what type of coke it was. I muttered something about how people shouldn't do drugs. Now coke is a drug I will never, EVER try—like I want to stick something up my nose that's gonna make me feel like a superhero for about fifteen minutes, and then I'll need to go find more of it? Screw THAT. When you see me jumping around like an idiot on stage, that's all ME. Not drugs.

And then I spent the rest of the night worrying that all our fans probably thought I was on crack.

"I'm a Man and I Have Needs"

Tonight we drove to the very outskirts of Los Angeles, to Palm Springs to escape the traffic tomorrow. While we drove we heard a story on the radio about a man who put his penis through a knothole in a two-by-four because he had seen an Asian woman with large breasts. He was suing the wood company for not putting a warning on the wood—he got splinters—and he was suing the lubricant company, Joe's Wood Putty or something like that, because he had been very uncomfortable. People called in to the radio show to yell at this man and scold him for putting his penis into the wood knothole, but he just kept repeating, "I'm a Man. I have Needs."

Driving to Palm Springs: It was unusually foggy for the desert. Very odd. But gorgeously warm.

Friday, May 5, 2000, Tucson, AZ

Hey! Guess what that fog was? A plume of hydrochloric acid (HCL) has wafted over I-10 east of Los Angeles, and the entire highway is shut down between two north–south freeways, and people are being evacuated from their homes! It's a Don DeLillo book! The plume came from a leaky train. We are lucky that we drove last night, even if we probably drove through the plume. The newspeople are not making such a big deal out of this toxic event; they are pushing the story of a motorcyclist that got run over by a school bus in front of a school, or something like that.

PART FOUR

1997

Post–Major Label

Wednesday, December 10, 1997, on Tour
with Superchunk (We Are Playing as Salaryman)

OSLO, NORWAY, DUELING PENISES WITH SUPERCHUNK

Jim, "Nature Boy," notifies us that we are very close to the 60th parallel North, way norther than I've ever been in my life! The sun woke up with us today at around eight a.m., and it began setting yesterday on Stockholm at three p.m. It's about 40 degrees (F) outside though, and very foggy, with a light dusting of snow on the fields we're driving through. The lakes we pass are strange milky-silver colored; mirrored because the water on top has melted over the ice. We pass mostly farms and pine forest with what looks like a whole lot of birch trees interspersed with the pines. The road we're on is a two-lane highway, but the lanes are wide enough for cars in the same lane to pass each other. In Scandinavia, there seems to be a lot more English than in France and Germany; here everyone knows English and seems proud to speak it to you. I remember when I was young, thinking along with everyone else about *Star Trek* that it is unrealistic that everyone in the universe speaks English, and now I'm wondering if that isn't part of a joke.

We were a bit worried about this border crossing because sometimes you have to have a list of your equipment or something like that, but either inadvertently or not, Keith, our tour manager and driver, sort of blew past the border probably around fifty miles per hour, without stopping. No one came out to shoot us, so we made it into Norway fine!

Today, as we walked into the club, Keith informed us that the local big radio station had been announcing that Supertramp was playing and playing Supertramp songs all day long today. Not Superchunk. Supertramp. Glad this happens to other bands too.

There was a graffiti drawing of two penises "battling" on the dressing room wall; one of the Superchunk guys called it "dueling penises." We treat it like we're digging in a cave and finding ancient hieroglyphics. I remarked that I had never seen that before; I usually see just one penis with balls and sometimes it's spurting. The "dueling penises" is a very rare find; as Laura said, "Yeah, you don't see two of them together like that too often."

There is a quick announcement about us leaving Sire on the pkids listserv, assuring our fans that we would be fine, and no mention at all in my tour reports. At this time, we were touring Europe frequently, as Salaryman, our electronic alter-ego, but with same Poster Children band members. Salaryman had come about by request of Jenny Toomey, who was touring around the United States and asking other bands to back her, doing "something different." Now Salaryman was signed to one of the most sought-after independent German labels, City Slang, and though it was a totally different type of music, it was fun to spend time in Europe. When we came home, we freelanced computer programming and graphic design, and found ourselves working in labs at UIUC, and then, back in graduate school (free if you worked there!) learning to critique what we'd practiced on our own Sire enhanced-CD releases.

With our recording advances and the money we'd made on tour we'd amassed our own computer lab, recording studio, and video cameras so we could make our own records, cover art, and videos. The internet was becoming a place where anyone could distribute anything. We'd also started doing multimedia for other bands, other labels like Thrill Jockey, Touch & Go, etc. Howie Klein at Reprise had let me work on multimedia samplers—I did a *Friends* (the TV show) sampler with info on it in exchange for more computer equipment—so I even had a resumé. Whereas leaving a major label killed most bands due to new lack of busses and tour support, having shunned those offerings, we were ready for the future.

Tuesday, September 30, 1997, Boulder, CO

TESLA MUSEUM + URANIUM SPILL

Today I went into the record store across the street from this club and bought every Poster Children CD it had so I could sell them at our shows. It'll be a cinch for us to sell those at a show, but probably impossible for the record store to sell them, buried in with the rest of the million bands. Ha! We have completely run out of a couple of types of CDs, especially the new one. I found two *Flower Plower* CDs at the store! Those are out of print, so that was really exciting! We're still waiting for a shipment of CDs from the label.

Also today we visited the Tesla Museum in Colorado Springs, CO. It was awesome. It's a couple of rooms in a building, full of old electronics stuff that I don't know what they are—big huge coils and capacitors and "over-unity" machines, which is the new name for a perpetual motion machine (a machine that puts more energy out than you put into it; something that's not really supposed to exist). There was a glass of water with a silver-shedding device in it; you put this battery attached to two strips of metal and the silver one flakes off silver into the water and then you drink it. It's supposed to be healthy. The guy showing us all this stuff, Dan, said he drinks the silver-water whenever he feels like he's coming down with a bug. He looked very healthy.

The best thing in the Tesla Museum was a huge six-foot-tall coil that I guess was used in the Frankenstein movie! This was connected to a capacitor the size of a kitchen stove. Dan had Rick and Jimmie stand about five feet away from this thing, each holding a fluorescent light bulb, and as he charged it up the light bulbs began to glow. I was scared of it, so I stood back with the camera. "There's 1.5 million volts coursing through your body right now," he told us. The discharge made such a loud noise, it was incredible, and lightning flew all around the room.

After this we ate at a huge, empty Chinese food restaurant and then took a huge side-road curving around the city back to I-25 to get to Boulder. We found out the next day that we missed a huge uranium spill—a truck carrying a WHOLE lot of uranium turned over on I-25 and it was closed for miles and evacuated as firemen sprayed water on the dust, attempting to keep it down on the ground so it could be cleaned up. We just missed this by accident.

CHAPTER 17

Online Participation

SOMEONE TAPED A CIRCUIT BOARD FOR A MODEM TO THE BACK OF OUR VAN!

That is the funniest, most awesome thing I've ever seen! I came running out to the van after the show last night to grab some t-shirts for people and there, taped with a huge amount of black electrical tape onto the back door above the license plate, was a circuit board—it looked like someone taped a bomb to the back of the van! AWESOME!! I wanted to get a picture of it but the guys took it down; I can't for the life of me figure out why they took it down! I would have driven like that for the rest of the tour! Jim got a picture, but he doesn't have a digital camera, so we have to wait for the film to be developed.

Afterward we collapsed back at our good friend Liz's house, which she'd donated to us for the night. She rules; I remember her writing to us back years and years ago, telling us that she was "about to graduate." We had been corresponding for like a year, I think. I congratulated her; I think I told her how brilliant I thought she was. I asked what her degree was going to be in, and she replied, "Oh, I'm just finishing high school now!" She runs a zine called *Wind Up Toy*. She did the most brilliant interview once with Steve Albini's cat, Fluss.

This tour report marks the first time there was an obvious community of people who were following our tour online. Someone had to have planned this beautiful present before the show, someone who knew we were into computers, hacking, etc., and probably wouldn't have been able to deduce all this just from our albums. It was also the beginning of our participatory culture online.

Now, "RO (Read-Only) Culture" was giving way to "RW (Read-Write) Culture," terms coined by Lawrence Lessig. Kids sampling. Communities researching. Fans participating. Individuals were becoming empowered, and everyone could now be a distributor. Along with this new online world of sharing came the unfortunate fact that there was no longer any reason for people to purchase what Lessig called "physical tokens of RO." Albums, CDs, etc., now converted to bits, were copied losslessly and flowing free on the internet. CD sales plummeted. Regular rock had finally caught up with alternative rock—no one wanted to buy any of it anymore.

Now with our newfound freedom and the onset of quick two-way and multichannel communications, Poster Children became vibrant, alive. The old timelines were shortened. Previously, we'd be writing and recording songs for a year, pressing records or CDs with a three-month wait for printed press to catch up, and then spending a half-year on tour, which would be the only time we could communicate with fans (save for fan mail). Now, with digital technology, we could exchange ideas spontaneously and continuously.

For us it became easier—and imperative—to give fans more of a dedicated experience. Henry Jenkins notes that when brand communities move online, numbers grow and casual consumers can move into a more intense engagement with the product.[1] Our online work combined with our constant touring made it possible for us to easily continue making music and flourish without a major label.

Usenet and Tangents

Date	Subject	# of posts
9/27/97	David Lynch: What the Crap?	8 posts
8/23/97	*Gravity's Rainbow*	3 posts
3/18/97	Who's up for some Ayn Rand bashing?	4 posts
3/6/97	PKids & I. M. Pei	6 posts
1/25/97	The current state of American politics	4 posts

1/21/97	WEB PAGE UPDATE. GET QTVR PLUGIN + CHEQ IT OUT plz	4 posts
1/4/97	I May Be from Columbus, Ohio, But I Can Give a F**K about the Rose Bowl	1 post
11/4/96	A conversation with Matt from the Archers	1 post
10/30/96	Punk rock on NPR in 15–20 years	6 posts
10/30/96	Michigan PC fans meeting, of sorts (if you're interested)	4 posts
10/24/96	Ralph Nader excommunicated from Tom Snyder show	3 posts
10/22/96	Clinton wants to drug test kids	8 posts
10/21/96	PXL2000	2 posts
10/20/96	What video would you like to see on the CD+?	12 posts
10/9/96	Hot doe gel	2 posts
10/4/96	Jackie Chan movies	1 post

In October 1996, Matthew Miller, a fan from Boston, had launched the Usenet group alt.music.posterkids for us, and thus began the online Poster Kids community. We were ecstatic and are eternally grateful. Normally, Usenet band newsgroup posts were mandated to be on-topic, but for our group, we specifically requested that postings *not* be about our band. Random, non-sequitur topics, for me, illuminate the space in between, like when you want to see the Pleiades constellation, you need to look away from it.

The purpose of the group was stated in the read.me file: "To further the Poster Children cause of spreading knowledge throughout the galaxy and of course, to help save the world."[2]

A3. What's on topic?
Rose says: "I'd love for [alt.music.posterkids] to be a place of semi-intelligent conversation, especially not about band stuff, but about things people have learned each day, etc. . . . ."

A selection of early community postings on alt.music.posterkids clearly displays the success of that philosophy. I am quite proud of the variety of topics displayed here, and the dialogue around them.

There would generally be three to five variously themed postings per day, with a couple of responses (denoted "posts" here). Alt.music.sonicyouth (a much more famous band) at that time had around twice as many postings per day, but with about the same number of responses per post. Alt.music .smash-pumpkins had around twenty to thirty posts per day with usually one to three responses, but the posts were more confrontational. Around two to three exceptionally bellicose posts per day would get much more responses; for instance, "Most hated song from albums" (December 16, 1997) had eighty-eight responses by forty-five authors. (As of this writing, these Usenet groups can be found archived in Google groups, and there is a body of academic fan writing [aca-fans] available for further investigation.)

Nancy K. Baym, who was researching online communities at UIUC during these years (and also has an extensive list of every band she saw in the 1980s), provides a fascinating ethnographic study of soap opera fans on Usenet.[3] In her book, she describes the rules, rituals, and boundaries of text-based, online friendships centered around a common theme. She notes that off-topic posts (TANS, short for tangents) "offer participants a space in which to broaden their discussion and, when it is called for, to provide one another with social support."[4] Perhaps the pkids community grew so strong because it was built entirely on TANS, a shoutout to our years as students bonding over off-topic posts on our courses' PLATO forums.

In research on communities, a concept called consensual validation speaks of people's need to feel as though their crazy thoughts, ideas, are agreed upon and supported by others, thus the community serves and protects them. Note that in 1996, the internet was still a novelty for our relatively unknown midwestern band, and to have our own little communication space visited and responded to by people we didn't actually know, from towns we'd never been in, was very exciting to us. The variety and intensity of early postings still amuses me, one simple post quoting a fortune cookie escalated from profanity to Bible quotes.

<jgne . . . @freenet.columbus.oh.us> 10/30/96

Hey you, Bubba Bo Bob whatever the fuck yr name is, watch the flame shit. It will not be tolerated around here, you will get flamed ten times as hard. This is a newsgroup based on free thought and dialogue, and Mr. Howard will interpret his fortune cookie however the fuck he wants. If yr myopic little brain cannot comprehend that, then I suggest that you go back to alt.sex.fetish.siblings or wherever the fuck it is you usually hang out.

So take that, you backwoods goatfucker. You picked the wrong day to fuck with us.

Love and Muchas Smooches,

Joe =^. .^= :)

Henry Jenkins writes, "Rather than being morally debasing, ethically dubious on-air conduct frequently encourages a public discussion of ethics and morality that reaffirms much more conservative values and assumptions. In a multicultural society, talking through differences in values becomes a mechanism by which different social groups can learn more about how they each see the world, so there is real value in gossip that extends into virtual rather than f2f communities."[5]

The group of people we met online and only saw at shows followed us from platform to platform for the next two decades plus and were the backbone of our Poster Children community. I assume this loyalty arises from the nonrestrictiveness of off-topic posts. *Looking outside oneself.* Usenet was the beginning of the phenomena of interpersonal relationships in online communities and the precursor to our thousands of "close" Facebook friends, where people feel they have a social support network. It was wonderful to be able to find the few odd people just like us all across the globe. Those who had computers, anyway.

An email from Joe 2.0 about *alt.music.posterkids:*

Monday, June 19, 2017, Joe Sumrall **<j*********@gmail.com>** wrote:
I discovered Poster Children in junior (citizen) high from my friend who had older brothers. By high school I had made other friends who also liked Poster Children. Not an anomaly, exactly; we lived between Chicago and Champaign and UIUC was the school of choice. This was right at the time of the crest of the band's "commercial success." I went to Lollapalooza in hopes of seeing them but it was a touring production and cruelly, Poster Children did not play the IL stop.

I collected CDs where I could find them, the first being the "Just Like You" EP. It was a scorcher. I was into punk rock but punk rock, ironically, has the MOST rules and this record sat outside of all the constructs of punk rock but was still punk as fuck, but smarter. The angular guitars and nerdy vocals of "Sick of It All" appealed to my nerdy academic self and it managed to rock so much at the same time. I was listening to Sonic Youth by then but the noise solo in "Tell Me What You Want" was a revelation. But the lead track "Not Like You" was my anthem. As a judgmental angsty punk teen I couldn't get enough of looking at the people around me and thinking *I'm not like you.*

My friends and I drove to the Metro in Chicago to see PC for the first time 20 years ago. We camped out in the first row through two opening bands and my best friend swooned when Rose touched his hand, giving out cassette singles from the opening act Summercamp. He claimed he would never wash his hand again. New to the Adult Rock Show scene I got annoyed by the surrounding audience. Some drunk girl, some guy smoking a joint. "I'm not like you."

When the crowd was at full tilt the band launched into my anthem and it was almost ruined by a big-muscled meathead bro smashing into me. Around the time that the chorus changes from "I'm not like you" to "I'M JUST LIKE YOU," I saw a *Junior Citizen* tattoo on the arm of this guy I had written off as a lunkhead fratbro. It moved me so much that I wrote the band an email to share my story.

Then something crazy happened: Rose wrote back. The internet was still young and even major companies didn't have websites. There wasn't much to do with this new technology. But Poster Children not only had a presence but an album with an interactive CD ROM!

I'm not sure how I found out about the listserv, probably the website. I signed up immediately. After lurking for a few days I realized there was an established "Joe" so I introduced myself as Joe 2.0, thinking it fit with the bands' brainy sensibilities. Essentially a group chat via email, I would get hit at times with hundreds of emails a day. And it was fascinating.

Of course we talked about the band but most of the discussion was about everything else. Our bands, our lives. It didn't take long until I felt connected to a lot of people on the listserv. I was turned onto music I would have never found. Oddly, a regional band led me to support nonregional bands in a way that wasn't typical before. I discovered PC because I lived in IL and they hailed from CHAMPAIGN, IL. But now I could learn about the hidden gems from all over.

Our fanaticism eventually led to a tribute concert, or, as we called it, "P-CON." Enough of us had bands that we organized sets at the Gallery Cabaret in Chicago. Each band or person played a PC song. My band, Candygram, chose "Dream Small." That's how I got my greatest guitar lesson.

I emailed Rick, as the band had proved accessible. I did not realize he was more misanthropic than Rose, but most are, right? So I asked for the chords and never got a response.[6] While waiting I worked it out on my own, and have been able to do so ever since.

The PC show that was the hub of P-CON was a terrific time and it was great to put a face to folks I've interacted with for years. The tribute show was a bit more dr.awkward [another alt.music.posterkids fan] just because we were playing a set, one band at a time for an audience who, outside of ourselves, was not interested.

Later, while attending school in Champaign, I worked at a video store. They were places you could go and rent VHS and DVD and Laserdisc movies. This one was very good so of course Rick and Rose frequented. I introduced myself and eventually asked if Rick would record my band. He did and it was a fantastic experience. They played our song on their podcast and asked us to open for them. So to be clear: After seeing my favorite band when I was 17 I got to record with and open for them a few years later. And I'm not the only one.

The listserv eventually petered off. Rick and Rose were growing a family and the band became dormant. The internet was changing quickly and no one wanted a chat room in their inbox. Zach, from our former band, told me to get on the Electrical Audio forum. It had the same balance of rock talk with an anything-goes level of discussion that similarly forged a community atmosphere, which resulted in a strong and organic society for underground rock that has managed to stretch much further. The community has grown into multiple local festivals that highlight members' bands and friendships that don't fall into the category of "it's a friend from the internet." When asking for travel advice I had a forum member reach out, saying he lived near Amsterdam and could meet up. We spent the whole day with him and he regularly buys my wife teaching supplies and sends gifts to our children. We spent one day with Martin, and he lives on the other side of the world, but he's our rock buddy. I consider it a gift brought on by the culture of the listserv.

It seems appropriate that the Poster Children were able to play a PRF BBQ. There are still fights and drama but as we've all learned the language of internet courtesy the heart of the concept has grown into something that I'm happy to be a part of. I'll forever link Poster Children with technology. In the case of the listserv in particular, there is a movement that deserves great credit, and they got the ball rolling.

Listservs—Time to Push

alt.music.posterkids: July 24, 1997, 2:00AM: Who wants to read *Gravity's Rainbow* with me?

EVERYONE who wants to do the _Gravity's Rainbow_ read-a-thon, go to Poster Children's Web site and follow Rose's instructions on getting added to their Listserv. Don't delay!

Uncle Tony

AFTER THE DAYTON SHOW

I've noticed a wonderful trend lately; people we know really well from coming to our shows so often are starting to meet each other at different shows; they're starting to drive to neighboring cities (well, they've always been doing that) but it's really, really neat to see two people who we meet in different cities and who we talk to all the time on the internet talking to each other! I only hope you people can handle the fact that all Poster Children fans LOOK different. Like, some of you are tall, black vampire-goths, and others of you have sideburns and pigtails, and others look like total indie rocker geeks (me too?!) and others look like frat boys! But you all discovered us, scary enough, you all have something in common, so be nice to each other when you meet each other.

Alt.music.posterkids gave way to the pkids-list which was a listserv, served from prairienet.org. Listservs worked in a different way than Usenet; you'd *push* your text out to people's email addresses, so your message would be sent to a central location that would then broadcast it to everyone on the list. There was a good amount of soul-searching for me and Rick, before implementation of an actual Poster Children listserv, because this was us "pushing" informational materials directly from our band, instead of people coming to "visit" us, and therefore this would be more egotistical than we would prefer. Listservs still allowed for flat-level communications where no one was in charge, though, and we left ours unmoderated. We continued to request that pkids-list content would be unrelated to pkids. Later, we implemented a separate pkids-news list as people requested information about our own band and tour dates.

From Chris Schneberger:

The List Itself

I remember that we almost never discussed Poster Children directly. I think it was in part because you, Rose, were on the list and it seemed too fanboy to do so. Instead, I recall discussion of political stuff, computer stuff, and sometimes offering advice on awkward relationship issues. Also, discussion of every other band and album out there. After a while we got to know each other through our style of discourse—some being more combative, some more conversational. I don't remember the topic now, but at some point I got into a very heated argument over a week or more, and it gave me such stress. Every time I checked my email I was nervous for how the other person would have responded, and how I had to keep coming up with new and better-worded defenses of my position. But it felt like I knew everyone at a certain point even before we had met. I won't remember everyone now but some of the main people I recall are: DJ (dr. awkward), Joe Lemur (=^. .^=), Andy (always signed xoxo, Andy), Victor (xray something), Marcus, Guti from Germany, Amanda (mandroid 2.0), Laura (Kate M. Blood), Tarik, Emily, Conan, Josh, . . .

I remember it was exciting when you or Rick would comment on something on the list. If it was something I said I was so proud, unless you disagreed or disapproved, and then I was worried that I wasn't cool. One time as an April Fool's joke I pretended to be other people on the list by changing the username or whatever and I did this spoof conversation that was kind of imitating the voices and signatures of the main people. I think you were upset about it. I thought it was funny and harmless but then I felt bad.

In Real Life

I remember Poster Children playing in Chicago, maybe at the Empty Bottle, and I told all the listers who were coming to Chicago they were welcome to stay at my place. Then I thought, "I don't even know these people! What if they're weird and sketchy? What if they steal my stuff? What am I going to say to the cops? "Well officer, they were a bunch of random people I met through the internet!" It turned out mostly great, although it was kind of awkward at first because we realized we were mostly introverted nerds and didn't know what to talk about in person. I remember joking at one point, "Hey, so you like Poster Children, huh? Me too." (Followed by awkward pause.)[7]

We were on tour during the Myspace years and so the pkids community jumped to Facebook and all of Facebook filled in the void that we left as we went dormant in the mid-aughts. We are Facebook friends with many of the heroes from the pkids digital community and follow their lives in their feeds. As we began playing and touring again in 2016, we remet friends from Usenet and the listserv, people talked to us about how much their lives had changed, and sometimes what role we'd played; we re-created ten-year-old photos; everyone looked older, wiser, and (mostly) happier.

From DJ Hostettler:

Poster Children were on Sire/Warner Bros. by the time we met them, but their ethos was still DIY/punk rock all the way. They eschewed the tour bus lifestyle of so many other 90s alternative bands swept up in the Nirvana feeding frenzy, and toured in a humble van. They still slept on people's couches and floors. And Rose and Rick, through their computer savvy and early embracing of the internet, created their own punk rock online community inside the larger punk world by starting one of the earliest listservs and posting tour diaries online long before the word "blog" evolved into the zeitgeist.

I learned so much about the importance of community in punk/DIY music from being a part of the pkids list crew. When the Pop Machine started playing shows, Poster Children invited us to open for them at the Empty Bottle. HiFi ended up sharing the stage with them a ton. And on our own, we glommed onto any like-minded people we could find across the country and made sure they all ended up knowing each other too.[8]

Forums

Website forums were another way to share knowledge, the advantage being that you'd have a record of all posts saved on your own website, like your own Usenet. Here we were able to direct topics, so various inception of posterchildren.com contained a fan-driven recommended book list, a list of radio-zero topic requests, news, and even a quotes database where fans could contribute quotes and add new categories for them (this was before tags). There was always an open forum where anyone could post any thoughts without fear of it being off-topic, as off-topic posts still garnered anger on other forums, even in a post-flame-war age.

As of this writing, the Electrical Audio forum from Steve Albini's studio is strong and healthy, having been incepted in June 2003, and runs on the same phpBB software that we used for our forums. Topics began in 2003 are still relevant (crap/not crap polls, any type of science or politics, etc.) and still very active to this day. Still active threads that are around ten years old (or more) are "Scientific Consensus & Global Warming" (2005), "What Are You Listening to Right This Second?" (2004), "Little Details from Your Day" (2005), "Post While You Are Depressed Thread" (2007), "Let Us See You" (2005) and a thread named "You Fat Bastard" (2010) in which, on Sunday, July 25, 2010, 11:47 p.m., dontfeartheringo has put out a call for weight-loss buddies.[9]

Spawned from the Electrical Audio forum is the PRF, which can stand for "Premiere Rock Forum" or also "People's Rock Forum," is a community of rock fans who support each other and meet up face-to-face a couple of times a year at BBQs and play music together. Poster Children was lucky to play at PRFBBQMKE17 (the 2017 PRF BBQ) and you could feel the love and caring among all individuals there. Everyone was very supportive and, at least to a somewhat outside observer, the atmosphere felt really safe.

Dixie Jacobs:

> I've met a lot of wonderful friends that have carried over from pkids list to PRF. It's the misfits each in their respective towns wanting to meet like-minded people, trying to challenge and create, wanting to share and push boundaries, each having similar goals as a band—see how much we can do ourselves on our own terms, and not caring about being famous 'cause that shit is gross. Meeting musicians like this has saved my life and motivated/inspired me to continue creating music![10]

1999: Radio Zero Podcast

> Basically we are sick of music. We started thinking that everyone we know should have their own talk radio station, because everyone we know talks a lot, rambles on about their lives, and we find it really interesting. . . . We figured that if we just sit here and talk for a long time, other people will [think], . . . "hey maybe I could do it too," and all of a sudden there will be 100,000 people . . . with their own little radio stations and maybe something interesting will happen.
>
> —From "The Concept," an early *Radio Zero* episode, September 2, 1999

We had finished touring for the year of 1998, and had decided that the conversations that went on in the van and with others (we'd been staying at people's houses, meeting other bands on tour, etc.) were so fascinating (imagine the self-importance!) that we needed to continue them, and record and archive them online so others could listen to them at their leisure. We called the collection of sound files *Radio Zero*. There were four episodes featuring other members of our band in 1998, but the official online archive starts with Episode 1, August 24, 1999, five years before the word "podcast" was coined. Other internet radio shows began popping up around the same time, but we were not aware of them at the time. Our inspiration for *Radio Zero* came from our great love of talk radio.

Tuesday, June 19, 1997, on a drive from Boise, ID, to Boulder, CO

TOUR REPORTS WHERE I MENTION ART BELL

We're all listening, rapt, to Art Bell. He is a crazy survivalist-conspiracy-minded radio talk show host who lives in a trailer in Nevada and broadcasts from there. The show is amazing; it's on all over the US on AM radio in the middle of the night. You can listen to it anywhere.

Tuesday May 25, 1999, Drive to Oklahoma City

The last time we played Oklahoma City was the day of the bombing. Tonight on the fifteen-hour drive to Ardmore, OK, we are once again entertained by Art Bell. His first guest reports on the new form of life he's discovered—they are called "Rods" and they apparently exist around us, moving very, very quickly, and hardly ever bumping into us. He complains on the air that no one will give him funding to study the Rods more closely. A guy calls up and says that a princess from another dimension spoke to him over the cable access station. Interestingly, Art doesn't believe him.

July 15, 1997—A woman called in to say she saw an Elf.

In *Radio Zero*, Rick and I had a weekly decompression, almost therapeutic session where we would talk about all we'd learned and experienced over the week. On the few weeks when we had a fight, we would skip the show, because we weren't talking. Sometimes, during special events, like scary elections or Y2K, we'd say we were broadcasting from our bunker and play a Clash song at the beginning of the show. Growing up in Chicago, I remember listening to Steve Dahl and Garry Meier talk about interpersonal relationships with family members at Thanksgiving and thought it seemed comforting. I wanted to bring that to others.

For a few years, we broadcast the show on WPGU, the local Champaign radio station, but I disliked the openness. Originally, you'd have to work to find our podcast. On WPGU, it was like playing in a shopping mall, and anyone driving down I-57 scanning their broadcast radio dial could potentially be smacked in the face with the odd Poster Children fan arguing with the fifteen-year-old much-beloved regular known as "the Lord and Master," a local high-school student who would call in to pick fights with college students about underground music. During the WPGU years, though, we interviewed some of our more illustrious friends—for instance, Ian MacKaye, Steve Albini, Mac McCaughan (Superchunk, Merge Records), and Alex Borstein, who I grew up next to—and they graced the Champaign airwaves with us.

Over the twenty-plus years of our podcast, we've had segments such as "Talk like David Mamet," "From the Bunker," tons of film critique, Rick's famous political rants, and the newish "Sourdough Update." I feel like dialogue has become a bit less cerebral since 2005, and I don't know if our children or social media are to blame, but I suspect it's the latter. I do not keep track of our listenership, but we have a few online patrons. We are honoring the addendum to the childhood fairytale of the "The Long Tail" where everyone will be famous to fifteen people. In 2005, the year we celebrated our 100th show, a *New York Times* article introducing the podcast concept lists "couples capering" as one of the "best" three categories of podcasts,[11] so as a genre, we are definitely not alone. We must be one of the first, though, and will strive to be the longest running. Perhaps we can one day contribute to a dataset on how podcasting has changed over the years.

Zero Stars Crowdsourcing

> The ifihadahifi guys opened my world to lots of interesting music, and would not shut up about how the poster children were about to put out a new record and play shows and I absolutely had to go! I prepped for this excitement by watching the zero stars doc, and had a revelation—oh my god I can totally be in a band! look at these guys being totally awesome and normal with healthy perspectives on what it means to make art instead of making "it." This was a big deal for me to realize. Also, I thought the DVD was super funny.
> —Dixie Jacobs[12]

Rick endeavors to covertly set up a tripod in the middle of Marketplace Mall, Champaign, in 2001. He, Jim, Howie, and I sit around the food court, pontificating for the camera on the wide selection of food available to us. Rick switches the camera angle a couple of times. It was the year that the first Macintosh DVD burner came out, and Rick now realized he'd be able to make and distribute a feature-length film.

The film is comprised of vignettes from my tour reports interspersed with video of us playing. To shoot video of reenactments of tour stories, Rick would use either the tripod or whichever of us wasn't in the scene at the time as the cameraperson. For the live show recordings, since we were all busy playing, Rick had the great idea of distributing tapes to any fan who wanted to help us record, then collecting and compiling them. *Zero Stars* was shot at two locations, Champaign, and Chicago at the Metro. Crowdsourced! It seemed we were on to something. Five years later, the Beastie Boys crowdsourced *Awesome; I Fuckin' Shot That!*, a movie comprised of footage shot by fifty fans at Madison Square Garden.

Earlier than our foray into crowdsourcing was the Berkeley SETI@Home project, (Search for Extraterrestrial Intelligence), which was a distributed computing system wherein signal analysis software in the form of a screensaver was available to the public, which could crowdsource their computers to search for narrow bandwidth radio signals that would indicate alien life during the downtime on their computers. Groups would sign up to compete for who had the most processing hours. We all ran the software on our home computers, and Jim, once, noticed that during his processing an alert came up on his computer saying it had detected something in the data that needed to be sent to SETI immediately. He pressed "next" to continue, but we never heard anything after that. (Jim is still with us.)

To those of us with open minds, the impending music industry tsunami was an exciting time. Being a Gen-Xer, I had always been prepared for the world to end. Being a computer nerd during this time was kind of comforting. Everyone knew a change was coming. Those who were going to survive suddenly became interested in computer science.

Monday, April 26, 1999, Columbus, OH
THE BUBBLE—SELLING PRICELINE.COM

Man, I never realized what a hellhole some parts of Columbus really are! What we've seen so far are really dirty, not like the kind of sexy, laid-back dirty you have in Louisiana, but more like a junky, junkie, gasoline sort of dirty. I'm sure that there are beautiful parts of this city, but in our travels to places safely zoned for punk rock clubs, we have never seen them.

So since we have arrived in town early and can't request a floor to sleep on from the stage, and I need to upload new tour reports, we decide to splurge on a hotel room. We pick up a free motel coupon guide from Waffle House[13] and found a "BRAND NEW RENOVATED" Travelodge, for only thirty dollars, one to four people. With an INDOOR POOL!! Sounds great, doesn't it? Well, when we found it, the office of the Travelodge had a bright orange, triangular roof, reminiscent of another hotel brand. I think they were still renovating it.

We were given a room in the "back building" of the motel, which had graffiti and gang tags all over the outside of it. I became terrified, not for our lives or safety, but mostly because I was thinking that if my dad saw any of this, he wouldn't let me tour anymore. The sign in the office of the motel had said, "Time limit on refunds: 10 minutes." Our VingCard let us into a jail-looking building, and we walked up the stairs. All of the doors had scuff marks and it looked like some of the doorknobs had been pried off at one time or another.

When we got to our room, we opened the door to find an almost completely dark room, save for a red, pulsating glow in the bathroom. A forty-year-old heat lamp was the only light on in the entire hotel room. "Do you want to stay here?" inquired Rick. "NO!!" I screamed, and was halfway down the hall already, but it was too late. Jim and Howie had already gone into the room and were ecstatic. "Do you know how much blood and sperm have probably been spilled in this room?" asked Jim. They are in reverie, some imagined glamorous previous times that the room might have seen. Howie plops down on the bed, peeks under the covers, gleefully: "There's probably a dead dog hidden somewhere in this room!" They've already set up camp.

Later on as we left the Travelodge to go to our soundcheck, we noticed two guys scuba-diving with full scuba gear in the indoor pool. Also, a man was going through the trashcan inside the building we were staying in. When I was checking out, I saw a flier taped to the wall that "Suite 17" contained "Mademoiselle June" or something like that who was a "Certified Show Girl" and also a Swedish massage therapist. The head maintenance guy was having a discussion with another gentleman about how he didn't want to smoke crack anymore, prompting the second gentleman to offer to take the unused amounts he had off his hands.

A skinhead in a Korn shirt was asking the woman behind the desk to "not give nobody a room key to room 457 please, if they ask." Another woman appeared with a half-empty highball glass and asked to have her card run through for another room. "He said it was OK," she assured the desk.

I am not making ANY of this up. I do not have that good an imagination.

There were some good points to the motel. I like to look on the bright side of things. The woman behind the desk had at first mistakenly lost our credit card slip but then found it while I stood over her and waited. She had insisted that we had been moved out of our room and also, that the original people from that room had also been moved out. It was all very confusing. But this room contained one of the top five showers on the North American continent.[14] Also, the mattresses were of a much higher quality than the Motel 6 mattresses, and the sheets were made of some kind of natural fabric. Interesting.

The next morning, I hunted around the premises of the hotel until I found a private payphone outside the lobby, because I didn't want to wake the rest of the band. I had to call my "bookie," my online stock robot, because I decided it was time to sell all of my shares of Priceline.com. It had gone up 50 points since I bought it a little while ago, and that was enough for me. I felt slightly out-of-place, on tour with my rock band, at a payphone outside this motel selling Priceline stock, but I wasn't exactly sure which place I felt "out of."

Friday, March 17, 2000, Austin, TX

STARVING: A GOOD HOTDOG STORY

It pains me to tell this story but I know I have to do it. You can all laugh at me now after I tell this.

We're waiting outside the Atomic Cafe last night, and I keep complaining "I'm STARVING! I'm STARVING!" Like a broken record, I'm complaining. Everyone else had eaten earlier and for some reason I decided not to. So I'm "starving" now. The club isn't going to open for hours, we're just trapped here, waiting to load in, on this empty street in the van.

Anyway, up ahead of us, I see a food van pull up; you know, one of those metal vans that stops and sells food. So I tell the others, "I'm going out to that food truck to buy a quick snack!" and I amble out the van door and down the street to the van. When I get there, I tell the guy standing outside of it, "I'm STARVING!" I think I forgot to mention that we are also parked in front of the bail bonds store; this is the only corner of Austin that looks very shady. Lots of people are loitering around here.

You already know what is going to happen, don't you? The guy says exuberantly to me, "Oh, that's WONDERFUL! We can help you!" and I say, "Great! What do you have?" and he says, "Hot-dogs and hamburgers!"—I notice out of the corner of my eye that the truck is full of McDonald's hamburgers—which was my first inkling that something was wrong—and so I say, "Great, I'll take a hotdog," and he hands me a toothbrush and says, "Do you need a toothbrush?" and I say, "Oh, no, I'm fine with toothbrushes" and I see there are hotel toiletries also being offered here. . . . And then a lady hands me a plastic bag and says, "OK, here is your goody bag!" and I look inside and there's an apple and milk and other things, and I say, "Oh, no, I don't need this, I just need a hotdog," and the guy says, "OK," smiles, and hands me a hotdog . . . and I say, "How much" and he says, "Oh, it's free! Everything is free here! We're a church donation bus!" and my stomach sinks to the floor. I'm eating a homeless person's hotdog!! I'm going to hell! Think fast—how do I rectify this situation? I say, "Oh, please, at least, let me make a donation," and he says, "Oh no, you don't need to do that, we're fine!" and by now there are people milling around the bus waiting for their goodies. So I thanked the guy and left and walked back down the street to the van, head down, terribly ashamed, and gave the rest of the band something to laugh about.

CHAPTER 18

Life as a Woman

Saturday, May 1, 1999, Columbia, MO, with the Urge

FAGGOT!

. . . I put on a pretty shirt so they would be able to tell I was a girl and wouldn't start yelling "FAGGOT" at me . . .

In 2016, on the stage at DC-9, Washington, DC, I finally had an epiphany. For years I'd downplayed the importance of women in rock. Women in science are learned, scholarly. Women in business are mentors, vital. Women in rock jump around on a stage, smile, and look sexy. I don't ever practice bass, so there is not much mastery involved.

So normally, when women come up to me after a show, complimenting me, I feel bad, almost an imposter. Please don't make a big thing out of this. Please don't make women special in this role. But this night I had a realization.

Maybe it was the half-hour of Ian Mackaye pep talk before the show, another buoyant exchange of ideas, this time about parenting. Tonight after the show, a woman brings her daughter up to me to meet me, and I decide

Poster Children—Jim, Rose, Matt, and Rick. Photograph by Scott R. Munroe (@scott.munroe.54).

not to reply, "I'm nothing, my actions are unimportant, I'm just jumping around on a stage." I decide to be gracious and accept the compliment. It's time to take responsibility.

A memory from my childhood, a fearless babysitter during a tornado watch. I thought at the time, "Why is she not terrified, like I am?" and then I thought, "Maybe she's just as scared inside, but she's not telling us." So comforted, I realized, her power made me less afraid. This is how I must act when I grow up.

Leading up to this epiphany, though, I had years of experience to build upon. I have certainly learned from my mistakes.

Friday, October 20, 1995, Lubbock, TX—On Tour with Sponge
I HEARD A GIRL YELL, "A FEMALE?? OH NOOOOOOOOO"

So when we finally got on the stage tonight, the audience looked alarmed and then started booing. I heard a girl yell, "A Female?? Oh NOOOOOOoooo" and a bunch of people started yelling, "Sponge! Sponge!" Then the Sponge Stage Crew told us we had to wait for fifteen more minutes before we started playing. "WHAT DO YOU MEAN?" I screamed, "These people will be rabid in fifteen minutes!" and they explained that if we went on early than there'd be forty-five minutes changeover between Sponge and us, and that would be bad. They were right. People were still sort of booing intermittently.

So for the next ten minutes, I lay on my back, on the huge stage, completely visible to the audience, while people yelled "Play! Play! Come ON!!!" and then I sat up once in a while and stared at them as they screamed. The fifteen-minute eternity passed, and Chris said we could go on. I got up to the mic and people actually started clapping, but I didn't want to hear any more complaining, so this is what I said:

Rose's Patronizing Dialogue with the Audience in Lubbock

ME: (speaking clearly, enthusiastically, and extremely slowly, with dramatic pauses between sentences) "Two months ago, we got a call from our booking agent. She asked us if we'd like to play some shows with Sponge. She said Sponge had ASKED US TO GO ON TOUR WITH THEM! We said, 'Wow, that's pretty cool! We like Sponge, we'll DO it!' What do you guys think, DO YOU LIKE SPONGE?"

AUDIENCE: "Yay!!!!"

ME: "Well then, for the next forty minutes, we are going to be playing some songs. Then after we finish, SPONGE [I pause here for more clapping] will go on!! Yay!!"

Then I threw out a bunch of free tapes into the audience, and I think all the complaining stopped, as people smashed into each other to get at the free stuff.

whew

There was plenty of moshing. I think it went fine. An added bonus: Someone from the crowd even yelled, "I WANT TO JUMP YOU." I think it was "jump." I hope it was.

Comparisons

Thursday, April 27, 2000, Portland, OR—Email from a fan: "I just wanted to say you are one of the most energetic people I have ever seen on stage. Also best looking just kidding. Besides the music, your energy got me into the band. . . ."

Inevitably there are comparisons. Many years ago, Poster Children was invited to play with an up-and-coming four-letter-named female-fronted band, but when the singer found out we had a girl in the band, the offer was rescinded. Fuming mad, I remember it being explained to me that perhaps the woman had a certain image of how a female should be portrayed on the stage and having me in the opening band might have ruined that. Damn straight it would have.

Megan Krecji, a Taekwondo sister, instructor, and folksinger who lived in Champaign, tells a story of being one of two female vocalists in a band, where one had a more sultry style. "When we had a gig she was dressed way more sexier than me and I felt like a dusty potato in comparison. It looked silly too, I thought, as we stood next to each other, for one to be so dolled up, and the other so not. So I felt pressure to amp up the sex appeal just because I knew we would be standing next to each other all night and that it just seemed incongruous."[1]

Thursday, July 24, 1997—Headlining after a six-foot-tall, fire-breathing ex-model female bass player kisses her female guitarist

NASHVILLE PUSSY

I am actually sitting in our van now, crying, perversely. There is no one to talk to, and stupid or not, I have decided to write about it and post it online for the world to see. These are the ups and downs of touring. The band who *opened* for us tonight was called Nashville Pussy, and they had a six-foot-tall, fire-breathing female bass player who used to be a model. And another female guitarist with huge blonde hair, wearing a leopard-striped bikini, who could REALLY play the guitar, and a biker lead singer guy who kept yelling Mutherfucker in between lyrics. They kinda sounded like the Didjits with more tattoos. They were phenomenal, and the audience loved it!

But we had to play AFTER them! I tried to get us on before, but the promoter was totally patronizing about it! The audience waited, too, until we started playing and THEN walked out on us. It was humiliating! On top of it, those girls came up and talked to me after their show, they were so sweet! I was embarrassed and horrified, as if I was some sort of egotist who needed to headline.

I was very disturbed to find this tour report. The current me would be standing in front of this band cheering and inspired. But that isn't what had happened. I had hidden in the van and cried after the show. Onstage, all I could think of was embarrassment that I couldn't breathe fire, only had four strings, and that there was no other girl in my band to kiss onstage, so I had no business headlining after that band. It was horribly presumptuous. Now, was there really need for comparisons? Unfortunately, with such few women on stage back then, there really was no escaping them. You had to work hard to transcend it. Liz Phair backs me up:

> I didn't run into that many women doing what I did. And when we did run into each other, there was kind of a weird sense—and maybe this was me, because I was young and insecure—but it felt like people would pit

the girls against each other. It would be like, "Do you like Courtney or do you like PJ?" And the sales forces, the market forces, were gross. It was like, "Look hotter! Get more naked!" Like as if it was a Jell-O wrestling contest. Like, "Let's put this female icon up against that female icon. Which do you like better?" It was a tokenism, and it was gross.[2]

As Marion Leonard, in *Gender in the Music Industry*, writes: "The very phrase 'women in rock' . . . usually works to peculiarize the presence of women rock performers. . . . Rock discourse thus normalises the male performer and so deems the activity of women in this field as worthy of note."[3]

Of course, having a token female in the band is hard for men too. Being "worthy of note" has its perks. We may get added to a festival because there aren't enough women on it, or get ahead just because our boobs beguile and bewitch. Kim Deal "hasn't done any of the things that we expect girls to do onstage—she never preened, confessed, flirted, demurred, or compromised."[4] "The flirting stuff wasn't available to me," she says. "I would have felt ridiculous."[5] Yet Kim still gets charged with using her feminine wiles, by her own bandmate, Charles Thomas, who remarked that all Kim would have to do is smile, and the crowd would erupt in cheers. This statement infuriated Kim, but I understand how Charles could be upset. "Just smiling" means so much more when you're a girl. " . . . 'All I had to do was smile, and the crowd was behind me'—how incredibly sexist—I'm sweating, almost passing out with the heat, threw up in my mouth, tour bus driver didn't buy tampons, probably bleeding a little down my leg. . . . You're discounting my years of work, toil. . . ."[6]

In 2019, Mary Cullen and Jon Norton, reporters for WGLT, our local public radio news station in Normal, Illinois, did a story on female representation on local stages. They found the total number of female-led bands playing Bloomington–Normal ranged from 5 to 11 percent at the major venues, with their best estimate of 30 to 35 percent of musicians in the nation identifying as female. Jon and Mary had interviewed me and I'd told them there were many instances on tour when I'd not been let into the club until I proved I was a member of the band. I'd be stopped even if I was walking with my bandmates. I told them that nowadays, I just say I'm the tour manager of the band, and this usually allowed me entrance without having to discuss what instrument I played. I was very comfortable with this solution, but Jon and Mary were not happy about it at all. But at this point in my life, I choose my battles. At least a working woman is perfectly acceptable in the music industry.

"WORKING"

At check-in tonight, the front desk man at the Budget Inn Motel on "O" Street asks me if I'm working. I say "no," confused. Doesn't he know who is an employee and who is not? Five minutes later when I get up to the motel room, the guys help me realize what he has asked and I am mortified. Baby Matt (our new drummer, #7) is my knight in shining armor who goes down to ask the guy what the hell he meant by that, and we apparently now have a six-dollar discount because we're "affiliated with some sort of working group." Rick is sure that the desk man just asked if I was a whore and now is freaked out about it so is giving us a discount. Geez. Do I look like a whore? (Was I standing like this?) Maybe we should stop staying at the motels that the promoters suggest, the ones that are in the center of town. I never had this problem back when we were staying at the Motel 6s.

The Baggage

It has taken me a while to acknowledge that life is different for women in some of my chosen fields. I don't believe in complaining, and excuses feel like a crutch. Whether teaching in higher ed, practicing martial arts, playing music on stage, or working in computer science, I've encountered a bit of baggage that comes on stage with my equipment. Recently, right before we are going to play, I put my purse in front of my massive eight-by-ten cabinet. The guys don't have purses, so they put their baggage on top of their amps. They have carried their keys and wallets in their pockets, scraping their thighs. Their baggage isn't stored in an extra thing that they can remove. It's with them all the time.

On stage, I'm known for high energy, jumping around, punching, and beating myself up, all delivered with a smile. People have asked what goes into my performance. I've not explored it, mostly because I don't believe in revisiting and dwelling upon old wounds. When I do allow myself time to think about it, I know it has something to do with what's been written in this chapter. Frustration, irritation, and things I cannot change. But I truly believe in letting go and being grateful for what one has. And that is why you see me smile.

AS WARM AS A HEART

Inside the 7th Street Entry it is as warm as a heart. People we recognize are here and they are kinder to us than our parents would even be. I feel like I'm in the presence of beloved older, caring siblings. I don't think any club is as nice as this one to us. And many clubs are very nice to us, so this is saying a lot. I'm wondering what we did to deserve this, but I don't spend too much time thinking about it. We get to work setting up our equipment and doing our soundcheck.

Old friends come to see us play this show. And old fans, people who have been with us since *Daisychain Reaction*. Texas Kevin is here to help us with our t-shirts tonight, and we realize this is probably the closest we've ever played to where he is currently living; this kid has traveled over the past five or six years to see us twelve hours away from his house. Maybe sometimes even further.

I think we got three encores tonight and played two songs for each encore. I wonder if that's a new thing for new drummer Matt. I hope he's enjoying himself—the audiences sure are enjoying his playing. At the end of the last two encores, I get myself into a little "energy problem"—that's what I'm going to call it when the energy builds up into a bottleneck and then your body does stuff without your mind's consent. When I see Mark Baldwin, who practices tai chi (and is the lead singer from Lovecup—now the Mezzanines) kick over his guitar amp, I think to myself, "Oh, Mark is having an Energy Problem." When that happens to me onstage lately I have just screamed (not into the mic!); in the past I would start shaking really badly. It's never really painful. Everything just gets really vivid for a little while.

Like a Heartbeat

The next morning: I notice that I have bruises on my left arm. I guess that's from playing bass yesterday; we had a coda at the end of our set. I found myself pounding my arm rhythmically on my bass, trying to emulate a heartbeat, I guess. I think I was crying. I wanted to write about it but I just cannot find the correct words. I don't even know what to write about it, I don't really know what the story was. Maybe someone in the audience figured it out. It wasn't a sad thing at all. Rick was still on the stage too; I remember realizing that this had probably been going on for a while, and Rick was by the amps ready to turn them off, so I looked at him and we counted to three and then shut all off.

I'm sorry I can't describe what I was feeling then. Maybe it's better that I can't. I guess I just felt like I was channeling pure energy. I don't really have a lot of feelings about it. I have bruises, though.

Relationship goals. Photograph by Tarik Dozier, 2017.

Interpersonal Relationships

Monday–Tuesday, April 24–25, 1995, Pensacola and Orlando, FL

MUSTACHES

The guys (except Jim) have all decided to grow mustaches, as a male-bonding thing. I am disgusted at this. I just don't associate Poster Children music with mustache rock. I have threatened to do everything from grow my own mustache to wear really heavy-metal, sexy-belly-button-showing clothes on stage. The guys don't understand this; they say it makes no sense, but I say that they are showing off their testosterone levels, so I can show off my femininity. The guys hate it when I wear revealing clothes on stage. I think they think it's degrading to me, and I guess they're probably right. I haven't carried out any of my threats.

I thought about this while I was looking at myself in the mirror in a Pensacola restroom that had the best graffiti—a picture of a guy frying in an electric chair and it said, "You can't burn an American Flag, but you can burn an American." Think about that for a while.

At our wedding, Rick's brother Jim said, in his toast, that it should be no problem for Rick and me to succeed as a married couple, since we'd already been living together in a marriage of four people. Two should be easier. It was really funny and brilliant, and correct. I'm sure our relationship/fighting—when surfaced—was hard to take, but I hope it wasn't too predominant during tours. We certainly didn't snuggle in public, and this helped me feel equal to the other men on the tour. I'd not seen any of my Midwest Bass Sisters snuggling their husbands on tour either, although I'd heard of some breakups and switches within other bands and could never imagine being on tour with that going on in the van.

I was in my very late forties when I heard that Kim Gordon wasn't married to Thurston Moore anymore, kind of like if you've graduated college and have moved away and then your parents divorced. I felt a bit sad for them, but I tend to think if people are going to use up that much energy for something, then it must be for the best. I'm glad they were together for all the years that I enjoyed their music, because it did set some sort of precedent, a royalty-like structure that I felt safe emulating—Thurston and Kim as king and queen. I even hoped that if couples came to see our show and saw how Rick and I navigated being together in work and in play, that it would instill some sort of strength and stability in others' relationships.

Playing Like a Woman Offstage

I now teach computer programming while female and am still very alert about the push-pull, mom/female boss, authoritarian/bitchy line that I have to navigate while I deliver my lessons. Female instructors are consistently evaluated on a different scale than their male peers—along with their students, of course. While I'm careful to be diplomatic with certain male (and female) students when making corrections to their work, I'm lucky to have chosen to teach a gender-neutral science.

2000+: MY FRIEND ANNA NESBITT'S RULES
FOR TEACHING WHILE FEMALE

1. **Be exceptionally organized.** Much more so than your male colleagues. The students will probably still call you disorganized.

2. **Never correct a student without employing the sandwich method.** A) Make a compliment. B) State the counterevidence. C) Make another compliment OR minimize their mistake by saying,

"This has been a tough concept for students. I am probably not communicating the idea well enough. Let me try another way."

3. **Dress professionally with makeup if possible.** Otherwise, you might be considered unprofessional. Students may still call you unattractive on your evals or, worse, give you hot chili peppers. This observation links to "Attractiveness Bias," and makeup can help close the gap.[7]

4. **Be confident.** Apparently, you're not an expert without total confidence. That 95 percent confidence interval and too many caveats just confuse students. Although it is a genuinely terrifying experience, practice saying wrong stuff with certainty. However, NEVER be overly confident. (That's bitch territory.)

5. **The quiet female students can be your worst detractors.** Make sure to provide lots of opportunities for extra credit, allow students to redo assignments, and a mid-semester climate survey doesn't hurt. My three worst SETs were from such students. They each gave me all 1s in classes where I averaged 4.0+ out of 5.0.

Too anecdotal? A 2016 analysis of a previous study where an online teacher taught two identical sections but masqueraded as a teacher of the opposite gender for the second section found that the female students were much more likely to rate their "male" teacher higher.[8]

6. **Recognize your strengths and weaknesses.** If you're frumpy, be a nurturing Mom figure; most students like this approach. If you're gorgeous, be the outrageously fun aunt. And mitigate like hell to fit student expectations, but always be authentic.

This may come back to bite me one day, lol.

Anna Nesbitt, Ph.D., former teaching assistant professor, Department of Atmospheric Sciences, University of Illinois

Punching on Your Period

This is a tour report from in between tours—when we had to pull rank to get haircuts and were angry about it.

Thursday, March 14, 2002—Where the HELL
Does a Seventeen-Year-Old Learn This Stuff?

SHOW OFF! STILL STUCK IN CHAMPAIGN!

Jane, my seventeen-year-old kung-fu sister, was marveling at my problems with the haircut appointments, trying to find the best haircutter for my hair. I told her that since she has straight, fine hair that it's easy to cut her hair. She still said she couldn't believe Rick and I spent so much time worrying about the haircuts, and so I said, "I guess we might be a little vain." Here's her response.

From: Mxxxxxx@xxx.com (Jane)
Date: Thu, 14 Mar 2002 08:23:54 EST
Subject: Re: ugh
To: rose@posterchildren.com
<< I guess we might be a little vain. >>

The dictionary definition being, "having or showing undue or excessive pride in one's appearance or achievements," I think my haircutting agenda shows more vanity than yours. I'm the one who is convinced I'll be pretty no matter who cuts my hair. You're the ones with a tiny flaw in self-confidence which has you convinced that you are dependent on good haircuts to look pretty or cool or well-groomed or whatever. Maybe one day we'll all realize that even if we don't look pretty, cool, and well-groomed, we'll still be beautiful. And then we can throw away our cosmetics and haircutting appointments and be our naturally beautiful and radiant selves, or we can keep on getting good haircuts and be beautiful AND pretty, cool, and well-groomed. Then everyone will love us.

Well, I need to go to school and be beautiful for all my classmates now. I hope you have a wonderful day.

—jane

Where the hell does a seventeen-year-old girl learn this stuff? In HIGH SCHOOL?? And to interject exactly the right amount of facetiousness at the end? This is why I think she is going to be president someday.[9]

New Female Black Belt!

Tonight a new female black belt appeared at our Taekwondo Academy! She is from another academy. She is really, really freaked out about being called a black belt, though, because she hasn't practiced in four years. You can see from her body movements though that she is very well trained.

She wasn't sure what rank our head instructor would put her in (she is wearing plain clothes, humble and commendable for someone who has already achieved a black belt), but I was pretty sure he'd honor her black belt. It's pretty hard to get a black belt, and once you do I think it should be honored by anyone respectable. Then if you have catching up to do, you are challenged not only to improve for yourself, but for others around you watching you and deciding for themselves if you are a black belt.

Master Hyong paired her up with me (because I'm a black belt also), and she was so apologetic! "I'm SO sorry!" she told me as I moved myself to the left of her in line, signifying that I believed she was higher rank than me—she looked so sad and worried that I was angry with her. I declared, "Nonsense! I will have NONE of that! We are here to work out together! I have no problems with where you are in your training!" Why should her place matter to me? Actually, as we started doing our form together, all of a sudden I felt so strong and happy and I wanted to be better—I've been uninspired in TKD for a while, and am now inspired again. I felt great!

When I taught MY TKD class today (I also have an hour when I teach TKD—Jane is my assistant), I called attention to one of the kids who was doing the splits perfectly. "Show-off!" another kid replied. "NO," I said, "She is not showing off! She is just doing her 'work.' When I see someone doing something perfectly like that, I say to myself, 'Wow, that's SO COOL! Look at her doing that! That means that I will be able to do that someday, too!'" The class was silent after that and continued stretching. They all looked like they were hard at work. I was in such a good mood today, from Jane's email.

·   ·   ·

Saturday, August 10, 2002—The Day before We Left for Texas and Breeders

CANDLE

So I had Mastery Class (in Taekwondo) the day before we left for our Breeders tour. In this class, only about seven of the black belts showed up, and this was the day that Master Hyong (our head instructor) has decided we were going to learn how to punch out a candle. He said he never does this kind of weird, shamanistic stuff, because he is a practical man and doesn't believe in this kind of crap. But he feels like we will be able to tell if we have good strong punches by seeing if we can punch a couple of inches away from a candle and put the candle out with the air flow from our punch.

So the night before, Nam (one of my best friends here) and I stood in our dining room while Rick tried to watch TV, punching at a lit candle set up on the dining-room table. The damn candle would not go out. We kept punching, kung-fu punches and Taekwondo punches, and the damn thing stayed lit. Punch, punch, punch, flicker. I finally ended up punching the damn thing off the table by accident, candlestick, candleholder, and flame, causing hot wax to fly everywhere. Rick yelled at us, comically. The candle went out, though.

So now at Mastery Class, the next morning, everyone practices punching out the candle. By the end of a half-hour, everyone can punch out the candle, except me. My punch will not put that damn candle out, because my punch has a slight wobble at the end of it. I know this too. I've known this forever. So then I had an extra half-hour lesson with the head instructor with his hand on my stomach, yelling at me to tighten my lower abdomen at the end of my punch. I thought I was. TIGHTEN HARDER! he yells. During this part of the month, my lower abdomen is not going to tighten any harder. I am not sure how to tell him this.

It's kind of depressing that there's something fundamentally wrong with my punches. They wibble at the end. And that's the way I learned it back in college. Damn it. I have to practice this now. And I feel an aversion to wanting to practice it because I am worried that I am not going to get any better, even with practice. How's that for logic. No. I'll just practice it. Because I know from this class that practicing will make me better, inevitably. I guess that's what "indomitable spirit" is.

CHAPTER 19

How to Look at Things

Sunday, August 11, 2002, the Drive to Texas

A FIREWORK SHAPED LIKE THE EARTH!

I love going down I-57 to I-55 South in Illinois. It's like I'm connected to the South in this weird way; I can step on I-57 outside my house and know that someone on the end of it is in a weird southern place where people talk funny. Is it weird that I feel like the roads are living organisms, like, they have a head and a tail? They are holistic beings; they can feel me on one end and some strange dude with a cowboy hat eating grits on the other end.

Today in Boomland, Open 24 Hours, near Sikeston, MO, at the corner of I-57 and I-55, I bypass the Black Jesus with Mary and Children Family Statues (only $6.99!), the ubiquitous Unicorn Ashtrays, the clear paperweight globes with roses embedded in them, and the Elvis, Jesus, and Trucker decoupaged wooden tree-stump clocks on the walls and head straight to the half-mile-long fireworks section where I purchase a bunch of baby sparklers and two blue Globe-shaped Caution Emits Shower of Sparks fireworks. It will be really cool to blow up the Earth into a Shower of Sparks. I probably won't even blow those up, I'll just sit them somewhere in the house for a year. Imagine a firework shaped like the Earth!

A State of Constant Total Amazement

Driving across continents for decades, meeting people, sleeping on their floors, and playing small stages each night to possibly no one profoundly changed me. For one, I'm forever provided an extended timeline. Patience develops following years of daily six–ten-hour drives. Moving to a new place each day helped me to practice letting go and to acknowledge that situations arise and fall just as the next sunrise renews each day. Leisurely roaming the United States and Europe with the simple job of playing music that I didn't even have to learn was part of a very lucky and privileged life. I made the most of it by trying to live in a state of constant total amazement. Now, I know I cried a lot, but I don't think it was for any reason. When your brain discharges at night, it causes the random thoughts you shape as dreams. When you cry randomly, it's probably just your heart dreaming.

July 2, 2002—We Are Back on the Road! Driving from Champaign to Phoenix. We Have Two Days to Do This. Begin.

ROUTE 66

The Mercator projection of the world makes you think that it is faster to drive down Interstate 57 and go across to St. Louis than it is to go across 72, then down 55. But it's not a parallelogram. We freaks, who know the world is not flat, who are aware of the centripetal-forced love-handles around its waist—and also, who have been through Effingham so many times—know that you can cut an hour off your four-hour drive to St. Louis if you take 72 West. It's like we know a secret wormhole through space, tesseracting the two cities together.

Leaving for a tour, for me, was always a playful replay of the scene from *Apocalypse Now*, where Martin Sheen gets collected for his next mission. He's been lying in a hotel room, drinking, murmuring "Saigon. Shit." He stinks from liquor. He hasn't showered in weeks. He hasn't left for his tour yet.

Now, however, after seeing the movie *Donnie Darko*, I have a new movie metaphor; I feel more like it's *The Last Temptation of Christ* that I'm leaving for tour again. Let me explain. I have spent the past two years completely ingraining myself into Champaign life. I have grad school classes, work, kung-fu classes, Taekwondo students, Sangha meetings, friends who are like family to me, too many houseplants, and a garden, and these things connect me to the earth in Champaign. I want to go on tour, I want to feel that huge concrete slab lift off my back as my responsibilities fall one by one out of the van on the way out of town again, but my Champaign life clings around my back and won't fall off, and it hurts and it's confining and it's weighing me down. I feel like it's not good to be this attached to things if they are hurting me like this.

I'm so attached to my life here that it's Monday night and we are practicing before we leave on this amazing tour with the Breeders, and all I can think about is, "if I finish practicing before 6:30 p.m., I get to decide between Taekwondo, kung fu, or my Sangha meeting." I keep thinking about this and it's hurting my chest to not be able to decide where to go and hurting it more that we're still practicing and I'm going to miss all this stuff anyway.

When did anything ever take precedence over making music? Rick scolds me for looking at my watch. I am supposed to be mindful of where I am, here and now at this time. I am supposed to live in the moment. What the hell am I doing? I guess we just haven't been touring enough so I've had to learn to live without it, and my mind can't even let myself believe I'm really going on tour again. It's being cautious. But I also think I am living too full a life here.

It's taking a while for that other life to dissolve so I can become part of the road again.

So now we're driving through Missouri, and there are so many different shades of green, I can only stare out the window in awe. I keep a watch out for when it starts raining and when it stops, notify everyone in the van of this. "It's raining again." "OK, it stopped." "Oh, it started raining again."

There was such a sense of urgency as I left Champaign, worry and insistence that when I return, everything might be different. When I get back, people will be gone. Life will be different. Maybe I'll go back to where I was three years ago, before I started to live in Champaign again, no good friends, no attachments. What if things are never the same again between me and my friends? I guess that I just have to wait and see what will happen. Everything changes, always, anyway. That's the way the world works.

Now the skies are starting to look really scary, huge dark clouds. Jim is still driving, and I am on Tornado Patrol now. I am combing the skies hopefully for anvil clouds. But I know deep inside I will never see a tornado, at least not today, because my video camera is loaded with film and ready to shoot.

ROSE: "What about that one, is that an anvil cloud? It kind of looks anvilesque. . . .
    Could be an anvil."
JIM: "That's just a bunny cloud."
ROSE: (turning around to face Rick, excitedly) "What if there's an EARTHQUAKE when
    we play in Los Angeles?!!!"
RICK: "What if there's one before?

The Largest McDonald's in the World

It's pitch-black night outside now and I am irritating Rick by reading the Dao to him, while he's driving. To him, it's poetry, and he hates poetry.

ROSE: "Rick—check this out: 'Why do I call honor a contagion deep as fear? Honor always dwindles away, so earning it fills us with fear and losing it fills us with fear.'"

ROSE: "Rick: 'Forcing it fuller and fuller, can't compare to just enough, and honed sharper and sharper means it won't keep for long.'"

ROSE: "Rick, oh, check this out: 'Once it's full of jade and gold your house will never be safe. Proud of wealth and renown you bring on your own ruin. Just do what you do, and then leave: such is the Way of heaven.'"

RICK: (driving) "We are about to pass 'The World's Largest McDonald's.' In fact, the sign says, 'Still the World's Largest McDonald's.'"

ROSE: "That cannot fucking be the largest McDonald's in the world, the sign has to be lying. What about that one in Austria?"

> I continue with the Dao until, in the distance, approaching at 80 mph, too close to get the camera out in time, a lone, behemoth golden arch over the highway appears, a controlled electronic bonfire in the night. The Largest McDonald's in the World.

ME: (dropping the Dao book on the van floor and fumbling for my camera and missing the shot) "SHIT!"

We wake up in Motel 6, Oklahoma City, it's about 68 degrees outside and the pool is locked. I've been looking forward to this tour so I could at least go swimming once, and now it's cold out and the pool is unavailable anyway.

We eat very cautiously at a Waffle House, no one spending over three dollars for breakfast. It's tough to live on ten dollars a day if you are not getting fed a free dinner; these two days we have no shows, so no free dinner, and all we do is drive and spend money on garbage food. Last night we ate at an Olive Garden, if you can believe it.

The Largest Cross in the Western Hemisphere

Somewhere along Route 66 is the Largest Cross in the Western Hemisphere. I tell Matt to pull off the road because we have to visit that. It goes in with my tour diary metaphor, anyway. The cross is HUGE and encircling it are something called the 14 Stations of Christ, sculptures of different things that happened to Christ as he was on his way to getting killed. I'm pissed off at those Romans now for killing him, and I tell that to Matt, who is a Catholic and believes in God. Matt informs me that the Romans were killing lots of people. Compared to the size of the cross, these sculptures of Jesus make him look like a small man. I think it's sad that he tripped a couple of times while he was carrying the cross. Imagine the kind of person that can put another person to death. You'd have to be very, very sure of yourself.

Rick went out and peed somewhere in the Portapotties they had set up out here, but didn't spend too much time doing research. It's really cool that we've seen the Largest McDonald's in the World, and now the Largest Cross in the Western Hemisphere, because later on we might visit the Largest Stupa in the United States. It's a whole religious tour theme!

. . .

We're driving toward Amarillo and I have been staring at the landscape for the entire day now. I want to be completely aware of when it changes; the terrain will change from dark green, deciduous tree-covered lands to brown dirt and dry shrubs and it will do it within the next three hours. I want to see the line where it happens.

"We have to stop at Cadillac Ranch," Jim and Rick say. "What the hell is that?" I ask, and they say, "You'll see." If they're not telling me what it is, it's going to be good.

Damn. It's an ART PIECE, made by a collective called "Ant Farm" in 1974, ten Cadillacs half-buried at about an 80-degree angle, all in a line like the Very Large Array. They are covered with spray-paint. I feel like I am in France all of a sudden, where there's Art all over the roads. This is completely amazing! And there's no sign, no billboards about it at all—you're just driving down I-40 west of Amarillo and all of a sudden, in the middle of a farm-field, you see ten Cadillacs half-buried, almost vertically, in the sandy ground. Wow. That is COOL.

Here's what it says on the plaque on one side of the art piece:

Cadillac Ranch©
Created by Ant Farm
Copyright 1974 (Lord Marquez, Michels)
All Rights Reserved
Stanley Marsh 3, Owner

In May 2002, Cadillac Ranch, one of the most recognizable landmarks on Route 66, became the eleventh landmark to be restored as part of Hampton Hotels Explore the Highway with Hampton© Save a Landmark Program

"The people's art is not for sale . . . or is it?"

Flooding in the Desert

Now we're driving through the desert in eastern New Mexico, in the worst flashflood rainstorm I've ever seen in my entire life. This storm is of biblical proportions! In addition to blinding floodwaters streaming down the van, hail is pelleting down, making a terrible noise, and I feel like I'm driving a boat. When we stopped at a gas station, the locals told us this was the first rainstorm they've had all year. This has been the worst drought they've had for 100 years. As I drove through the rest of the storm, I felt very happy for the people who lived around these areas.

2016: Reprise Repress

Dear [Reprise],

My band Poster Children would like to re-release [*Daisychain Reaction*] for its 25th Anniversary. We can do this by ourselves, we just need permission from you.

I cc'd every high-up email address I'd collected at Warner Bros. and signed this with my Illinois State signature, just in case they had children looking at colleges. It took a couple of tries and months, but someone from Rhino Records finally responded to me.

The WMG policy is to make manufacturing/finished goods deals for full album reissues and not license deals. This is where we manufacture the product . . . and sell you the finished goods. . . . [The] deal is 3,000 unit guarantee over 3 years; 1,500 unit initial order and any reorders need to be ordered as minimum 500 unit orders over the 3 years for the U.S. only.

What this meant was that we guaranteed that *we* would buy 3,000 records from *them*. We had originally just wanted to press up a couple hundred. At around seven to nine dollars an album, this would cost a lot more than we could afford. It also seemed that being a professor at a state university in Illinois didn't have as much pull with Rhino Records as I thought it might.

Chris Garibaldi, owner of Lotuspool Records and lifelong friend of Jim and Rick, helped us procure the rights to rerelease the record for a twenty-fifth anniversary release, and signed us for another new record, *Grand Bargain!* The music you love, that enters, buoys, and changes your life, comes to you because of people like Chris. His (and his family's) generosity is to be revered. I marvel at the fact that someone can believe so deeply and be so supportive of an artistic endeavor that will not recoup monetarily. To me, actions like this come from the highest order of being.

Rick redid the cover art (remember that is the only album without our own design) and we were lucky to peg author Jon Fine (our friend from Bitch Magnet) for commentary text. Bob Weston did the remastering. We assembled 1,500 copies of the album on our dining room table. We then began to regroup for playing live shows.

By this time, Rick and I were teaching as professors of music in a small program called "Creative Technologies" at Illinois State University, forty-six miles west of Champaign. Rick had been producing other bands' albums and videos for years, and also had begun a new career under the name "Thoughts Detecting Machines," which he describes as himself, "armed with only a guitar and laptop, building loops into songs that are simultaneously emotional and mechanical."[1] He had begun releasing albums and playing shows. Everyone's lives had been filling up with other interests, but somehow we were able to get ourselves together to practice, write a new record, and tour.

Grand Bargain! (2016) is another very political album. To create longdistance, some of the parts of the songs were exchanged over the internet. I may have even helped with some notes—songs with Jam or Buzzcocks chord progressions were probably influenced by me. I don't know how anyone writes music without perfect pitch. When I hear notes, I translate them into the name of the chord in my mind, and then I filter what chords could go next. It's not an organic, writerly process for me. It's more like amateur scientist hour. We recorded with Steve Albini at Electrical Audio quickly. Then we went on tour and brought our kids with us so they could meet our fans.

Touring as an "adult" with real-life responsibilities was invigorating, and also made for an incredible vacation. There was still the angst of worrying people wouldn't come to shows, but again the payoff of seeing my roads again. Only one aspect was very different. Now all the technology I'd ever used to communicate and create was in the palm of my hand, and it made me realize how numbing cellphone life could be. Compare this tour report to the previous "Route 66" one from 2002. Now everyone was constantly connected to their screens—even our kids, on tour with us, would not remember the East Coast I-90 boredom or the California fires, or the fact that they had driven through every perimeter state in the United States.

The Machines

2016 US Tour Supporting Rerelease of *Daisychain Reaction*

THE HOT ELECTRIC GLASS BURNS MY HAND

Touring is completely different now—before our break in 2002, I would sit in the passenger side of our van with the giant road atlas blanketed on my lap, tracing the orange double-lines with my fingers for hours as we drove, calling out the mile markers every so often. That's all gone now (probably not missed by my bandmates). On tour in 2018, I yank my smooth, black, hand-held device that's plugged into the rented van; it's tethered by too short a power cord. I strain my back to reach it, it flashes on, and a tiny map with me in the center tells me how many minutes to tonight's venue. There are also thirty or forty new messages, distractions for me to follow from all over the world and all over my life.

Also gone is the final descent into the city, the hunt for a payphone to call for directions and then the nightly adventure we likened to the "Don't get off the boat" scene in *Apocalypse Now*, our river being Mass. Ave., East Hennepin, or MLK. Today our phone-robot chants directions, and at the same time, I text the venue, implore them to leave a parking spot for the van, and order our food. As the phone sucks in cellular data, I continue the descent, but into my online world, the digital soap-opera of my friends, and I click to refresh every so often, looking for more likes. I have to attend to the guest list! The hot electric glass burns my hand with who knows what type of radioactivity and we continue the last part of the trip to the venue. The road passes me by, the giant fir trees in the Northwest, the California fires, the Texas desert shrubs, or what remains of the American landscape, the distinct personality of each city center.

But I know what's happening, because I straddled the centuries, and I constantly remind myself to stop staring into my little black mirror and look outside the windows. But how would you know to do this if you never had to, in the past?

While I'm proud of all the early-adoption we've done using the internet, the enhanced CDs, blogging, podcasting, now with decades of use, I can comment on their detriments, and on how I'm late-adopting different practices. Certainly, the internet kept us viable post–major label. But misuse of technology can harm. With great power comes great responsibility.

I noted in the above tour report a loss of peace, spaciousness, the emptiness that usually filled me as I traveled in the van. Nicholas Carr warned that with a phone we will never be bored, never have unanswered questions, and our thinking processes will become shallow and impatient.[2] Decades before this tour, a member of Six Finger Satellite was educating me about hypertext, and I remember thinking, "The link in the middle of the text takes us somewhere else, but when do we go back and read the rest of the article?"

Thursday, July 17, 1997
MUSEUM HOPPING

We have a day off in New York City, so of course we went museum-hopping. Jim and Howie went to the Museum of Modern Art, while Rick and I went to the Museum of Television & Radio, a library full of 75,000 TV shows. For six dollars you can choose four and you have two hours viewing time. Rick chose "Art of the Future" (technology and art, with Walter Cronkite, 1961), "Famous Moments in Interview History" (Jack Parr interviewing Fidel Castro, Tom Snyder interviewing Hitchcock, and

Richard Nixon being interviewed by everyone), and an episode of an English TV series featuring Penn & Teller. I chose a *Nova* episode about the unified field theory; a Bill Moyers show about lying, featuring Richard Feynman testifying about the O ring on the space shuttle with ice water; and the *Ellen* "Coming Out" episode. It was good.

We were ecstatic! Eight years before YouTube, it would have been nearly impossible for a layperson to access these materials. Now, normally in the van (and out) we consumed and regurgitated pop culture, but fuzzy recall would result in stimulating cross-pollination. Having 24/7 access to all cataloged culture changes how we create, and missing are ambiguity, obscurity of reference, and the boredom to fuel our projects.

Tuesday, April 18, 1995, Boulder, CO—Snow and the Garden of Eden

OKLAHOMA CITY BOMBING

We left the show (a wonderful show by the way; over 300 people on a heavy-snow Tuesday!) in a snowstorm, and we had an over-fifteen-hour drive to Norman, Oklahoma, near Oklahoma City, with a stop in Lucas, KS, at the urging of James Nature-Boy Valentin, who wanted to stop at the Garden of Eden. This is a person's house and yard in a teeny rural town in the middle of Kansas. A man had created concrete statues all along the perimeter of his yard, statues of dogs, cats, people, American flags, and so on, all in some weird array. He and his wife are buried in a tomb in the center of the yard, and rumor has it that you can look through a glass porthole and see them. Apparently, the house was built in 1907, and the guy died in 1930? This decade, his tomb has started leaking, so he is decomposing. When we arrived at the Garden, early in the morning, just a house next to a little yard with the Garden in it, the house was closed, and there was a phone laying on the porch for people to call to request a tour, but we were all about to fall asleep, so we drove on.

Oklahoma City, Wednesday, April 19, 1995—Explosion in Oklahoma City

As we're sitting here in our hotel room, we are watching footage of a terrible explosion that just occurred in the middle of this city, today. This is the sort of thing that happens to us a lot while on tour in the South. A couple of tours ago, we drove through the city with the Luby's Cafe Massacre, the day after (for those of you who don't know, some guy opened fire at a Luby's restaurant). For the next couple of days, we were in Texas, there were armed guards outside all the restaurants we ate at. In fact, I remember Stella, the keyboardist from Glass Eye (who also played that girl in *Slacker* who had been to a mental institution), telling us that her chiropractor had died in the Luby's massacre. She told us the list of dead people that she knew; she had started keeping track because there were so many. Later on tour, we drove through Detroit as a postal operator shot his fellow ex-employees. Today, we arrive in Oklahoma City right after a huge bomb exploded in a Federal Building in the middle of the city, killing "at least 20." Check our tour-dates to know when to hide.

The Priests Are Up for Reelection

Last night, we left right after the show in Boulder and drove fifteen hours to get to Oklahoma City. We have two hours to rest before we have to be at the club; this'll be the hardest drive on the tour, we hope. We are sitting grumpily in the cheapest Motel 6 on the planet, south of the brand-new crater, aghast at the news coverage of this explosion, yelling at the TV set. They are saying that the suspects of the bombing are two middle eastern men, driving around in a pickup truck, and even have artists' renderings of what they look like on the TV. There is no end to the parade of elected officials on TV, repeating the words "EVIL" and "CHILD-KILLERS," taking every advantage of the situation. It even seems like the priests being interviewed on the news are up for reelection.

Sample hotel room chatter:

TV: " . . . and this Evil, terrible tragedy has caused horror and terror to not only people but Children, here in the heartland and I personally, as your elected official am completely speechless and . . ."

RICK: (yelling at the TV) "grateful that this has happened during a reelection year"

Try to watch a newscast one day just to see exactly how much information they actually give you. Write down the information you gain from the top news story. We *watched* this incredible video before we left called "Manufacturing Consent," which was interviews with Noam Chomsky, a guy who you'll never see on American TV because he cannot make his point in an eight-second soundbite. He has important, informative things to say, not Spielbergian quotes to make a news story sell.

Cafe 66 in Norman, Oklahoma, Home of the Flaming Lips

Rats, no Flaming Lips to be seen; they have just returned from Australia and are probably too tired to come check out their labelmates, "The FOSTER Children," playing tonight. This will be the first time in eight years that we are billed as the Foster Children. I wonder if this will affect the attendance of the show. This will be the first time we ever play in Oklahoma!

Fake News

When I juxtaposed real-life onto a 3D model in *RTFM*, I felt arty and empowered (obviously this was before I went to art school). In that CD, I taught html so anyone could use it. Now anyone can create, which means anyone can create news. Mixing reality and the fabricated is now so accessible that "fake news" and "deep fakes," have confused the public into what Aviv Ovadya calls "reality apathy," where, beset by a torrent of constant misinformation, people simply start to give up.[3] And fake news or not, we still click in horror and rage and our free-speech DIY social media converts our anger into revenue.

In the music industry, you can buy robot-likes to increase your perceived audience numbers. In 2018, heavy-metal guitarist Jered "Threatin" was able to create a phony record label, management and production company, and enough info on his digital profile to book a tour in Europe.[4] After a week of playing to empty theaters, the prank was exposed, making headlines in *Rolling Stone* and the *New York Times*.[5] There was also the fascinating "Fyre Festival" whose organizers focused more on the advertising and target audience than the actual planning of the event, which yielded a somewhat comical disaster, social media influencers and rich kids trapped on an island without the level of accoutrements to which they were accustomed. The entire farce started with a mysterious logo, a plain orange rectangle, strategically placed in Instagram feeds.[6]

Addiction

In 1995 as I endeavored to create multimedia that would keep people's eyes on our site and CD-ROM, Don Norman was setting parameters for the study of "User Experience"[7] at Apple. Fifteen years later, Google would adopt one of forty-one shades of blue, chosen via data collection, that was most "clickable." The selection process caused a war between graphic designers and data collectors, "But . . . we made an extra $200m a year in ad revenue."[8] Over the next two decades, keeping users' eyes glued to websites became a profession and then a software. Boundless Mind AI boasted a product that used "neuroscience and artificial intelligence" to increase user retention,[9] at the same time selling an end-user app that "finds the perfect moment of zen to give you. It's the same math that we use to get people addicted to apps, just run backwards."[10]

The constant need for affirmation worries me most. In 2004, Facebook was born and the term FOMO was coined. Slowly, people began to realize that the gift of knowing what others were up to didn't exactly lead to the inclusivity they desired. It also led to jealousy, feeling left out, and anxiety about one's own choices in life.[11] I reflect on my own practice of taking pictures of audiences at shows, which I started in 2000. Originally it was to include people. What did it do for those who weren't there?

As someone who lived before social media, I can still view it from outside. I see that likes have moved from commerce to life-essence. Teenage depression is rampant, and almost everyone I know is always on their phones, checking their stats. There are apps to beautify our selfies and better popularize our profiles. In perhaps the most horrifying turn, people are actually showing up at plastic surgeons' offices requesting to physically modify their bodies to look more like their smartphone-enhanced images.[12]

In the end, our social media usage has become the opposite of that of the PLATO educational community. We are not existing to add to the knowledge base anymore, we are instead our own billboards, profiles to dress, to embellish. Our egos are to be visited. We are focused on our own selves now, not the greater good of society. Countless studies show cyclical depression leading to social-media-seeking leading to depression, but the lessons go back to the Buddhist teachings about dharma and self-absorption, that ego causes suffering.[13] As an amateur practitioner of design, I find a punchline in the fact that the orange rectangle, the "graphic vacuum" intended to attract attention through a millions-of-colors Instagram scroll for Fyre Festival, is coincidentally the same icon as the PLATO cursor.

Recently a website with AI-generated faces called "This Person Does Not Exist" made its rounds in my social addiction circle.[14] Each refresh of the site provided a newly generated face. I spent a much longer time than usual, clicking, as did many of my friends, and upon researching, saw a quote on Reddit by someone who also couldn't stop refreshing the images: "I keep looking for myself."

In Adam Curtis's documentary *HyperNormalisation*, there is a segment about Eliza, the first AI program ever built, a program that spewed back your sentence with a psychiatrist's twist on it. "Why do you suppose you feel that way?" Student researchers, with full knowledge they were communicating with a computer program, still became instantly hooked, and asked to spend time alone with it. "What Eliza showed is that in an age of individualism, what made people feel secure is having themselves reflected back to them, just like in a mirror."[15]

Friday, April 7, 2000, Columbus, OH, with Kelly 18
WHAT CAN MAKE A TOWEL SMELL LIKE BACON?

Do you think that James Woods has ever done heroin? I mean, he's in all these drug movies, and you know he's gotta be one of those Method actors. I wonder if he's done heroin. I'm sure he's probably done coke. I worry about him.

Tonight we had a lovely audience, a guy climbing on the ceiling as we played, hanging off the rafters like it was twentieth-century Montana, back in the good old days. Guys screaming "HEY HEY HEY" while we played "Revolution Year Zero." People jumping around like crazy, a guy taking off his shirt. I have to watch out that the microphone doesn't bang me in the mouth. I love this kind of audience. Oddly enough, tomorrow in our hometown, I know we'll be playing to a much more sedate, bored audience. In our own hometown. How funny.

This town is one of the gates to hell. I mean this in the best possible way, really. Please don't take it as an insult. It's just a town on the edge of chaos or something. Just go to White Castle here on a Friday night and you'll see why I say this. Kids dressed in all different types of costumes and uniforms meet here, in various stages of fucked-up-ness, and insult each other's haircuts, and they all look like characters out of a Martian movie. Howie tells me that three college kids die here per month, from drinking themselves to death. I saw a t-shirt in the University Bookstore window that said, "You can always retake a class, but you can never relive a great party." And the club, Bernie's, is such an incredible dive, and it's such a great place to play. It's so unbelievably grimy, and I absolutely love playing here. This is what touring is all about, even if the whole town is probably going to sink into a huge gaping hole in the earth, like in *Poltergeist*.

The towels in the hotel room today smell like bacon, and actually, the room smells like an ass. "No," Howie corrects me, "it smells like ass." I can't even imagine what has gone on in this room before we got here. What can make a towel smell like bacon?

What Can Be Done?

I asked Rick what made him so ready to accept and adapt to the changes in the music industry, and he answered, "Probably from being a computer nerd. All the big changes in the music industry (and the world) over the past thirty-plus years have been because of the computer. So being into the technology as much as being into music made the tech look like an opportunity rather than a threat." Now, as a martial artist, I've been taught to pay attention to what was coming and face obstacles head-on, so my mentality fits in great with this outlook.

So knowing the dangers of these new technologies, how do we continue to create and interact, digitally, but skillfully? At the university level, in teaching about music business and interactive digital design, we incorporate ethics and critical thinking into our courses. We employ civic engagement when teaching computer programming. We think about diversity, equality, and inclusiveness in our curricula, even (and especially) when courses seem solely technical in nature. At home, with our children and community, we question and converse about how much time is spent on devices. We read "surprising" news stories about how tech billionaires limit their own children's computer and social media use. It's important to recognize what is hurting us, what we're addicted to, and what is unsustainable for our own futures. It can all be boiled down to the Buddhist teachings on ego and attachment. Don't spend too much time Googling yourself.

> "The only way to make peace with technology is to make peace with ourselves."
> —Tristan Harris (Center for Humane Technology)[16]

> "Take good care of the machines or the machines will take care of you."
> —Rick Valentin, *Thoughts Detecting Machines*

Friday, April 19, 2002, New York City

BROWNIES, NYC—SOMEDAY A REAL RAIN WILL COME

We are traveling in a heat wave, a protective bubble that is going to keep us warm and safe through this entire week-long journey and then we'll get back home to reality and it will be freezing again. I am watching the weather reports.

We drove past the hole where the two buildings [the Twin Towers] used to be. There are people everywhere, butt-to-butt, milling around, and t-shirt booths up everywhere. There are sheets with words painted on them, monuments to people lost. We are driving really fast, and Matt keeps saying, "Can't you see the hole?" and I keep looking but it takes me a while to see the hole. I finally did see it.

Rick takes a nap in the van. Jim goes somewhere. Matt coerces me into walking around what I think is called the East Village with him. There are at least two Tibetan stores on every block in this area of town. I have never seen anything like it in my life. Not even in Tibet. We go shopping into used-clothes stores. There seems to be something very exciting about buying used shirts, to Matt.

It's still hot outside, like in the 90s, here. You know that this is my dream temperature. Although there is some weird kind of glow today in this city, like the sun is a fluorescent row of lights. Air looks green now and the wind is picking up. In this city, I only know there is wind now because I see trash and leaves moving. Otherwise I am encased in steel and window and cars and concrete everywhere I look. There really is no weather or atmosphere here.

I look up from St. Marks Place sidewalk across the street from Mandala Tibetan Store and see someone I know from Champaign. The last time I saw her I was actually leaving for Tibet the next day; this was a year ago. She is visiting NYC from Ohio. I invite her to my show, with her friend, an artist who it turns out has drawn a flier for us from the Grog Shop about six years ago. So many coincidences! She asks me about my typography teacher. It's like a people vortex.

Now I look up and in a one-inch crack between two buildings I see green sky. I see clouds moving in a way that would cause me to be very afraid if I was in Champaign. Dorothy! It's still really hot here, the kind of hot that you know is going to be followed by a world-ending storm. And it's obviously coming. Do they have weather here? Am I going to get to see weather in New York City? It seems like there are too many people here to have weather. The people outnumber the weather, so there is just not enough for everyone. You get a much smaller ration of weather here than you would say, in Nebraska.

I'm thinking this, and then I mention to Matt that I'd be really afraid if I saw this sky in Champaign, but since there's only one inch of it here, I'm not scared. But wind is whirling around us now, and someone's voice is shaking, I can't remember if it's mine or Matt's. Then we are soaked, running into the nearest shelter, yet another Tibetan store, poking at overpriced satiny Nepalese trinkets. Now we are running through dark gray streets of Alphabet City, Matt on the phone with Rick, assuring him that we're OK. Rick has called Matt's cellphone from five blocks away, Rick safely tucked inside the van. Think about what your life was like before the cellphone. I could call someone directly from the stage from my cellphone before we start playing. I think about the first cellphone call I ever got, sitting on a public toilet. Rick is safe inside the van in the pouring storm, five blocks away from us, and we are caught in this deluge. Someday a real rain will come. . . .

Somehow the wind gets through the huge buildings here and blows paper all over the streets. It's exciting, but I am just not seeing enough of the storm. I'd never live here. You have to share the atmosphere with way too many other people here.

We are playing with a band tonight who are about to be signed to RCA, by our own Joe M., the guy who signed us to Reprise about ten years ago. How do you like that? I was wondering if he'd say hello to us. I was also wondering if this band wanted to ask us any questions about the path that they are about to take, since we've been down it, but none of them asked me anything. They were too busy being told by a man in black about what cars were going to pick them up, or whose cameras were going to take pictures of them. Or whose money was buying them dinner tonight.

Joe M, our ex-A&R agent, talks to us after the show. How many bands are still around from your time? How many bands are still playing after being dropped from a major label? How many bands got famous and are now miserable? According to Joe, lots of famous bands are miserable. He's happy that we are still playing and still happy, and he hugs me. Damn right we're happy. And healthy. And alive! I have a mental image of a crayon drawing of the stick figures of us and Fugazi and a bright yellow sun, holding hands, playing together tomorrow in Boston. Fugazi! Tomorrow!

People are fucked up and wasted tonight. All four of us drive home, through the rainy streets of NY City, back home to East Brunswick New Jersey, where the giant yellow trucks are waiting in the motel parking lot to disturb our dreams.

Monday, July 15, 2002
I HAVE BEEN DERIVED, DRIVING THROUGH WYOMING

A couple of days ago, while I was driving overnight, I scrawled "My home is a velocity vector" on my receipt for my Red Bull. I used to have this happen to me, where after I'd been on tour for a while, my mental image of "home," the picture that comes up the instant I think of that word, would start moving backward in time; for example, after two weeks of touring, "home" means my normal house. After four weeks of touring, "home" looked like the house I'd lived in previous to the current one. One time we'd been on tour for so long that "home" meant my bedroom in my parents' house. It's the weirdest thing that happens to me on tour.

Now, I don't feel like my home is a point anymore, it's a vector in space, a moving from one point to another. My home today is a horizontal vector moving east at 80 mph on I-80. (I ought to win some sort of medal for that synchronicity, no?) My home is a vector, I have been derived.

Little by little I'm letting my mind think about what it will be like to be Home. At this point, I feel like I could stay out here forever. You can let your mind be as free as you can get it when you're home, but there still is no replacement for this constant moving through space.

Full Circle

Saturday, July 22, 2017, Chicago, IL,
ACLU All Tomorrow's Impeachments Benefit with Tar and Others
ALL TOMORROW'S IMPEACHMENTS

Tom Zaluckyj, the bass player from Tar, is nervous. He is dressed in the aluminum colors of his bass,[17] in cotton and gray, and is pacing backstage in the dressing room. He is not a happy kind of nervous, either; it is a physical, biological kind of nervous, and he tells us about it. He also says he doesn't want to be outside in the more public backstage area because there are too many people there. I hope that there are not too many people in here with him, because there are just me and Matt and neither of us want to be around other people right now, either.

It's 2017, August, and we are hiding backstage at the Bottom Lounge in Chicago, where a bunch of politically minded bands are about to play an ACLU and Southern Poverty Law Center benefit. It's the First Year of Our Trump, and we've progressed through the Stages of Grief from the first, Shock, then through Denial and Anger, and now to the fourth, Bargaining,[18] and thus, are hoping to raise some capital, to fund the Good Fight, via our fans and by touting the names of Shellac and Tar, also scheduled to play tonight,[19] to get our fellow rich and educated, angry white men to help the cause.

I fantasize a world where Tom Zaluckyj would be strutting around backstage, wearing that gorgeous aluminum bass, with his strikingly matching clothes and hair, playing those brilliant bass parts for us. For a moment, I wish he could be a stuck-up, arrogant rock star, so he could know how great it feels to love the band Tar.

But this will never happen. Tom is one of those shy guys you find so much in this genre of rock. He would never strut. An audience twenty feet outside the dressing room exuberantly awaits his playing and he is definitely not reciprocating by simply being happy about the whole thing. I can only hope that he feels comfortable enough to sit down in this dressing room that I, alone, brazenly decided Tar should share with us Poster Children.

The backstage area of this ACLU benefit is filled with people who probably are uncomfortable around a lot of people. Minutes ago, Steve Albini, from his broken-collarbone-resting chair, looked up at a group of us standing around and shook his head and murmured, "Man, is this a nerdfest." A couple of days later, in our recording session, he explained to me the difference between a nerd and a dork—a nerd is someone who can focus upon something and be good at it, and a dork is a nerd who is socially inept.[20] I'd asked him to classify bands such as the Afghan Whigs, Naked Raygun, etc.

Meanwhile, as Tom Zaluckyj paced and felt nervous, I sat stewing about how to best represent a female on a stage, because I was going to be the only person with a vagina on this stage these two days of this ACLU benefit, and it was 2017, and it was liberal politics, and there should be a lot more vaginas around. I spent a good three to five minutes wondering if Poster Children were added on this bill for my lack of penis. But Rick's lyrics are probably the most consistently political of all bands in this area, Steve once called us "old friends and comrades in the fight," and also, we were old. So I could make a case that we weren't necessarily picked because I'm female.

After those three to five minutes, I spent probably a total of three to five hours laboring over what to wear on the stage, which is three to five hours longer than I've ever spent laboring over what to wear anywhere. I was already one half-hour into fretting, and around twenty minutes into the fretting about the fretting, when one Eric Mahle sauntered into our nerd-filled dressing room.

In 2000, we played with his band Kelly 18, and I wrote an entire tour report about how much they blew my mind. They even recorded in the basement of our house. Tonight I don't recognize him at first, and wonder why he's backstage. He's less shy and more exuberant than the others, maybe because he's not playing. He is wielding an impressively expensive bass that he bought for all the "rock stars" to sign, and he's going to auction it off to help raise money for this benefit.

He used to run sound at this club (among others), so this is how he has gotten backstage without being someone's girlfriend.

He clears out the dressing room and then closes the door, sits me down to perform a psychiatric intervention with me. I must be driving everyone else crazy audibly ranting about my appearance; maybe that's why there aren't a lot of females in bands. Why is it anyone else's responsibility to dress me? Everyone else has enough to worry about. We haven't played out in years, and we're all old.

"What are you going to wear?" he repeats after me. He is chivalrous, wants to stop my worrying. Men still care. He sits down facing me. "Where is the Pink Dress? When I pay for a ticket to see Poster Children, I want to see the Pink Dress," he reasons with me, the same voice I shut out in my head when I packed for the show. "The Pink Dress is not here." I try to say it nonchalantly, but in my mind, I hate myself, I have let my audience down. Since it was not the 1990s anymore, at home, I had purposely touched, held, and then did not bring the Pink Dress. It is back in the coat closet 100 miles away in Bloomington, Illinois, hanging next to my wedding dress. The Pink Dress is made of lace, tulle, pink and black, full, like a dolly birthday cake. I used to wear it with my black, lace-up Doc Martens boots. Juxtaposition of girly and war.

I think about showing him my current clothing options; what I'd stuffed into a ridiculous, sequined backpack (what little girls think Rock Stars carry) to bring to Chicago with me. There aren't many options. Eric goes off on an easier mission, to find more self-effacing rock stars to sign his bass, and I am left with my backpack to choose from the B-list, second-guess bag of clothes. I end up wearing a hippie dress that's unfashionably long, and overcompensate by wearing a Tar shirt over it, like a shield. I look homeless, but I won't trip onstage, I definitely do not look like I "tried," and my boob won't accidentally come out. Most of the other men are all dressed elegantly in their work shirts and twill pants, the Chicago indie-rock uniform of bourgeoisie gas-station attendant.

Rick reminds me that we've now come full circle. We're playing in Chicago, with our buddies Tar, Steve Albini is there, and we're still fighting the good fight, only we're now much more experienced. Steve, who wrote the definitive music business article in *The Baffler*, has now written an essay about his charity work in the *Huffington Post*. Steve's partner Heather Whinna had discovered letters to Santa mailed at a Chicago post office and Steve, a journalism major reading the words of the masses, had been deeply moved. "People let down by the remnants of a social safety net, without families . . . suffering sickness, poverty and abuse . . . addressed their problems to Santa Claus at the North Pole and sent them by mail into the vacuum of humanity that had left them so desperate."[21] The couple began delivering gifts to people in need on Christmas Day, a practice that ballooned into something

Poster Children at Café du Nord, San Francisco, 2018. Left to right, Jim, Matt, Rose, and Rick. Photograph by Patric Carver, @pc.photo.rock.

larger, including a fundraiser marathon with Second City and other stars. At the time of this writing, Heather runs Poverty Alleviation Charities, a non-profit organization whose mission is "to use Art as a conduit to transform passive compassion into immediate assistance through the distribution of money given, without expectation or judgment, directly to families suffering poverty."[22] In a 2020 article in *Inside Higher Ed Jobs*, about passion during the pandemic, she describes artistry in improvisation as "art is the process not the product."[23] This should hearten any artist still chasing "the Golden Nugget." There is much more to do with art than to just "get famous."

In fact, the "getting famous" thing never did much for me. Bands will get famous for a short window of time, and then the audience will move on. There is a time before and after the fame. Those who have a lasting impression on some will still be unknown to others. And the fame does not necessarily make you happy. Here is a favorite quote from David Foster Wallace's *Infinite Jest*: "There are feelings associated with fame, but few of them are any more enjoyable than the feelings associated with envy of fame." When you are jealous of someone, they do not enjoy the reciprocal feeling of pleasure. They are also constantly worried about losing the fame. I'm sure Wallace learned this from the same place I learned about the anticipation being better than the payoff, and the journey transcending its endpoint.

Backstage at All Tomorrow's Impeachments, my sequined bag held t-shirts and costumes from the past, and I probably had trouble deciding what to wear because I didn't want to look backward. Rick's influence, again. His lyrics are purposely timeless, in that he doesn't fixate on one particular event and is great at expanding and abstracting his content. Because of this, we can pull out any of his most political songs from any of ten to twelve albums, and the lyrics are unfortunately, always relevant. He deeply understands societal cause and effect.

One of our songs, "Clock Street," comes from an experience that I had when, driving alone, I'd picked up an elderly lady on the side of the road in Champaign who needed a ride home, to "Clock Street." She was slurring her words and could barely sit up in the seat. Clark Street is a residential street that runs through campus, so I assumed she lived there, and it was the only residential street with that same-sounding name that I knew of at the time. At Clark Street, she sobbed, "No, Clock Street. Clock Street." We drove around seemingly aimlessly, she whimpered more directions to me, and I was scared we'd never find her home. Finally, we came across a gray street, opposite the factory on the other side of town, where I'd never been. Clock Street. I dropped her off. Rick contextualized this story so poetically that years later it still gives me a history lesson.

> Clock Street doesn't have a clock
> Clock Street's doors are always locked
> It's where you'll start, it's where you'll stop

His words, his chords, and his delivery made me understand our place in all this. All I did was tune down my E string.

I am grateful to have been along on this ride.

Wednesday, September 10, 1997, Kalamazoo, MI
THE NEW ASCETIC

People have been asking me lately, "So, how's the tour been going?" and I can't even answer them. I feel so detached from any calendar and any ground markings. We've been on tour for so long I'm completely cut loose from space and time. I think we were in Europe a month(?) ago? and then in New York, but as a different band. I know we were off for a week just recently too. This is the New Asceticism. I am completely without any possessions except my contact lens solution,

Rick and Rose. Photograph by Jason Young.

case, and glasses and these little Synthroid pills I have to take or I get depressed and gain weight. Those are the only four important things I need each day. Even clothing doesn't matter anymore. For food or entertainment, there are always the equivalent of an ascetic's nuts and berries he finds in the forest for nourishment; mine are Jay's "Hot Stuff" potato chips, a Hershey bar, and a can of Coke plucked straight from branches of the nearest Shop-n-Go. I know I am like an ascetic because I am beginning to feel purified in some weird way.

CHAPTER 20

Teaching

Best Show Ever

A standard interview question over the years has been "What was the best show you ever played?" It may have been answerable in the first couple of years of playing shows, but after ten or fifteen years, the static indices of shows blend into a waveform, and there are multiple filters for the experience of the travel to the show, the place where we stayed, the audience, the climate, the compensation, the change between the previous and the next shows. So when I'm asked the Best Show Ever question, I do what all good politicians do: I answer the question I want to answer and hope it's better than what the interviewer expected.

I used to handwrite all answers to our fan mail. This was before the internet, and a band even as small as ours received fan mail. A lot of it was from disaffected youth, teens wanting to quit school. Most letters weren't happy, but all were beautiful; the different handwritings, pictures, the slant of the penciled words on the light-blue staves of the page, rhythm now lost to the immediacy of email.

One particular fan wrote to me over the years, letters described hating high school, thinking it was worthless, and wanting to drop out and join a band. I answered back with my own stories of being bullied in high school, even in college—does this even help, to hear that someone else had your own experience? But stay in school, I implored. It doesn't even get better the first years of college; you have to wait until the 300-level courses, I explained, because that is where you'll find teachers and other students who actually care about what you care about. Please stay in school, I begged, because your life will be better afterward, no matter what.

A decade passes. My band is sitting in the Courier Cafe, distraught. This is an 1800s diner in tiny downtown Urbana, filled with ornate wood and antique lights, a place you bring your parents when they visit you, for sandwiches and old-fashioned ice-cream sundaes. We are in the middle of recording *RTFM*, and Reprise has just informed us that, for our own benefit, they will be delaying our record. This will help us get more attention, they explained, since we won't be having a record out at the same time as Filter, or some other band on the label that they probably heard a "hit" from. (It's never good when your label wants to delay your record, no matter what they tell you.)

So we were in the back of the Courier Cafe with our heads in our hands, sitting with our producer, when a young man walked up to our table. "Are you Poster Children?" he asked, quietly excited. "Yes?" I grumbled, trying to look worthy of being recognized. It is very rare that someone will notice us here, as we're a known quantity in our hometown. The man introduced himself and told us that he was from New Mexico (I think, my memory is waning) and he was visiting graduate schools around the country. He was visiting UIUC because this is where we came from; this is where Poster Children studied. He'd stayed in school because of my answers to his fan mail. Now he was going to graduate school. He thanked us. When I tell this story, I always mention that Rick cried at that point. I was stunned. The delay of our record didn't matter anymore. We made someone stay in school. I still tear up when I think about this story.

So that's my answer to "What was your best show ever?" Kids hanging off the lighting rafters in Bozeman, my younger sisters crowd-surfing from the stage at the Metro in Chicago were definitely runners-up. But it wasn't Lollapalooza, Nulle Parte Ailleurs in Paris, or even the Terrace in Madison with Mercy Rule. It was when I made someone want to learn.

Art or Hobby—"Day Gig" Redux

Sunday, April 2, 2000, NYC

HOW CAN YOU HATE MUSIC?

As we wait at the Holland Tunnel, we sit on the brink of the number 1, most awesome City in America. We make up statistics and each call out the following:

At least one person is killing another person right now.

100 people are shooting up heroin right now!

One person is beating another person into a bloody pulp right now.

Someone is crapping on someone else's face right now.

Someone is ODing right now.

Someone is killing themselves right now.

and Jim says something like,

and right now, a little girl is sitting in her room, petting a cute little puppy dog

to which Rick replies,

and her dad is breaking down the door to her locked room, to grab the puppy dog and stuff it into a plastic bag and drown it.

We go on like this for quite some time. The wait for the Holland Tunnel is very, very long.

Brownie's Sunday Night Crowd, New York City

I don't feel so well, but it's OK. I guess the show went well, although it seemed really, really quiet to me on the stage. The really fun part about this show was I heard people laughing as I did funny things on the stage. I announced that I had just been informed that someone had peed on our van, and that I had thought that was illegal now in New York. Then I mentioned that perhaps the man was trying to clean the van; perhaps it was too dirty for the city. That got a chuckle. I even made some sort of connection between Giuliani, saying that perhaps it was the mayor himself that peed on our van to clean it, and still people laughed. You have to be careful with your midwestern sarcasm in New York City, because many times these people just don't get it at all. Maybe the audience was giving me the benefit of the doubt. Anyway, it was nice to hear laughter.

Our crowd in New York City seems very warm and nice, contrary to what you'd think. (Someone even brought me some Kleenex, which I am using right now in the van, thank you!) And, for some odd reason I feel really safe just leaving stuff lie around in Brownie's, the club we played at tonight. New York City seems cleaner than I remember it—there were only a couple of spots where I smelled urine, and one of them was on the stage.

Rick tells me that the people of NYC are trying to get Giuliani out of the mayor's office by making him into a congressman, and when I ask why, Rick says that bad things are happening. I think in order to clean up the city, they are making drastic changes each week and not following through the next week. I hear that one week they ticketed double-parked cars along a street for the entire week, but didn't continue doing that after that week. And Rick says that the police are just starting to shoot people. And they're not supposed to do that without getting in trouble, I guess. It actually sounds a lot like Los Angeles—maybe that's why the New Yorkers are getting mad.

Monday Morning, Three a.m., New Jersey

We wander red-eyed and sober through a hidden twenty-four-hour A&P city-sized grocery store at three a.m. in the New Jersey suburb of East Brunswick and run into a short, stocky drunk guy with a New York accent wearing a bicycle helmet and biking gloves. He decides to follow me around the store and talk to me about music. He asks, "What was the last record you bought?" and I say, "It was ten years ago, I believe." He says, "how can that be?" and I say, "I hate music," and he says, "How can you hate music?" and I say, "I'm in a band."

We visited lots of art museums when we were on tour, so many that in *Zero Stars*, Rick filmed a segment with Jim visiting a museum (also a loving shout-out to *Ferris Bueller's Day Off* and *Chicago*). I had always felt uneasy in art museums because I don't have Art History dates and movements memorized, but that all changed when I did some work for an art education curriculum named VTS (Visual Thinking Strategies).[1] In VTS, facilitators elicit an honest rapport with a painting by simply asking civilians, "What do you see in this picture?" and all answers are valid, because they come from your own experience. So I'm on tour as Salaryman, in Lausanne, probably depressed, and staring at a Jean Dubuffet painting.

Whenever I look at art, I have a mental conversation with my dad. Dad grew up in a family that appreciated art, and his sister, Verna Sadock, was the courtroom artist for Chicago's NBC. It was classic art, though. Dad steps out with Renoir and Van Gogh (and now, at ninety-two, has begun to paint voraciously). When my aunt asked what type of art I was studying, I said, "Conceptual Art," and she replied, "Oh, so, painting."

The Dubuffet I was entranced with was covered in a thick, brownish-black paste of tar, mud, and broken glass. "This looks like shit wiped on a canvas!" Dad says angrily to me in my mind. "Yes, but look at how the broken glass glitters!" I reply. Later I realize it's my Gen-X echo to his own words. I would call him, even as an adult, crying about some first-world injustice done to me, and he'd patiently listen and then laugh, "It's not so bad." He was always right, and it made me consider my privilege.

The Dubuffet really does look like shit wiped on a canvas. I think some of our music might sound like that to the uninitiated, pop or classical music fans. Pop or Poop? There was a reason for this shit, it was a reaction, anti-intellectual art "for the people." (Though it's not the greatest example because it *was* hanging in the museum, and Dubuffet was a Nazi sympathizer.[2])

Not everything you create will appeal to everyone, and you certainly don't need a goal or an audience to give purpose to your work. I finally had the privilege of bringing my two great mentors to speak to my own students at ISU. At University Galleries, Steve Albini elevated the concept of "hobby." It's not something to be ashamed of, just because you can't make money at it. On the contrary, "hobby" is what gives your life meaning. You do whatever menial job it takes to be able to support your art-making, Steve told my class. Ian MacKaye spoke to my Music Business class, and when a student asked about "pursuing the dream" of making music even during the "bad times," Ian retorted quickly, "making music isn't a dream, it's a fucking reality."

Sunday, March 26, 2000, Asheville, NC

A BEAUTIFUL DRIVE

I had the weirdest thought the other day when we were driving through Louisiana; it was so strange that I decided not to write it down. This is what it was—I actually felt that the countryside that we were driving through was so beautiful that I wanted to be cut open and have my blood poured out onto the fields. You can see why I didn't write that down or tell anyone what I was thinking at the time. I get these thoughts of beauty and feel so touched by them that I sometimes want to cry. And it's not because of how the place looks, either. It's some kind of feeling I get.

Anyway, why have I decided to write this now? Because I just bought this book called *Shambala, the Sacred Path of the Warrior*, by Chogyam Trungpa[3] and started reading it. Let me quote from it.

"Basic goodness is very closely connected to the idea of bodhicitta in the Buddhist tradition Bodhi means 'awake' or 'wakeful' and citta means 'heart,' so bodhicitta is 'awakened heart.' Such awakened heart comes from being willing to face your state of mind. . . ."

Then it talks about the search for the awakened heart and notes that upon finding it you will find a genuine heart of "sadness" and "tenderness."

"Your experience is raw and tender and so personal. . . ."

"The genuine heart of sadness comes from feeling that your nonexistent heart is full. You would like to spill your heart's blood, give your heart to others. For the warrior, this experience of sad and tender heart is what gives birth to fearlessness. . . . You are willing to open up, without resistance or shyness, and face the world. You are willing to share your heart with others."

Monday, July 22, 2002

EACH NOTE IS A PRAYER

I went to work today at the university. I work in a lab where no one else works, where I think about landscape architecture, urban planning, and parkour, and put it into Virtual Reality.

Then I went to the chiropractor. I've only been there a couple other times. I think they're all quacks. I paid thirty-nine dollars for this guy to spend about three minutes with me, cracking my back. I don't think I feel any better. I think the terror of hearing your bones crack overpowers the terror of "why do I hurt" and that makes you feel better.

Then I went to Tibet Night and learned how to Non-Meditate. I think I did it right, actually. It is said that if you do this type of Tibetan non-meditation correctly, that even if the Buddha comes down and tells you you were doing it wrong, you'd say to him, "No, I was doing it right." It was nice to see everyone in my little group there.

Then I came home and my wish has come true. We are going on tour again.

"Greetings Poster Folk,

"I wondered if you ever thought of doing a show where you had to deftly unravel yourselves from various chains, ropes, and other binding apparatus in Houdiniesque fashion, before your audience got tired or freaked out and left? Just wondering. Please send me your dental charts? Thanks.

"Love it,

"P.S. Each note is a prayer . . ."

—Anonymous fan letter

*   *   *

Each note is a prayer.

*   *   *

List of Poster Children Alumni

Rick Valentin (guitar, vocals) 1987–
Rose Marshack (bass) 1987–
Shannon Drew (drums) 1987–1988
Brendan Gamble (drums) 1988–1989
Jeff Dimpsey (guitar) 1989–1991
Mike Rader (drums) 1989–1990
Bob Rising (drums) 1990–1991
Jim Valentin (guitar) 1991–
John Herndon (drums) 1991–1993
Howie Kantoff (drums) 1993–2001
Matt Friscia (drums) 2001–

Opposite: Rose on stage, 2016.
Photograph by Christopher Schneberger.

Poster Children Band Members (1987–2021)

	'87	88	89	90	91	92	93	94	95	96	97	98	99	00	01	02	03	04	05	06	07	08	09	10	11	12	13	14	15	16	17	18	19	20	21
Rick Valentin (guitar, vocals)	/	/	/	/	/	/	/	/	/	/	/	/	/	/	/	/	/	/	/	/	/	/	/	/	/	/	/	/	/	/	/	/	/	/	/
Rose Marshack (bass)	‚	+	+	+	+	+	+	+	+	+	+	+	+	+	+	+	+	+	+	+	+	+	+	+	+	+	+	+	+	+	+	+	+	+	+
Shannon Drew (drums)		+	+																																
Brendan Gamble (drums)			+	+																															
Jeff Dimpsey (guitar)				⟨	⟨	⟨																													
Mike Rader (drums)				+	+																														
Bob Rising (drums)					+	+																													
Jim Valentin (guitar)						⟨	⟨	⟨	⟨	⟨	⟨	⟨	⟨	⟨	⟨	⟨	⟨	⟨	⟨	⟨	⟨	⟨	⟨	⟨	⟨	⟨	⟨	⟨	⟨	⟨	⟨	⟨	⟨	⟨	⟨
John Herndon (drums)						+	+																												
Howie Kantoff (drums)							+	+	+	+	+	+	+	+																					
Matt Friscia (drums)															+	+	+	+	+	+	+	+	+	+	+	+	+	+	+	+	+	+	+	+	+

Poster Children Members Timeline

Notes

Part One. 1980s: College

1. Josh Gottheil Collection, Library and Archives, Rock and Roll Hall of Fame and Museum, http://catalog.rockhall.com/catalog/ARC-0150, accessed June 12, 2020. The first entry mentions Frances Reedy, Josh's and now also my children's violin teacher, who should be the subject of another book.

2. Tickets for this show are archived in the Josh Gottheil Collection, Library and Archives, Rock and Roll Hall of Fame and Museum, http://catalog.rockhall.com/catalog/ARC-0150/ref156, accessed June 12, 2020.

Chapter 1. Origin Story

1. Maureen Ryan, "You Call That Service?" *Chicago Tribune*, July 4, 2003, https://www.chicagotribune.com/news/ct-xpm-2003-07-04-0307040100-story.html, accessed January 12, 2017.

2. *The Note*, Episode 4, Red Bull Music Academy, September 21, 2016, https://www.youtube.com/watch?v=AiDYGlSJY1E, accessed June 28, 2021.

Chapter 3. Punk Bands in Dorms

1. "*Where It Begins 1977–2000* Extended Teaser-Trailer," video, 6:47, November 6, 2017, on *Where It Begins 1977–2000*, a film by John Isberg (Swede Films, 2017), https://www.youtube.com/watch?v=TDbufTuOCzc&t=63s, accessed May 21, 2019.

2. Gordon Pellegrinetti, Facebook direct message to author, November 8, 2021.

3. Matt Golosinski, Facebook direct message to author, February 10, 2018.

4. John Mohr, Facebook direct message to author, February 10, 2018.

Chapter 4. Computers

1. To verify this for yourself (I did), you can do the following in your TRS-80 Model III computer or an online emulator. "You can see them by jamming the character codes directly into video memory. FOR X=0 TO 255 : POKE 15360+X, X : NEXT X." Adam von Librikov, Facebook direct message to author, February 21, 2017.

2. According to many websites, modern updates on traditional prayer wheels are welcomed and accepted. "His Holiness, the Dalai Lama, has said that having the mantra on your computer works the same as a traditional Mani wheel. As the digital image spins around on your hard drive, it sends the peaceful prayer of compassion to all directions and purifies the area." Here are two: https://buddhaweekly.com/wheel-dharma-prayer-wheels-may-ideal-buddhist-practice-busy-people-benefits-self-sentient-beings-teachers-say/#ftoc-heading-4, accessed April 24, 2022, and http://oak.ucc.nau.edu/jgr6/tibet.html, accessed April 24, 2022; and here is a Wayback Machine archive: https://web.archive.org/web/20111010063517/http://www.dharma-haven.org/tibetan/digital-wheels.htm.

3. David R. Woolley, "PLATO: The Emergence of Online Community," *Just Think of It*, January 10, 1994, https://just.thinkofit.com/plato-the-emergence-of-online-community/, accessed February 14, 2017.

4. Nancy K. Baym, *Tune In, Log On: Soaps, Fandom, and Online Community* (N.p.: Sage Publications, 2000).

5. "PLATO @ 50: Seeing the Future through the Past," Session 6: "An Early Online Community: People Plus Computing Grows Communities," Computer History Museum, Mountainview, CA, June 3, 2010, https://www.computerhistory.org/collections/catalog/102702356, and https://www.youtube.com/watch?v=qmuN_RpXn6I&t=8s, accessed March 8, 2022, esp. 28:28; see also Woolley, "PLATO: The Emergence of Online Community."

Chapter 5. Play Like a Man

1. I'm so sorry, Ian!

2. Fugazi, "Suggestion," vocals by Amy Pickering, whose story inspired the lyrics. Gareth Hutchens, "Fugazi Sang an Anti-rape Message to Their Male Audience 30 Years Ago—What's Changed?" *The Guardian*, November 27, 2018, https://www.theguardian.com/commentisfree/2018/nov/27/fugazi-sang-an-anti-rape-message-to-their-male-audience-30-years-ago-whats-changed, accessed June 25, 2020.

3. Marion Leonard, *Gender in the Music Industry: Rock Discourse, and Girl Power* (New York: Routledge, 2017), 34.

4. Mary Ann Clawson, "When Women Play the Bass: Instrument Specialization and Gender Interpretation in Alternative Rock Music," *Gender and Society* 13, no. 2 (1999): 193–210, www.jstor.org/stable/190388, accessed January 12, 2020.

5. Conversation with Heidi, Barb, and Candice, Facebook direct message, June 24, 2020.

6. When I asked for verification, Steve responds, "Well there's just no way you didn't figure that out on your own." But he is wrong. It was the first I'd heard of it, and he doesn't have a vagina, so how would he know?

Chapter 6. The Indie Code of Ethics

1. John Kreicbergs, "The Quiet Curse of the Midwestern Work Ethic," American Advertising Federation–Kansas City, January 9, 2013, https://web.archive.org/web/20150317152624/https://www.aafkc.com/news/quiet-curse-midwestern-work-ethic.

2. Bruce Gibney, *A Generation of Sociopaths: How the Baby Boomers Betrayed America* (New York: Hachette Books, 2017).

3. Michael Friedman, "Steve Albini Shows That Punk Rock Ethics Are Good Business," *Psychology Today*, July 7, 2015, https://www.psychologytoday.com/us/blog/brick-brick/201507/steve-albini-shows-punk-rock-ethics-are-good-business, accessed June 7, 2019.

4. Friedman, "Albini Shows."

5. A good place to start on happiness and gratitude studies is "Highlights from the Research Project on Gratitude and Thankfulness," by Robert A. Emmons and Michael E. McCullough, https://citeseerx.ist.psu.edu/viewdoc/download?doi=10.1.1.520.4351&rep=rep1&type=pdf, accessed March 8, 2022, and the work of Ed Diener (from UIUC) and Martin Seligman.

6. Rick Sims told me Didjits were born in his mom's chicken shed on a farm outside Sullivan, Illinois. Facebook direct message to author, June 6, 2021.

7. Ward Gollings, Facebook direct message to author, May 7, 2019.

8. Santanu Rahman, Email interview with author, June 3, 2020.

Chapter 7. Local

1. Jesse L. Silverberg, Matthew Bierbaum, James P. Sethna, and Itai Cohen, "Collective Motion of Humans in Mosh and Circle Pits at Heavy Metal Concerts," *Physical Review Letters* 110, no. 228701 (2013), https://sethna.lassp.cornell.edu/pubPDF/MoshPits.pdf.

2. Michael Hann, "Sub Pop: 25 Years of Underground Rock," *The Guardian*, July 4, 2013, https://www.theguardian.com/music/2013/jul/04/sub-pop-25-years-underground-rock, accessed March 18, 2019.

Chapter 9. National

1. From Rick Valentin's history of Poster Children archived on earlier posterchildren websites.

Chapter 10. Mashed Potatoes

1. Heidi Ore, email conversation with author, May 24, 2018.
2. Leonard, *Gender*, 93–95.
3. Leonard, *Gender*, 95–96.
4. Lizzy Goodman, "Kim Deal Is Still a Punk," "The Cut," *New York Magazine*, April 2018, https://www.thecut.com/2018/04/profile-kim-deal-of-the-breeders-and -the-pixies.html, accessed July 4, 2018.

Chapter 11. Recording

1. Joe Taysom, "Read the Incredible Four-Page Proposal Letter Steve Albini Sent to Nirvana," Far Out, May 6, 2020, https://faroutmagazine.co.uk/steve-albini-letter -to-nirvana/, accessed November 26, 2020.
2. Angie Martoccio, "Nirvana's *In Utero*: 20 Things You Didn't Know," *Rolling Stone*, September 21, 2018, https://www.rollingstone.com/feature/nirvana-in-utero-trivia -kurt-cobain-722109/; references Keith Cameron, "MOJO #90—May 2001," https:// www.livenirvana.com/documents/mojoinutero.html.
3. Steve Albini, email exchange with author, July 2, 2021.

Chapter 12. Touring

1. "Sinead Criticizes Bob Dylan for Not Defending Her at Tribute Concert," AP, November 1, 1992, https://apnews.com/article/adf6a172198fb43f98f-baea55342a682; and Andy Greene, "Flashback: Sinead O'Connor Booed Offstage at Bob Dylan Celebration," Rolling Stone, November 19, 2013, https://www.rolling stone.com/music/music-news/flashback-sinead-oconnor-booed-offstage-at-bob -dylan-celebration-189352/, accessed November 30, 2020.
2. Mark Lanegan, *Sing Backwards and Weep* (New York: Hachette Books, 2020).

Chapter 14. Computer Experiments

1. Ann Bishop, Karen Fletcher, and Greg Newby, "Prairienet History," Prairienet Community Network, https://www.petascale.org/prairienet/pnet-history.html, accessed November 20, 2018.
2. "Greg Newby's Personal Pages," https://www.petascale.org/, accessed November 20, 2018.
3. Rose Marshack, "Building and Running Your Own Web Site: The Poster Children Go Hypermedia," *CMJ: New Music Monthly*, June 1995, https://books.google

.com/books?id=Ji0EAAAAMBAJ&lpg=PA51&ots=9HoLNm9EfU&dq=uiuc%20 poster%20children%20prairienet&pg=PA51#v=onepage&q=poster%20children%20 prairienet&f=true.

4. Jill Howk Gengler, Facebook post responses, October 22, 2018.

5. Sally van der Graaff, "Digital Participation and the University of Illinois: Prairienet, Community Infomatics, UC2B &CDI," Center for Digital Inclusion, https:// cdi.ischool.illinois.edu/files/2017/04/VanDerGraaffCDIPaper_2015.pdf, accessed March 8, 2022.

6. Peter Kirn, "Enter the Surreal 1995 World of Laurie Anderson Multimedia," CDM, March 6, 2017, http://cdm.link/2017/03/enter-surreal-1995-world-laurie -anderson-multimedia/, accessed March 9, 2017.

Chapter 15. Expectations

1. Balthazar De Ley, "The Real Congregation: The Greatest Band You've Never Heard—Menthol," *Soundcloud*, July 15, 2014, https://nerdyshow.com/2014/07/the -real-congregation-the-greatest-band-youve-never-heard-menthol-071514/, accessed May 11, 2019.

2. "Keith Brammer (Die Kreuzen)," episode 106, *Conan Neutron's Protonic Reversal*, December 17, 2017, 1:19:22, https://www.protonicreversal.com/2017/12/17/ep106 -keith-brammer-die-kreuzen/, accessed May 14, 2019.

Chapter 16. Big Changes

1. Michael Azerrad, "Inside the Heart and Mind of Kurt Cobain," *Rolling Stone*, April 16, 1992, https://web.archive.org/web/20080109140249/http://www.rolling stone.com/feature/nirvana-inside-the-heart-and-mind-of-kurt-cobain-103770/, accessed March 18, 2019.

Chapter 17. Online Participation

1. Henry Jenkins, *Convergence Culture* (New York: New York University Press, 2006), 79.

2. Alt.music.posterkids readme 8/Dec/96, https://groups.google.com/forum/#! topic/alt.music.posterkids/akXstk6G5M8, accessed March 8, 2022.

3. Baym, *Tune In, Log On*.

4. Baym, *Tune In, Log On*, 132.

5. Jenkins, *Convergence Culture*, 84.

6. Rick still has the email from 1999 and is mystified that he never answered it.

7. Chris Schneberger, email to author, June 23, 2017.

8. DJ Hostettler, Facebook posting (and personal conversation with author), November 29, 2021.

9. Electrical Audio Recording home page, https://www.electricalaudio.com/ phpBB3/, accessed November 25, 2018.

10. Dixie Jacobs, Facebook direct message to author, November 29, 2021.

11. Virginia Heffernan, "The Podcast as a New Podium," *New York Times*, July 22, 2005, https://www.nytimes.com/2005/07/22/arts/the-podcast-as-a-new-podium.html, accessed December 27, 2020.

12. Jacobs, Facebook direct message.

13. FEMA uses an informal metric that they call the "Waffle House Index" for measuring the degree of damage in disaster areas. The legend is as such: "Green means the restaurant is serving a full menu, a signal that damage in an area is limited and the lights are on. Yellow means a limited menu, indicating power from a generator, at best, and low food supplies. Red means the restaurant is closed, a sign of severe damage in the area or unsafe conditions." Valerie Bauerlein, "How to Measure a Storm's Fury One Breakfast at a Time," *Wall Street Journal*, September 1, 2011, http://www.wsj.com/articles/SB10001424053111904716604576542460736605364, accessed July 20, 2016.

14. The top shower in North America is located in the women's changing room at Master Hyong's HMD Academy, Savoy, IL.

Chapter 18. Life as a Woman

1. Megan Krecji, Facebook communication with the author, June 5, 2018.

2. Jessica Bennett, "Liz Phair Is Not Your Feminist Spokesmodel," *New York Times*, May 3, 2018, https://www.nytimes.com/2018/05/03/arts/music/liz-phair-exile-in-guyville-reissue-interview.html, accessed May 24, 2018.

3. Leonard, *Gender*, 32.

4. Amanda Petrusich, "The Remarkable Persistence of the Breeders," *New Yorker*, March 9, 2018, https://www.newyorker.com/culture/culture-desk/the-remarkable-persistence-of-the-breeders, accessed July 4, 2018.

5. Quoted in "The Breeders Are Back," *The New Yorker Radio Hour with David Remnick*, May 18, 2018, https://www.newyorker.com/podcast/the-new-yorker-radio-hour/the-breeders-are-back, accessed April 3, 2018.

6. "The Breeders Are Back."

7. Angela Cristiane Santos Póvoa, Wesley Pech, Juan José Camou Viacava, and Marcos Tadeu Schwartz, "Is the Beauty Premium Accessible to All? An Experimental Analysis," *Journal of Economic Psychology* 78 (2020), https://doi.org/10.1016/j.joep.2020.102252.

8. Anne Boring, Kellie Ottoboni, and Philip B. Stark, "Student Evaluations of Teaching (Mostly) Do Not Measure Teaching Effectiveness," *ScienceOpen Research* 0, no. 0 (2016): 1–11. doi: 10.14293/S2199–1006.1.SOR-EDU.AETBZC.v1.

9. This is the Jane from the Poster Children song. She was my martial arts sister for many years, and then I followed her to India one year while she was studying Buddhism. At the time of this writing, she's back in Urbana with an undergraduate degree in religious studies from Princeton and a graduate degree in architecture from UIUC, project managing and doing energy efficiency consulting.

Chapter 19. How to Look at Things

1. Thoughts Detecting Machines, https://tedium.us/, accessed December 30, 2020.

2. Nicholas Carr, "Is Google Making Us Stupid?" *Atlantic*, July 2008, https://www.theatlantic.com/magazine/archive/2008/07/is-google-making-us-stupid/306868/, accessed February 16, 2019.

3. Quoted in Charlie Warzel, "He Predicted The 2016 Fake News Crisis. Now He's Worried About an Information Apocalypse," *Buzzfeed News*, February 11, 2018, https://www.buzzfeednews.com/article/charliewarzel/the-terrifying-future-of-fake-news, accessed February 23, 2019.

4. Jonah Engel Bromwich, "The Story of Threatin, a Most Puzzling Hoax Even for 2018," *New York Times*, November 16, 2018, https://www.nytimes.com/2018/11/16/style/threatin-fake-band-tour.html, accessed February 23, 2019.

5. David Kushner, "The Great Heavy Metal Hoax," *Rolling Stone*, December 14, 2018, https://www.rollingstone.com/culture/culture-features/threatin-metal-tour-fake-ticket-sales-hoax-767580/, accessed February 23, 2019.

6. Davis Richardson, "Blame the Fyre Festival Fiasco on the Plague of Celebrity Influencers," *Wired*, May 4, 2017, https://www.wired.com/2017/05/blame-fyre-festival-fiasco-plague-celebrity-influencers/, accessed March 11, 2019. *Hulu Press*, https://www.hulu.com/press/show/fyre-fraud/, accessed February 15, 2019. Kenzie Bryant, "The Frye Festival, Built on Instagram, Dies by Instagram," *Vanity Fair*, April 28, 2017, https://www.vanityfair.com/style/2017/04/fyre-festival-disaster-bahamas, accessed March 11, 2019.

7. Donald Norman, Jim Miller, and Austin Henderson, "What You See, Some of What's in the Future, and How We Go About Doing It: HI at Apple Computer," CHI '95 Mosaic of Creativity Conference, Denver, CO, May 7–11, 1995, doi: 10.1145/223355.223477.

8. Alex Hern, "Why Google Has 200m Reasons to Put Engineers over Designers." *The Guardian*, February 5, 2014, https://www.theguardian.com/technology/2014/feb/05/why-google-engineers-designers, accessed March 11, 2019.

9. Boundless Mind AI, https://www.boundless.ai/, accessed March 11, 2019. Now part of Thrive Global.

10. Http://youjustneedspace.com/, accessed March 11, 2019.

11. Andrew K. Przybylski, "Motivational, Emotional, and Behavioral Correlates of Fear of Missing Out," *Computers in Human Behavior* 29, no. 4 (2013): 1841.

12. Allyson Chiu, "Patients Are Desperate to Resemble Their Doctored Selfies. Plastic Surgeons Alarmed by 'Snapchat Dysmorphia,'" *Washington Post*, August 6, 2018, https://www.washingtonpost.com/news/morning-mix/wp/2018/08/06/patients-are-desperate-to-resemble-their-doctored-selfies-plastic-surgeons-alarmed-by-snapchat-dysmorphia/?noredirect=on&utm_term=.7047e58798d4, accessed March 2, 2019.

13. For more info, read some of Mark Epstein's books on Buddhism and psychotherapy, most recently *The Zen of Therapy: Uncovering a Hidden Kindness in Life* (New York; Penguin, 2022).

14. Random Face Generator, https://thispersondoesnotexist.com/, accessed December 30, 2020.

15. *HyperNormalisation*, directed by Adam Curtis, video (BBC, 2016), at 1:25.

16. Tristan Harris, "Our Brains Are No Match for Our Technology," *New York Times*, December 5, 2019, https://tinyurl.com/srsq8zf, accessed January 5, 2020.

17. Tom plays an aluminum bass made by Ian Schneller.

18. From the Kübler-Ross model, I realize I am loosely defining "bargaining" as using money to bargain with.

19. Steve Albini had been car-doored as he rode his bike to work a week before (with a helmet on), so Shellac was unable to perform, and so he emceed the entire evening with a sling on his arm and a broken collarbone.

20. Steve Albini, conversation with author, July 29, 2017, before songs recorded by PJ.

21. Steve Albini, "Why I Haven't Had a Conventional Christmas in 20 Years," *Huffington Post*, November 23, 2015, updated November 23, 2016, https://www.huffpost.com/entry/why-i-havent-had-a-conventional-christmas-in-20-years_b_8614568?utm_hp_ref=impact&ir=Impact, accessed December 31, 2019.

22. Poverty Alleviation Charites, https://www.unconditionalgiving.org/mission, accessed November 22, 2021.

23. Andrew Hibel, "Is Passion the Antidote for Pandemic Work Life?" (interview with Steve Albini and Heather Whinna), *Inside Higher Ed Jobs*, 2020, https://www.higheredjobs.com/HigherEdCareers/interviews.cfm?ID=2525, accessed December 31, 2020.

Chapter 20. Teaching

1. Visual Thinking Strategies, https://vtshome.org/, accessed January 1, 2021.

2. Naomi Polonsky, "Jean Dubuffet's Highs and (Controversial) Lows," *Hyperallergic*, July 15, 2021, https://hyperallergic.com/660900/jean-dubuffet-brutal-beauty-barbican/, accessed July 16, 2021.

3. Noted for extremely problematic behavior.

Index

ROSE MARSHACK is a professor of Creative Technologies in the School of Music at Illinois State University. Her band Poster Children has performed over 800 shows in the United States and Europe.

Music in American Life

The Golden Age of Gospel   *Text by Horace Clarence Boyer; photography by Lloyd Yearwood*

Aaron Copland: The Life and Work of an Uncommon Man   *Howard Pollack*

Louis Moreau Gottschalk   *S. Frederick Starr*

Race, Rock, and Elvis   *Michael T. Bertrand*

Theremin: Ether Music and Espionage   *Albert Glinsky*

Poetry and Violence: The Ballad Tradition of Mexico's Costa Chica   *John H. McDowell*

The Bill Monroe Reader   *Edited by Tom Ewing*

Music in Lubavitcher Life   *Ellen Koskoff*

Zarzuela: Spanish Operetta, American Stage   *Janet L. Sturman*

Bluegrass Odyssey: A Documentary in Pictures and Words, 1966–86   *Carl Fleischhauer and Neil V. Rosenberg*

That Old-Time Rock & Roll: A Chronicle of an Era, 1954–63   *Richard Aquila*

Labor's Troubadour   *Joe Glazer*

American Opera   *Elise K. Kirk*

Don't Get above Your Raisin': Country Music and the Southern Working Class   *Bill C. Malone*

John Alden Carpenter: A Chicago Composer   *Howard Pollack*

Heartbeat of the People: Music and Dance of the Northern Pow-wow   *Tara Browner*

My Lord, What a Morning: An Autobiography   *Marian Anderson*

Marian Anderson: A Singer's Journey   *Allan Keiler*

Charles Ives Remembered: An Oral History   *Vivian Perlis*

Henry Cowell, Bohemian   *Michael Hicks*

Rap Music and Street Consciousness   *Cheryl L. Keyes*

Louis Prima   *Garry Boulard*

Marian McPartland's Jazz World: All in Good Time   *Marian McPartland*

Robert Johnson: Lost and Found   *Barry Lee Pearson and Bill McCulloch*

Bound for America: Three British Composers   *Nicholas Temperley*

Lost Sounds: Blacks and the Birth of the Recording Industry, 1890–1919   *Tim Brooks*

Burn, Baby! BURN! The Autobiography of Magnificent Montague   *Magnificent Montague with Bob Baker*

Way Up North in Dixie: A Black Family's Claim to the Confederate Anthem   *Howard L. Sacks and Judith Rose Sacks*

The Bluegrass Reader   *Edited by Thomas Goldsmith*

Colin McPhee: Composer in Two Worlds   *Carol J. Oja*

Robert Johnson, Mythmaking, and Contemporary American Culture   *Patricia R. Schroeder*

Composing a World: Lou Harrison, Musical Wayfarer   *Leta E. Miller and Fredric Lieberman*

Fritz Reiner, Maestro and Martinet   *Kenneth Morgan*

The University of Illinois Press
is a founding member of the
Association of University Presses.

————————————————

Text designed by Jim Proefrock
Composed in 10.5/14 ITC Legacy Serif
with Trade Gothic and League Gothic display
at the University of Illinois Press
Manufactured by Versa Press, Inc.

University of Illinois Press
1325 South Oak Street
Champaign, IL 61820-6903
www.press.uillinois.edu